EIGHT WORLD CUPS

EIGHT WORLD CUPS

MY JOURNEY THROUGH THE
BEAUTY AND DARK SIDE OF SOCCER

GEORGE VECSEY

TIMES BOOKS   HENRY HOLT AND COMPANY   NEW YORK

Times Books
Henry Holt and Company, LLC
Publishers since 1866
175 Fifth Avenue
New York, New York 10010
www.henryholt.com

Henry Holt® is a registered trademark of
Henry Holt and Company, LLC.

Copyright © 2014 by George Vecsey
All rights reserved.
Distributed in Canada by Raincoast Book Distribution Limited

Library of Congress Cataloging-in-Publication Data
Vecsey, George.
  Eight world cups : my journey through the beauty and dark side of soccer / George Vecsey.
    pages cm.
  Includes bibliographical references and index.
  ISBN 978-0-8050-9848-8 (hardback)—ISBN 978-0-8050-9849-5 (electronic copy)   1. World
Cup (Soccer)—History. I. Title.
  GV943.49.V43 2014
  796.334668—dc23   2013042574

Henry Holt books are available for special promotions and
premiums. For details contact: Director, Special Markets.

First Edition 2014

Designed by Kelly S. Too

Printed in the United States of America
1 3 5 7 9 10 8 6 4 2

To Marianne
For all the good times on the road—and at home.

CONTENTS

EIGHT WORLD CUPS

THE GOAL THAT CHANGES
EVERYTHING

PRETORIA, SOUTH AFRICA, 2010

The Americans were minutes from humiliation.

The long plastic horns of South Africa were blaring like klaxons of doom.

Landon Donovan and his teammates had been working for four years toward this day, but now they chased the ball around the field in a scoreless draw, needing a victory to stay alive. A good bit of the world was rooting for gallant Algeria to eliminate the United States.

Many World Cup matches end this way, with one team trying to kill the final seconds in a distant corner, with the other side as desperate as its fans back home.

In Italy in 1966, angry fans flocked to the Rome airport and threw eggs and tomatoes when the Azzurri landed after being eliminated—by North Korea. *Che peccato.* What a sin. In 2010, Americans were not yet at the stage of heaving produce at their lads but, still, expectations had been raised all over the States as a younger generation had become consumers—experts, in their own minds, about the world's sport.

Soccer was having something of a boom in the United States, helped by networks like ESPN, Fox, and Univision. In New York and many other places around the country, signboards were popping up in front of pubs and restaurants, proclaiming: REAL v. BARÇA, 2 PM. American players were going to Europe for the money and the experience. Rich Americans were buying European clubs.

People back home cared now—maybe not to the point of shooting out the TV or jumping off a bridge (which can happen) but enough to post cranky messages in social media, criticizing the starting lineup or the tactics. In summery time zones across the United States, anxious fans were convinced the Yanks really should be able to beat Algeria. They were begging for a goal, as the vuvuzelas blared. At the southern end of Africa, it was June 23, early winter. Getting late.

Keep an eye on the ball. The adage applies to soccer writers as well as athletes. At my first World Cup in Spain in 1982, I could not follow the ball because the skill of the players, the things they could do with their insteps and knees and foreheads, was beyond my comprehension. Over the years, in eight World Cups all over the globe, I learned to continuously take mental note of who touched the ball, and how, and where it went—creating an endless sixty-second loop of memory that could be erased when those touches led nowhere.

Goals are always precious, always unique, and often come out of nowhere because of a nifty steal and a laser pass at the far end. You cannot afford to let your mind wander between plays, as I do at American football games, when I read a few paragraphs of a newspaper between plays that Coach sends in. In soccer, you must watch the ball every second because you just don't know.

Was I rooting for the Yanks? Not exactly. American soccer writers are pretty independent; they criticize and report, but they also spend time around the players, and generally admire them for their pursuit of the game. The men's national team and the highly successful women's team are the sons and daughters of the hybrid nation—never more so than on the epic all-American romp that was about to happen in distant Pretoria.

Reporters and fans had watched the squad change kaleidoscopically from match to match, from year to year. The eleven players on the field were survivors of a long march, and some who had helped win qualifying matches did not make it to South Africa. "Good friends we had, good friends we lost along the way," as Bob Marley put it.

Now, as the vuvuzelas yowled like hounds of hell, I spotted Tim Howard, the latest in a pipeline of supple American goalkeepers, prowling the goal line, anxiety on his face.

A few weeks earlier, when the United States played a tune-up in Connecticut, team officials brought in Bill Russell, perhaps the most successful American athlete in history, who had won eleven professional basketball championships as the center for the Boston Celtics and who had previously led his team to two college championships and one Olympic gold medal. A rebounder-poet named Tom Meschery once described Russell as "an eagle with a beard." Now the eagle's beard was white, and he stooped a bit as he strode across the field, but he still looked like the man who could swat the ball out of Wilt Chamberlain's hands—fierce, purposeful, distant.

A few steps behind Russell was Tim Howard, part African American, part Hungarian, the nicest of people, who always talked civilly with reporters who covered the U.S. team.

Any fool can be a straight man. I knew Howard had been a star basketball player in high school back in New Jersey. I also knew he could handle my break-the-ice question.

"Did you tell Russell you could dunk on him?"

Howard looked at me quizzically, as if to ask, *Are you crazy?* Then he smiled and told us how Russell had talked about focus and intensity and pride. The main thing was, Howard had studied the aging eagle, up close.

Every four years, the World Cup moves to a different corner of the earth, becoming part of the history and politics of the host country. The spectators get a quick rush from watching the best-known athletes in the world march onto the field holding the hands of appropriately diverse and always appealing children. Giant yellow Fair Play cards are flashed, the pageantry so blatant yet somehow effective, making people around the world temporarily overlook the demonstrated venality and opacity of FIFA (Féderation Internationale de Football Association), the governing body of soccer.

Late in 1994, I wrote the script for a Brazilian documentary about the World Cup in the United States, just concluded. The title was *Two Billion Hearts*. I have encountered those thumping hearts in subways in

Mexico City, at wurst stands in Germany. In 2010, I was feeling the pride of the African continent; I could sense two billion hearts, all pounding, including my own.

The whole world plays soccer. Two hundred seven nations were registered and ranked as of May 2010, with Brazil ranked first, possibly out of habit, and surging Spain right behind. Six nations were tied for last— San Marino, Anguilla, Montserrat, American Samoa, Central African Republic, and Papua New Guinea.

The United States was ranked fourteenth going into that World Cup while Algeria was ranked thirtieth, which made for a delicious first world– third world matchup. Algeria, although at the opposite end of a vast continent, was representing Africa.

Organized soccer had talked for decades about Africa being the future of the sport. Now FIFA had belatedly honored that commitment, making South Africa the host—a mixed blessing of worldwide exposure and crushing cost. Either way, the world was watching a World Cup in Africa, and the event seemed normal in just about every way, except that the season was winter instead of summer, and fans had to bundle up.

This match was being played in Pretoria, the executive capital of South Africa, in Loftus Versfeld Stadium, built for rugby, named for an early player and administrator of that white man's sport.

During the terrible struggle over apartheid, officers on horseback had stormed through downtown Pretoria, lashing out at demonstrators. Films of that violence are shown at the Apartheid Museum in Johannesburg. In 1995, this stadium was used for several matches as South Africa improbably won the Rugby World Cup and Nelson Mandela donned rugby gear, setting a tone of unity and accommodation. Fifteen years later, a soccer team from North Africa was giving fits to the United States of America.

It was getting dark, and cold, and very late. The sideline official designated four minutes of supplemental injury time, every second a bonus to the desperate Americans. The red-clad American fans hooted, but many more fans cheered as an Algerian defender played the ball backward to his own keeper, a common stalling tactic.

The Algerian players worked the ball down the right side. Normally, one of the strongest players would dribble into the corner and kill some seconds by grappling with the defenders. However, one player saw an opening, set up a parabolic pass across the goalmouth, where a teammate met it with his forehead. Cristiano Ronaldo or one of the German strikers might have hammered the ball into the far corner to finish off the Americans, but the Algerian lofted it directly toward Tim Howard's chest.

Howard has a trace of Tourette's syndrome and normally displays no visible symptoms except perhaps facial twitches now and then. As the ball approached, the condition did not affect his dunker hands. He got the feel of the ball and danced a few steps forward, glancing downfield. In another time and place, the eagle with a beard would have spotted Sam Jones or John Havlicek streaking downcourt. Tim Howard spotted Landon Donovan going in motion.

There was no time for a buildup, only desperation. Howard dished the ball with an overhand motion, bouncing it up the middle, where Donovan, with his sprinter's stride, caught up with it, forty yards downfield.

Root for the story. That's the rule for any reporter. The obvious story of this day would be Algeria knocking out the Americans. Then I would write a column asking why Our Lads, with all that money, all those youth programs, were actually deteriorating as a world soccer power since their high point in 2002, when the U.S. team reached the World Cup quarterfinals in South Korea.

In our own provincial little World Series of baseball, back in 1986, I had the vague sense the Boston Red Sox were still haunted by some dank vapor, cursed for sending Babe Ruth to the Yankees. I would have enjoyed writing about their first championship after sixty-eight years of failure; instead, I wrote about the fluke ground ball that squiggled through some poor soul's legs. In baseball, there is no ticking clock, but in this sport of surprises the stopwatch was in the hand of the lone official on the field. Wracked by jet lag, I had no journalistic premonitions as I sat in Loftus Versfeld Stadium. The match was moving in real time, as Landon Donovan picked up the pace.

He was the most beautiful of athletes, with the grace of an 880-yard racer rather than the churning legs of a sprinter. In a sport of ethnics, among sons of immigrants and holders of dual passports, Donovan was a beach boy, happiest when he could smell the Pacific. He had tried the challenge of soccer in Europe but declared himself a homebody, a Californian. He was intense, private, but it was a mistake to underestimate his drive, his toughness. Donovan had learned the second language of California, Spanish, from growing up around Mexican kids, and he was not afraid of sandlot roughness or bilingual jibes from hostile crowds in arenas like Azteca Stadium in Mexico City. He almost seemed to like it.

Donovan was the most potent attacking force the United States had ever sent onto a field. He could take corner kicks or find an open seam on the field or fight off an elbow to capture a loose ball—or just outrun everybody. In a nation that has produced great athletes in many other sports, he was the closest approximation to a star. In World Cup terms, he was America's Maradona, America's Baggio, America's Zidane. Tim Howard made sure the right man had the ball.

Donovan caught up with the ball at full speed, opening up the field. In the past fifteen minutes, the United States had seemed to gain the edge in cardio fitness. Donovan raced past the Algerian defenders. All over the world, four billion eyes began to widen, the quick rush of this sport.

The temptation for Donovan, for any footballer, was to try too much. A basketball player knows he has enough energy and skill to race down the court and dunk, which is why scores often exceed one hundred points, from repetitive brilliance. Ninety-nine times out of a hundred, a soccer player might overreach, but Donovan found the incredible presence to lay the ball off to his right, where Jozy Altidore was racing.

A big striker of Haitian background, born in New Jersey, Altidore had traveled around the soccer diaspora, looking to be a star. Not known for speed or finesse, Altidore caught up with Donovan's ball, controlled it with a touch far beyond his norm, and took a swerve toward the goal, past defenders, making the run of his life.

Again, there was the danger of doing too much. Instead of getting fancy, Altidore drilled the ball toward the goal, putting pressure on the keeper, who had other distractions: Clint Dempsey, an intense kid from East Texas, who grew up playing with Mexican friends and had gone overseas to eventually become the all-time leading American scorer in England. He had had a goal taken away earlier by an offside call that looked spurious on the replay; now the Yanks were running out of seconds.

"When the ball got played out to Jozy, I tried to make a run," Dempsey would later recall. Altidore drilled the ball into the scrum in front of the goal and Dempsey got his foot on it, but as he tumbled forward he saw the keeper deflecting the ball and he thought, "Oh, no, this is not my day." The momentum carried Dempsey into the goalmouth, like a human cannonball, making contact with the Algerian keeper before tumbling into the back of the net.

Any Algerian player might have blasted the ball out of danger—as Kristine Lilly and Brandi Chastain had done so acrobatically in the Women's World Cup final of 1999—and back in the States those viewers not yet enchanted with soccer might have said, "But nothing happened!"

In this case, something did happen. That's why we hold our breath and watch. After passing the ball to Altidore, Donovan had kept running with his beautiful 880-yard gait. He put his foot on the ball from seven yards out and flicked it into the net. Then he dashed to the corner of the field and slid on his stomach like a very happy baby otter, with American players landing on top of him, followed by reserves and staff members and goodness knows who else, a whole nation, in a sense. Redemption in the ninety-first minute.

"I was one of the last people to make it to the dog pile," Dempsey recalled.

That goal, by young American players of vastly diverse backgrounds, immediately became the greatest single play the United States has ever made in the World Cup—considering the lateness of the hour, the distance traveled, the stakes involved, and the higher profile of the American program by 2010, its sixth straight World Cup appearance.

When I watched the video of the Donovan goal recently, I felt a surge of respect, all over again, for the sheer degree of difficulty. If Howard had distributed the ball in another direction, if Donovan had gotten giddy on his dash upfield, if Altidore had bungled his possession, if Dempsey had overdone his slide near the keeper and prompted a foul call, if Donovan had blasted the ball into the upper deck—all potential failures, an intrinsic part of this sport.

Instead, the American players killed off the last three minutes and celebrated on the field, still alive, at the center of their sport, at the center of the world.

2

THE MAKING OF A FAN

QUEENS, NEW YORK, 1954

My high school did not have a football team. That may be where it all began. I was a chubby junior, obscure in a school of five thousand, and I heard some friends talking about the soccer team. That sounded like something I could join.

Jamaica High School was in New York City's borough of Queens, a beautiful building on a glacial hill, serving a huge area that included Parkway Village, a housing development built for families connected to the United Nations. The soccer team was like one of those World War II movies—you, Lewin, you, Oliva, you, Lyon, front and center, we need you to run a mission!

The players had different styles, which led to chaos on the field, since some believed in short crisp passes and others had been raised on long booming kicks downfield. However, there was one unifying factor on the Jamaica team—our star player, Bob Seel. He could move the ball with either foot or take it away with a feint of his willowy body. He knew the game and was intensely competitive, coaching us on the field in a thin, reedy voice, which was a good thing since our coach, Mr. Harrington, did not do much except open the ball bag.

Nowadays, I drive past playgrounds where girls and boys are dribbling the ball around pink cones, and I think, "Why couldn't Mr. Harrington have run that drill?"

The first time I saw Bob Seel make a sliding tackle I thought he had invented the move. Of course, to slide on the Jamaica field was to invite gashes from broken glass and pebbles and bottle caps.

I gravitated to fullback because it sounded like a position in American football, that is to say, one where you would hit people. For a fat boy, fullback seemed to demand less running, less finesse. The starters were given first choice for shoes, so my leftovers were a size too small with nails sticking up into my feet. I went out to practice anyway and cut up my feet, and my parents sent the shoes out for repairs.

We began playing games, a noisy multilingual band taking the subway or bus to Bushwick, Forest Hills, Bayside. The journey to the heart of soccer was to Grover Cleveland High School's home field, the Metropolitan Oval, on a plateau in Maspeth near the Brooklyn-Queens border—near Bob Seel's old neighborhood of Ridgewood.

When we reconnected years later, Bob told me that his father, a German immigrant named George Seel, had learned the sport in Kaiserslautern, and after moving to America had become a star with the German Hungarian club in New York. "I never saw the man play," Bob told me sadly, but he did see his dad gambol in old-timers' games, where he was treated with great respect by other players of his generation.

Bob recalled at least five ethnic social clubs in the old neighborhood, all with a bar and meeting hall on the main floor and changing rooms for the players in the basement. He was not given to bragging but said that as a twelve-year-old in Ridgewood he had scored with each foot in the state championship game for his age group, before his family moved out to eastern Queens. This game was in his genes; it was a pleasure to watch him play.

On game days we would emerge from the subway, walk through the curvy streets of Maspeth, and find the Oval, mostly dirt and pebbles but what a view—the skyline of Manhattan towering directly behind the west goal. It was one of those holy places—Delphi, Kyoto, Cholula, the ancient Mexican town of 365 temples—where you feel in your bones that you are at the navel of the earth. Not only that, but the Grover Cleveland soccer team actually attracted fans—not just the occasional parent or girlfriend but real neighbors, kids, men and women, old people, shouting encouragement, knowing the game.

In my junior season I sat on the bench with the subs while Seel and our regulars gave Grover Cleveland a good battle, but ultimately we gave up a few goals, their players shook our hands, and we trudged back toward the subway, proud of ourselves for not giving up more. Sometimes I got to play in scrimmages, with the regulars cheering and shouting instructions while I lumbered toward a loose ball and booted it downfield. I had not learned to make tactical passes, and never did.

Defense appealed to me. Stop the sneaky bastards before they get too far. To this day, I enjoy watching defenders—football safeties who arrogantly swat away the long pass, hockey brutes who break up an attack with a hip check. On our pebbly home field in Jamaica, the afternoon sun in my eyes, I was the cop on the beat, however clumsy and crude. Whenever I run into people who play soccer, I ask, "What position?" It's a Rorschach test; it explains your personality.

In my senior year, many of our regulars had graduated, so I got to start. Sometimes Bob Seel would score a goal or two in the first half and then take over as keeper in the second half, but he couldn't save all my mistakes.

In our annual trek to Grover Cleveland, my chief tormentor was a curly-haired thick-necked forward named Reinhart "Bubbi" Herink, who faked me to Brooklyn, faked me to the Bronx, exposing me as a lumbering oaf.

My career came to an end against Brooklyn Automotive High School on the beautiful afternoon of October 4, 1955, in the Borough of Churches. Baseball fans have already sussed out that date. Up in the Bronx, the Dodgers were playing the Yankees in the seventh game of the World Series. Somebody had a portable radio in the stands, and I kept edging over toward the sidelines to catch the baseball score—something I never saw Franco Baresi or Andreas Brehme do. At halftime, Mr. Harrington said, "If you want to listen to the ball game, you can sit on the bench." Which I did, for the rest of the season.

Bob Seel went on to play soccer, basketball, and baseball at the

Philadelphia Textile Institute and had a long career as an agent for the Treasury Department. At our fiftieth class reunion, I thanked him for my first example of what this sport could be.

As for Reinhart Herink: a few weeks after faking me into Newtown Creek, he scored the only goal in the 1955 city championship match against Lafayette High School, with a great feint followed by a goal into the upper corner. When I learned that, years later, I felt a bit better. At least he terrorized everybody.

The sport had a hold on me. When I arrived at Hofstra College the next fall, I had lost forty pounds but was too busy working as a student publicist for the athletic department to even think about going out for soccer. However, I took my four semesters of gym in an autumn soccer class, run by the basketball-soccer coaches, Butch van Breda Kolff and Paul Lynner, terrific athletes themselves, who sometimes would jump into the game to show us a trick or two. They were scouting for athletes who could learn to play varsity soccer, but they never invited me.

I savored those autumn afternoons, sliding around on grass and mud, the wind and rain whipping off the plains of Hempstead. I must have played forty matches between high school and gym class, but never in my life did I get close enough to take a shot.

Soccer was still lurking inside me in 1967, when I was a reporter covering baseball for *Newsday*. I had never noticed the 1966 World Cup in England when it was taking place, but a year later a full-length documentary named *Goal! The World Cup* began getting good reviews. The film was playing at the Paris or the Guild, one of those charming little art houses in Manhattan, so one afternoon I slipped into the theater and was captivated by the teams from all over the world, the fans, the physicality of the sport.

I had covered Mickey Mantle's home runs and Bill Russell's blocks; these soccer players on the big screen were just as compelling. There was the effervescent Pelé of Brazil, being kicked by cynical defenders, and the dignified Eusebio of Portugal, being hacked, and there were the mysterious North Koreans, impassive and aggressive, in a shocking 1–0 victory that earned the Italian players that tomato barrage when they arrived at the airport in Rome.

The main theme of the film was the progress of the English and West German teams toward the final, at Wembley Stadium in London. World War II was still part of collective memory in 1966; the film did not mention the war per se but subtly made the point that these two nations had a bit of history between them.

The final was tied at 2–2 after ninety minutes, and the teams went into overtime. In the 101st minute, a shot by England's Geoff Hurst hit the bottom of the crossbar and bounced near the wide chalk stripe of the goal line. The officials conferred and ruled it a goal, although the rudimentary camera work of the day suggested that the ball did not actually cross the line. Hurst scored again in the 120th minute for the 4–2 victory, still the only World Cup championship for the nation that invented soccer.

In that dark movie theater in Manhattan in 1967, I was hooked.

A couple of decades later, in a World Cup press room, I was charmed by the prehistoric clackety-clack of an Olivetti portable (lightweight, built to last forever), recording the words of Brian Glanville, the great correspondent of the *Sunday Times*. I have come to think that soccer lends itself to great writing because it thrives in the imagination, like so much of life. Great writers put themselves into the possibilities of the sport— pondering, What if Sócrates of Brazil had passed to his left instead of his right? I suspect that poor doomed midfielder asked himself the same thing. Cervantes, Tolstoy, Dickens would have loved divining the choices of the costumed surrogate armies in our modern world of soccer. Over the years, I sought out the writing of Glanville and Gardner, Foer and Kuper, Galeano and Hornby.

In one of those media rooms, somebody told me that Glanville had written the script for *Goal!*, but in those Babel-like settings I could never muster up the courage to ask him about it. The documentary, directed by Ross Devenish, a South African, and Abidin Dino, a Turk—how international is that?—has more or less vanished in the United States because of rights legalities, but in 2013 a friend burned me a DVD, and I was instantly reassured as to just how wonderful, how seminal, the film is.

The camera catches not only the expertise of the best footballers in the world but also their tumbles, their gaffes. The musical arrangements by Johnny Hawksworth—the spare pace, the chimes, the stray horns—are the epitome of mid-'60s cool jazz. At one point, an Argentine player dawdles while leaving the pitch after a deserved red card, and Hawksworth supplies squawks of a burlesque horn to underscore the man's foolishness, like a circus background in a Fellini film.

Perhaps the viewer has come for a soccer documentary but is instead treated to an art film—quick shots of teams arriving in England, very '60s-ish, very Bond-ish, lots of birds in very short skirts. The Spanish team disembarks, and the narrator, Nigel Patrick, softly notes that Spain, for all that talent, somehow comes up short. This was 1966, and Brian Glanville was spot on. Only forty years to go, *compañeros*.

In one staccato segment, players hack away at one another, and the narrator alludes to "the football of negativity"—as if players of bygone decades had all been ballet soloists.

In an Iron Curtain intramural, the Soviets propel one Hungarian over a low wall, into the front row. The player steadies himself and graciously waves a hand to reassure the bobbies that he is well enough to continue. When the Soviets win, the narrator says, "The steamroller has crushed the artist." It is the closest the narration comes to overt political comment.

Early in 2013, I rang up Glanville in London, still chipper, now well into his eighties. He told me he had stopped going to World Cups after 2006, leaving him with thirteen, one behind the record of David Miller of England and Malcolm Brodie of Belfast. Glanville also told me that he was the second choice to write *Goal!* The original choice was Bryan Stanley Johnson, who called himself an experimental novelist. "I called him B. S. Johnson," Glanville said.

"I don't think England would have won anywhere else," Glanville said about the home-field advantage at Wembley. He fretted that the film might seem "chauvinistic" but was proud that the documentary does not dwell on the history between the two nations. "I mean, I'm Jewish, but I was on good terms with the Germans; it was a *football* match," Glanville told me.

The film is the work of artists who know how to pace themselves. It ends in littered, sun-dappled, and silent Wembley, after the queen and the hordes and the players have all departed the premises. Johnny Hawksworth tosses in spare notes from, of all tunes, "The Farmer in the Dell," and the narrator enunciates Brian Glanville's muted final words: "And at Wembley, Mr. McElroy locks up." Have you ever heard a better ending to a documentary?

I told Glanville that I hold him personally responsible for my fascination with the World Cup.

Maybe there was another reason I was drawn to soccer—all the foreign connections in my family. My mother was born in England to an Australian father and an Irish mother, and the family migrated to the United States after World War I. My mother's Irish aunt had moved to Brussels, and that aunt's daughter, Florence Duchene, died in Bergen-Belsen after being caught harboring Scottish soldiers.

My father had Old World ties, too. He had been adopted by an old Hungarian family that had long settled in Connecticut. (My guess is that my father was part Jewish, but we will never know.) His adoptive mother spoke with a thick Hungarian accent, and my aunt Irene sang in Hungarian nightclubs on the East Side of Manhattan.

In our first years of marriage, my wife and I loved visiting my Hungarian grandmother and aunt, who stayed up late into the night, sipping sweet Tokay wine and chatting about music and spirituality and the old days. One day, my grandmother proclaimed that my wife and I had the makings of good Europeans. I wondered, What does that mean?

All I knew was that I needed to live on the eastern edge of America, in the city of spices and noses and accents. When my family went to Jones Beach, I felt the Atlantic stretching across to England, where my mother was born. Did my European roots make me receptive to the sport of the world?

I got my first sense of soccer noise in the summer of 1970, when we were staying in a hotel near the Spanish Steps. There is no place like Italy for a family vacation. Italians made our three young children feel welcome in trattorias or museums or churches. "*Famiglia, famiglia,*" people said.

Very late one night, we were awakened by a mob below our windows—chants of "Ee-tal-ya! Ee-tal-ya!" People were massing in a square, waving flags and banners, milling around good-naturedly, cars honking. After an hour or so, the crowd dissipated, and we went back to sleep.

In the morning I asked the desk clerk about the demonstration. He gave me the short version: Italy won a soccer game in Mexico.

Many years later I looked it up: at four o'clock in the afternoon (local time) in Azteca Stadium, Italy and West Germany played an epic semifinal of the 1970 World Cup. West Germany equalized in the final seconds of added time, and then the teams scored five goals in the extra thirty minutes, with Gianni Rivera of Italy scoring the decisive goal in the 111th minute. Franz Beckenbauer finished the match with a separated shoulder. Given the eight-hour time difference, that match would have ended at two in the morning in Rome. No wonder people were out in the streets, cheering.

I was busy covering religion for the *New York Times* in the late 1970s and pretty much missed the brief glowing spurt across the firmament by the New York Cosmos, the legendary professional team that was known for Pelé on the field and Mick Jagger in the stands. When I came back to cover sports in 1980, entire franchises and ancient stars were flaming out from the North American Soccer League, but I was drawn to the spectacle of another of the Cosmos' aging stars, Giorgio Chinaglia, a stormy Italian who had grown up in Wales, who could plant his bulky frame near the goal and outmaneuver anybody, and who was hell on coaches. Giorgio had played on Italian teams that disappointed their fans in the World Cup; the Cosmos also had Franz Beckenbauer, the suave midfielder who had helped West Germany win the World Cup in 1974, and a smooth old defender, Carlos Alberto, who had played for Brazil's champions in 1970.

When he turned thirty-eight years old in 1982, Carlos Alberto retired in the most touching farewell for an athlete I have ever seen. The Cosmos, with their showbiz flair from their part owner, the record impresario Ahmet Ertegun, had the old master play half the match for Flamengo, his previous team, and half for the Cosmos. Afterward, he took a victory lap around Giants Stadium, with the loudspeaker playing Carly Simon's song "Nobody Does It Better." To this day, whenever I hear that version, I think of the grand old footballer slowly circling the field, waving at the fans in the gloom of a dying league.

The aging stars imparted the aura of the World Cup. I looked up the record: Uruguay won at home in 1930, Italy won at home in 1934, Italy won in France in 1938, Uruguay won in Brazil in 1950, West Germany won in Switzerland in 1954, Brazil won in Sweden in 1958, Brazil won in Chile in 1962, England won at home in 1966 ("*And at Wembley, Mr. McElroy locks up*"), Brazil won in Mexico in 1970, West Germany won at home in 1974, and Argentina won at home in 1978.

The geometry of the game, the space, the freedom of choice for footballers who suddenly come into possession of the ball—all of these made me love soccer. But even as my appreciation grew, I could not help noticing the disdain from friends of my generation, who clearly hated the idea, the very existence, of the sport. Soccer was not part of their childhood, they seemed to be saying, and therefore could not be part of their adult lives. If soccer was so important, why hadn't their fathers kicked a ball to them instead of throwing it?

Generations had been formed by the voices of Mel Allen or Vin Scully talking baseball or Marty Glickman talking basketball. I could easily understand a lack of interest from Americans who had other sporting diversions, golf or auto racing or whatever. *Chacun à son goût*, as they say in other parts of the world. But I am talking about hatred.

There was some deeper antipathy or fear that caused television comedians to toss off stale one-liners about scoreless ties—the old "nothing happened" criticism of this low-scoring sport. Soccer seemed to remind Americans of something they instinctively feared—foreign languages, foreign influences. I've seen the freaky reaction of Americans' renaming French fries "freedom fries" in the run-up to the war in Iraq—irrational, but not totally funny. Or the horrible stigma of John Kerry speaking French or Republicans' shock upon learning that Mitt Romney could also speak French.

In a country that was founded mostly by people who wanted to get away from the Old World, soccer seemed to bring out a defensiveness, an isolationist posture, a fear of mobs and stomping boots in the generation that was young during World War II and the Holocaust and the Cold War and nuclear proliferation.

This animosity to soccer has been abetted by many of the best sportswriters of the past generation. I have a theory: traditionally, when young people were breaking into what we used to call the newspaper business, they were assigned to take a crack at soccer. Somebody had to do it. Maybe it was some ethnic league in a funky old stadium, some touring world team with inscrutable names and languages. Go make sense of this, kid.

The strangers in shorts would then play ninety minutes, and nobody would score, and nobody could explain what just happened. What do you write when you have just witnessed a scoreless tie? You make fun of it. I suspect I did it myself once or twice.

Wacko theories abounded. Wise and witty and informed sportswriters predicted the sport would never catch on because, after all, Americans cannot possibly relate to a sport whose primary skills involve the pedal extremities. Soccer touched off footy phobia.

Another theory was: Americans need double-digit football scores and triple-digit basketball scores. Unless they can witness a series of acrobatic dunks, with the scoreboard digitally rising like the National Debt Clock, then Americans lose interest. We like things big, like American restaurants doling out super-size portions, even if they bring on diabetes. By that logic, soccer is tofu and bean sprouts. (I like tofu and bean sprouts.)

I have sat with colleagues at the 1994 World Cup in the United States, when Italy's Roberto Baggio—the sublime artist, Il Divin Codino, a Buddhist with a pigtail—controlled the ball in midfield with a few swoops and swerves, found a gap in the defense, and dished off a pass to a striker, who delivered a cannonball that soared just wide. The reaction from some colleagues was: nothing happened.

But look: just before the shot, a defender delivered a hip check that sent the striker slightly off stride, just enough to change the arc of the ball, not enough to merit a yellow card or a red card. That's what the game is about—waiting for the shocking moment when everything goes right for the offense, or somebody makes a mistake.

This is not an easy sport, but the skills are exquisite. My photographer pal John McDermott, who worked the World Cup sidelines for decades, once watched his friend Baggio practice free kicks. "He could make ten of ten into the corners," John recalled. But with a keeper protecting the goal and a wall of defenders bouncing around, hands cupping the most vital part of their anatomy, it was not that simple.

Why do some free kicks splat into the wall of defenders, like a moth hitting the windshield? Do the kickers get caught up in the moment and forget about fundamentals? This is why everybody celebrates goals. This is why billions of people love the improbability of this sport.

I have also read the theory that Americans cannot possibly relate to a sport with so many draws. We demand a winner. For the first four seasons of its existence, Major League Soccer pandered to this theory by conducting shoot-outs, but the home office of FIFA, located in Zurich, chastised the young league, so in 2000, MLS legitimized draws, and rightfully so.

Fans all over the world accept the dynamics of a draw. A team can go on the road on the final day of the season, needing a draw in hostile territory to avoid relegation. The tension in the closing minutes can grip an entire city or region. How hard is that to feel?

Maybe it's the British soccer vocabulary that drives Americans crazy. I once had a sports editor, a really good editor, who sent me to a bunch of World Cups but also mocked the sport because of foreign words like "pitch" instead of field and "draw" instead of tie. I always wanted to sneak up behind him and blurt "nil-nil" to see if I could make him levitate, but I refrained. As I said, he is a good friend and a good editor.

We've all got cultural gaps. I get distracted during American football games—all those time-outs and substitutions—and cannot remember who is playing. Still, I would never try to talk anybody out of loving helmetball. (I know a few sportswriters, bless their hearts, who actually coach youth soccer, as a civic duty. I will not name names.)

Traditionally, American sports editors would take note of world-level soccer only when they came across a photo of a soccer riot, death in the stadium. Horrors like Heysel and Sheffield and Bradford City are a quarter century in the past; hooligans have been minimized in western Europe as the sport became big business with high ticket prices and no-drinking, no-cursing, no-smoking family sections. But even in these kinder, gentler times, racist behavior has become more noticeable in Europe these days, and those who have observed from this side of the Atlantic have often blamed such racist chants on a sport that does not employ hands, a theory akin to birther prattle.

To me, with my European roots, soccer did not sound like tromping boots, did not smell like tear gas. It sounded like prayer chants and universal rock, it smelled like beer and empanadas, wine and wursts, and it felt like home. I listened to Chinaglia and Beckenbauer and Carlos Alberto talking about their World Cups, and I thought, I really need to see one of these for myself.

3

THE BEST GROUP EVER

SPAIN, 1982

The World Cup could never get better than this, but I had no way of knowing it, back then. Every World Cup has a "Group of Death"—the most competitive cluster in the first round—but in 1982 the tournament was expanded from sixteen to twenty-four teams, creating a second round of group play.

The wicked sense of humor of a higher power assembled the greatest talent ever seen in one place—Brazil, with three past championships, Italy, with two early titles, and Argentina, the defending champion. Only one team would advance to the semifinals. This was not a Group of Death; this was a Group of Mass Extinction.

Recently appointed a sports columnist, I had suggested to my editors at the *New York Times* that I cover a chunk of the World Cup. They knew very little about this strange sport and its emotional crowds, but they approved my proposal, probably from their superb instincts on international reportage. Since the United States wasn't in it, they told me to go for the second round and stay through the end. Cool.

I followed the first round on television, watching tiny figures flitting across the screen. There was no Internet in those days, but I gleaned a few basics from rudimentary wire service reports. Some days I would wander over to the Hotalings newsstand in Times Square and pick up European papers and clip snippets on soccer. In other words, I was unprepared.

The first round was nuts. In an episode straight out of "The Marx Brothers Go to the World Cup," the president of the Kuwait Football Association stormed onto the field to protest a goal by France after his players believed a whistle had been blown to stop play. In his robe, sandals, and kaffiyeh, the sheikh berated the Ukrainian official, who then stunningly reversed his decision. The sheikh returned to the stands, and France swamped Kuwait, 4–1. Neither Kuwait nor that official has been back since.

In another first-round match, tiny Algeria stunned West Germany, 2–1. People were calling it one of the biggest upsets in World Cup history, on a par with North Korea's victory over Italy in 1966 and the United States' victory over England in 1950.

Wait a minute. The United States beat England in the World Cup? This was news to me. I discovered the United States had indeed upset England, 1–0, on a goal by Joe Gaetjens, who was actually from Haiti. I also learned that newspaper editors of the time believed the score was a typographical error when it came clattering over the wires from Brazil, so they awarded the victory to England, until confirmation arrived later.

Plus, it was only soccer. In 1960, Americans would celebrate the Olympic ice hockey gold medal, and in 1980, they would celebrate another gold medal, but the nation had no collective memory of a soccer World Cup victory over England in 1950. It was as if it never happened.

I traveled to Spain by way of England, where I was introduced to the dark side of soccer. At Wimbledon, I saw Billie Jean King and Jimmy Connors, two geriatric icons having a grand run. During a rain delay, I stood around a hospitality tent watching the World Cup from glittering Spain.

On the screen, eleven players from West Germany and eleven players from Austria were waltzing with one another, as graceful as dancers in Vienna entertaining *Sacher-Torte-und-Kaffee-mit-Schlag* tourists. Hans from Austria would lead for a while and then Fritz from West Germany would lead. The Europeans in the hospitality tent were not amused and were directing the anger at FIFA.

FIFA, somebody explained, had scheduled the third and final matches of each group in the first round on separate days, thereby opening up a huge strategic advantage for the teams that went last. Algeria had two victories and one loss for 4 points (two for each victory) and a 5–5 goal balance. Twenty-four hours later, everybody had figured out the mathematics for this group: if West Germany beat Austria by any margin under four goals, both teams would advance to the next round, eliminating Algeria.

As the saying goes, *wunderbar*.

The ensuing match on June 25 between the two German-speaking countries was disgraceful. West Germany scored in the tenth minute, and the two teams waltzed with each other as most of the fans in Gijón whistled angrily. The 1–0 lead held up for the final eighty minutes of the match, and both countries advanced. Algeria was screwed.

By the next World Cup, FIFA would mandate simultaneous third matches, which made it harder to manipulate a result. However, FIFA would wait until 1994 to allot three points for a victory in group play, which served to reward more aggressive play. All of this was too late to help Algeria. In the swank hospitality tent at Wimbledon, I picked up a heady whiff of scorn for FIFA.

By the time I flew from soggy London to sunny Barcelona, everybody in the world knew that FIFA was stuck with a mammoth miscalculation. It had placed two second-round groups in the magnificent city that nurtured Dalí and Miró, the city transformed by Gaudí, but one group would play its matches in the grand stadium called Camp Nou, with its capacity of 115,000, while the other group was in a funky little arena named Sarrià, nicknamed La Bombonera (The Candy Box) which held only 43,000.

However, because Argentina and Italy had performed below expectations in the first round, they were now matched with Brazil in the little stadium while the stolid collection of Belgium, Poland, and the Soviet Union had qualified for Camp Nou. The stadiums were set in stone, with no room for flexibility.

The first World Cup match I saw in person was in Camp Nou, between Poland and Belgium. I learned to love the ritual of two national squads marching out for the anthems, exchanging banners, posing for the starting-team photo, and then whacking away at each other. Poland won that match, 3–0, with Zbigniew Boniek scoring goals three different ways—with his foot off a pass, with a header, and by dribbling and faking out the backup keeper. I also learned that Boniek was about to leave his Polish club to play for Juventus, the powerhouse of Italy, as part of the normal market of soccer, in which stars frequently move to larger clubs for larger salaries.

The attendance was given as 65,000, but it looked more like 30,000 to me. Polish fans did enliven the evening by waving Solidarnosc (Solidarity) banners, supporting the labor uprising going on at home, to taunt any stray Soviet fans in the stadium. Even with this nationalistic fervor, Camp Nou was tepid.

The next day, by comparison, Sarrià quivered with life. The stadium is long gone now, but I remember it as crammed into an urban neighborhood, a version of Boston's homey old Fenway Park, at least before Fenway was yuppified. Lucky Sarrià. On three mad days, it was home to the greatest group ever assembled.

Brazil had already won three of the first eleven World Cups, and this squad was considered one of its greatest ever. My assumption as a novice was that Brazil would surely win the tournament. But the first match of that group was between Argentina, the defending champion, and Italy, which had been wracked by a recent gambling scandal. Paolo Rossi, a fleet forward, had been suspended for almost two seasons but was conveniently reinstated just in time to compete in Spain. The Italian players were smarting over criticism from their performance in the first round— three lackluster draws. Rossi had failed to score, and there were calls for him to be benched.

The press seats at Sarrià were close to the field—maybe the tenth row or so. After watching from up high in cavernous Camp Nou the night before, I was thrilled to be able to see the features of the players, the long hair of the Argentines, as they stood for their nearly four-minute-long national anthem.

It is often a mistake to judge teams on the basis of their national stereotypes, but the fact is, the World Cup is an international event, with players representing their homelands and carrying all the baggage of whatever is in the news. The nasty skirmish between Argentina and Great Britain over islands off the Argentina coast, alternately known as the Malvinas or the Falklands, was fresh in everyone's mind. The war had begun on April 2 and ended with Argentina's surrender on June 14. The Argentine players would surely insist, fifteen days later, that the only thing that mattered was soccer, but who really knew how the battles, the sinking of ships, the deaths of fellow countrymen, affected the players?

As the anthem played, I watched Diego Armando Maradona, Argentina's tempestuous prodigy. He was famous for having cried when he was left off the 1978 Argentina team at the age of seventeen because the coach, César Luis Menotti, had thought Maradona was not ready. Argentina then won the World Cup without him.

Now Maradona was standing there in Sarrià, all five feet five inches of him, with thick curly locks—a marked man in every sense. As he looked off into space during the anthem, I could only guess what it meant to be Maradona, the hope of Argentina. With his pre-Columbian looks, he was a mixture of Italian and Native American. Maradona had moved as a child with his family from the outback of Argentina into a hard barrio of Buenos Aires. While still very young, he entertained fans with his dribbling and other ball tricks at halftime of club games, and then moved up rapidly through the youth system.

Shortly before this World Cup, Maradona had signed a lucrative contract with one of Spain's most venerable clubs, FC Barcelona, the powerhouse that played at Camp Nou, and was under intense pressure to justify his cost. Barça shareholders had already seen him play in his new home in the first round in a foreboding 1–0 loss to Belgium. Sarrià was enemy turf, the home of Barça's Catalan rival, RCD Espanyol; welcome to the World Cup.

Maradona was playing with a sore hamstring, but we did not know that. He would be marked by the Italian defender Claudio Gentile, who, I was told, was nicknamed Qaddafi because of his looks, his birth in Libya, and also his nasty tactics on the field. When the match began, I could hear—hear!—the thud of Gentile's boots on the shins of Maradona. The Romanian official waved a yellow card at Gentile in the first minute but that did not deter him from hacking away at Maradona, whether or not the ball was nearby. The cynical tactic was closer to the bullring than the soccer field, and Maradona began to retaliate in kind—and was shown a yellow card in the thirty-fifth minute.

Theoretically, the yellow cards meant that both Gentile and Maradona would have to behave or risk being tossed out of the match. Maradona began making outrageous flops on the manicured lawn of Sarrià and the ref awarded a free kick after one egregious foul by Gentile. The aggrieved Maradona took the shot but sent it over the goal. His knees bent. He clutched the back of his neck with both hands. He despaired operatically. The Barcelona crowd was not sympathetic. He was having a bad start in his new town, and he knew it.

Gentile's close-order combat was part of the gritty Italian defense, known as the *catenaccio*, the chain or bolt. Italy had not won a World Cup since 1938 and was mocked by fans of other teams, who said that Italy's methodical defenders did not know what to do with the ball once they stripped it from marauders. "Eventually, catenaccio became more than a style of play; it became a mentality that dragged Italian soccer down through boring negativity to almost total sterility," wrote Paul Gardner, the British-born soccer journalist, in his book *The Simplest Game*.

Italy was certainly slowing down the defending champions, but with skill beyond my comprehension. My most recent exposure to the sport had been to watch the aging Cosmos, former stars ending their days like beached whales on a foreign shore. I had never imagined the sport could be conducted at such a pace, bing-bing-bing, like a pinball on speed.

When Italy and Argentina were attacking and counterattacking, I was not able to follow the touches, the names and numbers, as they moved over more than one hundred yards up and down the field. Early in the match, I missed the sequence of a near miss and turned to a fellow reporter named Enrico Jacomini from the Associated Press, who politely reconstructed the quick progress of the ball.

In the second half, Italy unveiled its counterattack, scoring in the fifty-seventh minute and then springing Rossi in the sixty-seventh minute, with Antonio Cabrini putting in a loose ball after the keeper ventured out too far. Argentina scored in the eighty-third minute on a free kick while the Italians were arguing with the referee after yet another foul by Gentile, but Italy won, 2–1. The hacking of the little bull from Argentina had paid off.

"There is a rule, as I recall, it is Article 512, that says if you repeatedly foul somebody, you are warned and then sent out of the game," said Menotti, the slim and long-haired Argentine coach, who had won the Cup in 1978 after not choosing Maradona.

"Gentile must have fouled Maradona at least twenty times," Menotti added. "I think Italy was lucky."

Gentile's response was blunt: "Soccer is not for ballerinas."

After the match, I wondered why I found myself charmed by the brash intrusion of the Italians. Perhaps it was a memory of Mayor Fiorello La Guardia, who read the Sunday comics on the radio during a newspaper strike when I was a kid. Or perhaps I was recalling my neighbors across the street in Queens, who kept homemade wine in casks in the basement and spewed pungent Italian curses in their kitchen; plus, they often fed me a starter bowl of pasta before I headed home for my own supper. The beautiful girl in my homeroom in high school. The college bar, summer of '58, when the jukebox played Domenico Modugno warbling "Nel Blu, Dipinto di Blu" every other tune, and everybody in the warm beery night sang "Vo-la-re, oh-oh . . ." I'm a New Yorker. Therefore, I'm part Italian.

Of course, anybody who follows soccer also becomes part Brazilian. On an off day in Barcelona, I was taking a walk along the Ramblas, the ancient leafy streets with curved tile pathways that undulate like the river that used to trickle down toward the harbor. Hearing a rumble of drums and horns, the shuffle of feet, the throaty roar of Portuguese, I spied a moving mass of varied colors—twenty or twenty-five musicians and singers and dancers and fans, bobbing their way through the Gothic Quarter, in a slow samba beat. Carnival in July. Their hair styles ranged from blond to Afro, and many of the women wore abbreviated outfits. I was told that some female fans had a unique way of celebrating a Brazil goal—by shedding their halter tops. What a country.

Sports mobs usually annoy me—Americans, with their money and self-indulgent chants of "U-S-A" at the Olympics; fans from England and a few other countries, with their hint of menace. The newspapers said that in Madrid, sixteen English fans had been detained by police, with five of them deported. Brazilian fans do not fight. They shake their tambourines and their *bumbums*, making strangers want to dance in their wake.

Later, I learned that the Brazilian swarm was called La Torcida, a Portuguese word for something that twists. I had my epiphany: Brazil, with the warmth of Pelé, the three championships, the samba beat, *jogo bonito* (the beautiful game), was the heart of the sport.

I took myself to Sarrià on July 2 to watch Brazil vs. Argentina—the mystical globe of Brazil's flag, the three horizontal bands of *blanca y celeste* of Argentina's—the best soccer rivalry of the Americas. Their soccer history included racial insults toward dark-skinned Brazilian players in the late 1930s and two Argentine players having their legs broken by Brazilian players on the field in 1946. For the next decade, Argentina and Brazil stopped playing each other except in unavoidable tournaments.

The two nations exported their best players to the rich European leagues and their older players to the United States. Menotti, the Argentine coach, had played for the New York Generals in 1967, while Pelé and Carlos Alberto had gone to the Cosmos in their athletic old age.

Inevitably, Brazil and Argentina had met in the World Cup. The first meeting took place in 1974, in Hannover, West Germany, with Jairzinho of Brazil breaking a 1–1 draw in the forty-ninth minute. The second meeting happened in Rosario, Argentina, in 1978, in what the official FIFA site calls "a bad-tempered stalemate."

The 1978 World Cup still evokes hard feelings. In the third game of group play that year, Brazil beat Poland, 1–0, early in the day, leaving

Argentina in need of a victory and a four-goal differential to advance. Argentina promptly hammered Peru by a comfortable 6–0 score and eventually won the World Cup at home. Brazil still resents that friendly tango between the two Spanish-speaking countries.

Now it was time for their third World Cup meeting, my first glimpse of Brazil, with players going by soccer nicknames like Oscar, Junior, and Zico and, on the bench, Roberto Dinamite.

The gods came out to play in blue shorts and yellow jerseys. The ball came rocketing from the goal line to a willowy, shaggy midfielder named Sócrates, who sent a quick little tictac pass to a teammate, took a couple of slide steps, and received the ball in return. Then Sócrates dispatched a laser pass to a teammate with curly locks named Falcão, who raced forward for fifteen or twenty yards, dodging, evading, keeping the ball in front of him, before unleashing a long floating ball toward the goal, where it was met by the forehead of a human projectile named Zico, who sent a cannonball soaring a few inches above the crossbar.

This was some entirely new sport, a blend of ballet and geometry, quick triangles appearing and disappearing, instant decisions by athletes on the move, so graceful and independent, performing intricate maneuvers with a round ball, on the fringes of their feet.

Who were these people? My new mentor, Jacomini from the Associated Press, filled me in. Sócrates had graduated from medical school; his philosopher's name was not from soccer but rather had been given him by his classics-minded parents. I assumed that Falcão—"Falcon" in English—was also a *nome de futebol* in the Latin soccer fashion, but in fact his full name was Paulo Roberto Falcão. He played like a bird of prey and looked like a rock star; Jacomini told me Falcão had played two seasons for rich and powerful AS Roma after a long career in Brazil.

The Brazilians played with a style different than Italy's or Argentina's, flicking the ball back and forth, a form of love on the green grass. Clearly, these Brazilian players were not bound by definitions of position. They were footballers. In the eleventh minute, Dr. Sócrates, as he was called, slipped in front of the frustrated, lethargic Maradona and tapped the ball to Zico, who slammed it upfield to Oscar, who moved it to Serginho, who was stopped the only way Argentina could do it, with a trip. Eder took the free kick and hit the crossbar, but Zico headed the rebound into the corner of the goal. The globe on the Brazilian flag shimmered in celebration. Halter tops were removed.

Brazil scored again in the sixty-sixth minute, when Serginho stole the ball, forwarded it to Sócrates, and from there to Eder, Zico, and Falcão, who took his defender to the right side and lofted a cross high above the goal. Serginho, with the vertical leap of a basketball player, headed it home.

In the seventy-fifth minute, Junior scored on a pass from Zico. (Three decades later, I admit it, I still relish typing these names.) Then, finally, in the eighty-ninth minute, Ramón Díaz of Argentina scored past Waldir Peres, the Brazilian keeper.

By this time, Maradona was no longer on the premises. Having been kicked around by Gentile in the first match, he was a lost and lonely soul in the bear pit of Sarrià. He missed a few shots he could have made, and he gesticulated when he thought he had been brought down in the penalty area. In the eighty-fifth minute, he made a complete fool of himself by kicking Batista of Brazil square in the groin, with the whole world watching.

The Spanish broadcaster promptly included that foul among the *gestos feos*—ugly gestures—of any World Cup. ("Terrible," he trilled.) Maradona was expelled from the match minutes before the defending champions were eliminated. The jeers in Sarrià were a predictor that Barcelona was not Maradona's city, but it was surely a wonderful place for a World Cup.

Everywhere in Barcelona there was genius, particularly among the soaring spires of La Sagrada Familia, the unfinished cathedral planned by Antoni Gaudí, the dreamer and architect whose work is all over that city. My wife, Marianne, and I had been to Barcelona twice, once in 1966 when Catalonia was still essentially an occupied province under Generalissimo Francisco Franco and again in 1977 when Franco was dead and the Catalan culture had begun to reassert itself.

The change was as basic as renaming a thoroughfare from a Franco-era title in Castilian to Gran Via de les Corts Catalanes in Catalan—a revolution depicted in street signs. During the World Cup, folk dancers assembled in the plazas of Barcelona and performed a Catalan dance called the *sardana*, a sweet, dignified reflection of the ancient culture.

I've always had a soft spot for Spain, its regions trying to recover from the wounds of the civil war in the 1930s. Americans don't do politics very well, with our tea-party types blithely tossing around labels like "socialist" and "fascist" without the glimmer of an understanding of how the political needle points left or right. In Spain, politics had been lethal. Camp Nou was home to the powerful FC Barcelona, a communally owned club that represents the nationalistic Catalan impulse, while Sarrià was the home field of RCD Espanyol, a somewhat less successful team that was understood to represent centralist ties to Madrid.

On July 3, there was no game, so I bought a ticket for a concert by Maria del Mar Bonet, a folk singer from Mallorca. The concert was outdoors in a quiet plaza very late on a hot night, the air so still we could hear every ping of the chime, every chord of the mandolin, every syllable. The audience seemed to know the songs and hummed along at times. The next day I stopped off at the big department store El Corte Inglés and bought a Maria del Mar album called *Alenar*, the Catalan verb for "to breathe." When the World Cup was over, I carried the vinyl disk home with me. I play it still on my turntable—songs of love and revolution, songs of a summer night in Barcelona.

With Argentina gone, fans began to take seriously the onrushing and cranky Azzurri, as the Italian team was known, for its bright blue jerseys. The players had long since stopped talking to the media, proclaiming what is known as a *silenzio stampa*. So flamboyant in some ways—nobody can wear sunglasses with sweaters tossed gracefully over shoulders like Italians—the players were smoldering after being criticized for the draws in the first round, their negative reputation for the *catenaccio*, as well as the gambling scandal of 1980, known as Totonero. Now Rossi had come bounding on the counterattack like a bicycle thief to eliminate the casual Brazilians.

Some Italian journalists had made fun of the Italian players for being paid a bonus for advancing from the first round, after three wretched draws. The journalists claimed that the bonuses were $30,000 per player, but team officials insisted they were only $15,000 a man. Without access to the players, the reporters were thereby emboldened to write whatever crossed their minds—which was considered normal, as long as the writing was stylish.

The scribes also wrote about Italy's adherence to the long soccer (and cycling) tradition of enforced celibacy—keeping the lads away from their wives or girlfriends during the competition. Allegedly this makes men strong, gives them focus and purpose, but a lot of nations never won anything after keeping the boys locked up. Besides, it isn't the sex that weakens a footballer but rather the demand for tickets from old friends and relatives. With the Italian players sequestered in Spain, two to a room, one journalist wrote that Rossi and Cabrini were spending the World Cup "like man and wife." That snide and unwarranted phrasing did not go down well with any of the Italian players.

It was impossible to hear the players' version because locker rooms were (and remain) closed in world soccer, probably for good reason, given the swarms of journalists. American reporters were accustomed to some access to athletes, but FIFA had no clue how to showcase the great players in its signature event. Rare press conferences by coaches were stilted. Enzo Bearzot, the gabby pipe-smoking Italian coach, fancied himself something of a linguist and would quibble over the translation from Italian to other romance languages, thereby eating up most of the interview time. Team guidebooks were nonexistent; the primitive computers at the media centers contained little information. Soccer details were locked inside the secretive skulls of the correspondents. Asking questions was not cool. So people made stuff up.

With the Italian players incommunicado, my new friend Jacomini took the gracious step of asking Dino Zoff, Italy's forty-year-old goalkeeper, to grant an interview to an American outsider. To my delight, Zoff agreed. I showed up at the team's hilltop hotel, where I spotted several of his teammates, half his age, recuperating from the Argentina match in the hotel pool. I also noted that whereas the younger Italian players wore the skimpiest of bathing suits and sported deep tans and youthful muscles, Zoff kept on his floppy white T-shirt and wore baggy bathing trunks. He looked more like a middle-aged man who had put in a hard week at the office and was hoping to catch a few winks alongside the pool.

Zoff was tall and dark and angular, vaguely Dean Martin–esque, with none of the energy and gestures of his younger teammates on nearby lounges. His taciturnity was later explained as a trait of his home region in the Friuli, in northeast Italy, which is known for its good wine and earnest frugal laborers who gave a day's work for a day's pay. He did not speak English, and I was more confident with my poor Spanish than my rudimentary Italian, so we spoke two different languages, and sometimes Jacomini interpreted—a normal transaction in the polyglot world of soccer.

I had ascertained that Zoff was a mainstay of Juventus since coming over from Napoli. I asked him a series of questions—about his age, his diet, his workout, the Italian renaissance in soccer—and received polite, modest responses, which I took to be part of the Friulian calm. Plus, he was a keeper, a breed that sees the game and the world from a different angle. The taciturn man said he liked his job and hoped to keep playing for years to come.

I got just enough to write a column, and I felt proud that I had actually talked to the Italian keeper. I had no way of knowing how much this journey to the heart of Italy would stay with me over the years.

On July 4 in Camp Nou, Poland needed only a draw with its dear friends from the Soviet Union to move into the semifinals. The small number of Polish fans with enough money and freedom to get to Barcelona taunted the few Soviet fans who had come for the tournament. Still, police had to go into the two-thirds-empty stands to take down a Solidarity banner and separate the two factions.

This Iron Curtain intramural was not as vicious as the infamous water polo match in the 1956 Olympics. Known as the Blood in the Water match, it took place during the Hungarian revolt against the Soviets. The Poles were keeping the Soviets occupied in the match—and why not, inasmuch as the Soviets had been occupying Poland for years. Late in the match, the Poles were killing the clock, and the Soviets were hacking away at them, pretty much within normal range.

Zibi Boniek, the author of the diversified hat trick against Belgium, was clearly cut down by Sergei Baltacha, who was quickly given a yellow card. Then, as Boniek writhed on the ground, he directed a petulant kick in the direction of a Soviet player—hardly as punishing as the shots the Soviets were taking at the Poles. The referee, Robert Valentine of Scotland, who had passively observed the Austrian and West German waltz in the first round, suddenly became a legalist and unobtrusively booked Boniek—his second yellow card of the tournament.

As the Poles celebrated the 0–0 draw, Boniek left the field, his pale face doubly ashen as he realized he was now ineligible for the semifinal against the winner of the Italy-Brazil match the following day.

Bravo, arbitro. I was just getting some slight feel for the impossible role of the solitary ref. From observing umpires and referees in other sports back home, I knew that one trait of a good official is knowing when to look the other way. Valentine did not seem to know that.

And then, on July 5, the whole world crammed into Sarrià for the decisive match between Italy and Brazil. Brazil had a better goal differential than Italy, which meant that Italy had to beat Brazil in order to advance. A draw would do Italy no good.

I thoroughly expected Brazil to win. If the Italian press was still down on the Azzurri, why shouldn't I be? Brazil was one of the most beautiful teams ever seen—people still say that, to this day—but beauty generally refers to offense. Defense can be negative, even ugly, hence the general contempt for the *catenaccio*. Still, in a sport where one goal is crucial, taut defense can produce offense via the counterattack.

Early in the match, Brazil began taking jaunts down the sidelines, because that was the only way Brazil knew to play. Italy slammed the bolt shut, with Antonio Cabrini, a left back, racing down the left sideline, lashing a left-footed cross that hooked violently until it met the forehead of Paolo Rossi, streaking down from the right. Bizarrely open, Rossi had plenty of space to blast the ball past Waldir Peres for the 1–0 Italy lead.

The Italian press had been calling for Rossi to be benched, saying the nation had been patient enough with him following the gambling scandal. Now Rossi had scored his first goal of the tournament. The match was only five minutes old.

The Brazilian gods knew how to score. Sócrates put the ball under Zoff in the twelfth minute, but Rossi scored in the twenty-fifth minute. Italy led for forty-three ominous minutes, until Falcão stutter-stepped into the Italian defense, mesmerizing them and scoring past Zoff, who may have been screened.

With the match tied at 2, Brazil could not tighten its own bolt. In the seventy-fourth minute, Rossi scored again for a 3–2 lead. Brazil threw all its offense for the draw that would get them through. In the closing moments, Zoff had to stop a shot and then grovel on his belly as he snagged the squirming ball, inches from the goal line.

Zoff impassively cradled the ball as long as he dared, then released it, and soon the match was over. I was stunned, and so was everybody who believed in Brazil. John McDermott, who was working the sidelines that day, recalled how Brazilian photographers were crying as they clicked away. Several years later, Rossi published a book entitled *Ho fatto piangere il Brasile* (I made Brazil cry).

The Italian players, having taken gibes from their own nation, passed through the mixed zone, where hordes of reporters brandished microphones and cameras and begged for a few words. The players tossed their fashionable locks and delivered a patronizing sneer. Something smelled, they said. Like shit.

As I took a taxi back to my hotel after the Italy triumph, the city was silent. The national team of Spain—known as La Selección—was playing England in Bernabéu Stadium in Madrid. The cab driver, listening to the match on the radio, proudly asserted he was a member of La Raza Pura (he spoke Castilian, with its lisped *z*—"Ra-tha Poo-ra") and emphatically not Catalan.

Up to now, I had been so entranced by the two groups and Barcelona that I had overlooked the hopes of the host nation. Spain had been depicted as recidivist underperformers by the great Brian Glanville in the 1967 documentary; fifteen years later, it still was.

Language and regional divisions were a huge issue for Spanish soccer, seven years after the death of Franco. People paid attention to who was starting for La Selección, where the national matches were played, which flags and banners were waved. Did the differences detract from La Selección? In 1982, Spain was known for great individual talent and a strong national league including its two signature teams—Barça and Real Madrid—but little cohesion and durability in a long and demanding tournament.

The 1982 players had made a commercial for El Corte Inglés, the chain department store, wearing stylish suits on the field as they performed volleys and headers and bicycle kicks. Making commercials was much more fun than digging in against grittier squads.

Spain had to beat England by at least two goals to be assured of advancing, but in the long summer evening, neither team could score, which sent West Germany through to the semifinals. Barcelona remained silent, as if in mourning. I was getting my first taste of the angst of any host team. La Selección was twenty-eight years away from fulfillment.

We were in the first primitive decade of computers; almost all the reporters at this World Cup were still tap-tap-tapping their stories on portable typewriters. The *Times* had sent me to Spain with a rudimentary TeleRam Portabubble computer in a thick square case that made me look as if I was carrying a bowling ball. One night the electrician in the press box cut off the power and blew out my computer; I had to find a pioneer computer store in Barcelona to buy new fuses.

These were dangerous times. Dave Kindred of the *Washington Post* and Hubert Mizell of the *St. Petersburg Times* did not have the right plugs for the outlets at their hotel, but the electrician rigged up a connection between a live wire in their computers and a live wire in the air-conditioning unit. One wayward drip of condensation could have electrocuted either of them, but they lived to tell the tale.

Before the semifinal, there was a rare opportunity for reporters to meet the Polish team, sequestered in the jagged peaks of Montserrat, outside Barcelona. Because of the economic and political turmoil back home, the team was keeping a low profile. Poland was one of those mystery teams that occasionally infiltrate the semifinals; the coach and several players seemed stunned to be playing Italy instead of Brazil.

Zibi Boniek was hangdog about being ineligible for the semifinal because of his double yellow cards; later we heard he had been sighted in the Ramblas days earlier, nearly getting his car towed; the man has suffered enough, fans told the police.

When we got back to town, Kindred, Mizell, and I invited our translator, a charming Polish-born woman with a Scottish married name, now living in Barcelona, to a late lunch. We sat outdoors at a seafood restaurant and had a glass of wine and cracked shrimps and tossed the shells onto the sidewalk, as per local custom. Some things about the World Cup you always remember.

On July 8, Italy played Poland in the semifinal in Camp Nou. From a distance of time, I can imagine the disqualified Gentile sitting with the disqualified Boniek, discussing how cool it was going to be in a few weeks when they would be united as teammates at Juventus, the team of the Agnelli family and the Fiat empire. Juve collected stars the way the New York Yankees of the era accumulated the Reggie Jacksons and Dave Winfields. Gentile surely would have marked Boniek that day, presumably as physically as he had marked Maradona a few days earlier.

Poland had nothing left without Boniek, and Italy prevailed, 2–0, as the galloping Rossi scored both goals. Camp Nou was easily half empty, with attendance listed as fifty thousand.

Later that day, I repaired to the Ritz to watch the West Germany–France semifinal from Seville on television, along with my pal Dick Schaap, who was there for ABC. In the sixtieth minute, with the match even at 1–1, a French substitute named Patrick Battiston took a lovely pass from Michel Platini behind the German defenders but squibbed it wide to the right—a split second before the West German keeper, Harald "Toni" Schumacher, blasted Battiston in the jaw with his right hip.

Battiston went down, and some French players thought he was dead; ultimately, he would need extensive work to repair his jaw and teeth. The referee showed no curiosity as to why a player would suddenly need

extreme medical attention for a broken jaw; Schumacher was not penal-
ized. The collision remains the ugliest single act in World Cup history.

The teams remained tied, prompting a thirty-minute overtime with
no sudden death. France scored twice within eight minutes but was just
not geared for defensive posture. The bartender at the Ritz watched as
the French players blithely surged forward toward disaster, like muske-
teers storming a castle—because it is there.

"*Once tontos!*" the bartender blurted, pronouncing it "ON-thay tontos," in Castilian. I can still hear him.

Eleven dummies.

The bartender was absolutely right. West Germany took advantage of
the Gallic nonchalance—or maybe it was weariness. Because Battiston
had come and gone within ten minutes, France had no substitutions left.
West Germany's blond locomotive of a forward, Karl-Heinz Rummenigge,
who had not started because of a thigh injury, came on in the 97th minute and scored in the 102nd minute; another player scored in the 108th
minute; and West Germany won on penalty kicks, inevitably.

From casual comments from that bartender and other knowledgeable
fans, I was starting to get a feel for this sport. Things happen all the time—
but not the repetitious goals of basketball or strikeouts in baseball. In soccer, the game turns as one team finds a weakness (Italy on the counterattack
against Brazil) or one team shows foolhardiness (France, going for a needless third goal). One substitute—the hobbling Rummenigge—can make a
difference. Things happen. But you have to watch.

On Friday morning, the entire World Cup coalesced in Madrid for the
final that would take place on Sunday between Italy and West Germany.
Five years earlier, my family had lived for a month in a friend's flat fac-
ing the Parque del Oeste; the city felt like home. This time I stayed in a
FIFA hotel, where, waiting for the elevator, I noticed a security guard.
Then I spotted Henry Kissinger outside his suite down the hall.

Kissinger used to attend Cosmos matches in New York and loved the
sport, dating back to his childhood in Germany. Many years later, he
would tell me he kept a gift jersey from the team in Fürth, the town

he left just ahead of the Holocaust. "You know, my experiences in Germany were not that great," he would tell me in his gravelly accent, adding, "This town that I left seventy years ago, why should I care? But I do."

I found out later that day that Kissinger was acting as a liaison for the United States Soccer Federation. Colombia was about to default as host for 1986 because it could not meet its financial commitments, and the United States was eager to serve as host.

I got the distinct feeling that FIFA officials loved the money the United States might shake free but were quite nervous about the relative transparency required by American corporations, television networks, and government, as opposed to Europe, where companies (particularly nonprofits like FIFA) did not have to reveal much financial data. Meanwhile, Dr. Kissinger got to see the games.

Having covered a few Super Bowls of American football, I was curious how FIFA would promote its biggest event. The answer was, FIFA did not. At the Super Bowl, every player must show up for Media Day and answer questions both wise and foolish. Perhaps Media Day was overkill—or good business sense. FIFA did not expose its players to roaming packs of interviewers, and even canned quotes from coaches and packets of basic details were minimal. Generating zillions of dollars and francs and pounds and pesetas from the biggest sports event in the world, FIFA felt no need to inform. Everybody was going to watch anyway, so why bother?

Ninety thousand people packed into Bernabéu for the final. This event felt bigger, deeper, better than the Olympics, where all those exotic sports emerged once every four years for a worldwide television audience. This was a monthlong tournament for one sport, the one the world knows best, loves best.

Both two-time champions marched onto the field and stood at attention for the stately anthem "Deutschlandlied" and the merry tarantella of "Il canto degli Italiani" with its more dramatic lyrics ("We are ready to die"). Then the starting teams posed for separate pregame photos, six standing, five crouching.

A large banner hung from the grandstand, proclaiming: Colombia 1986. That was not going to happen.

Italy's coach, Enzo Bearzot, jacket slung stylishly over his shoulder, pipe in his mouth, looked like a padrone about to enjoy his *aperitivo*. I had more feel for Italy, having seen them three times and West Germany none.

Gentile was back for the final but had shaved his Qaddafi mustache, perhaps reasoning that the referee in the final would not recognize him. Must be some other No. 6 whacking away at people. Gentile had new company on the back line. Giancarlo Antognoni was injured and had been replaced by eighteen-year-old Giuseppe Bergomi, the youngest player on the squad. The kid, known as Lo Zio (The Uncle) because of his calm demeanor beyond his years, hounded Rummenigge, the best player in Europe during the club season, who was playing despite the injured thigh.

Italy was so deep. Franceso Graziani injured his shoulder when hit from behind and had to come out in the seventh minute, replaced by Alessandro Altobelli.

The Italians were aggressive and confident, but it took them fifty-seven minutes to score. West Germany was called for a foul, and the Italians took a quick restart, with Marco Tardelli racing down the right side, advancing the ball into the box, where Gentile, of all people, tipped it in front of the goal, and Rossi flicked it into the goal, his sixth score in three matches after the wretched start.

Italy had its counterattack in gear. In the sixty-ninth minute, the reliable sweeper Gaetano Scirea intercepted a sloppy pass and—a true footballer—saw the opening and took off downfield without a play being sent in from the sidelines. Moving the ball back and forth with Bruno Conti, Scirea calmly flicked the ball sideways to Tardelli, who shifted and fired a left-footed shot past the keeper.

Twelve minutes later, Conti took off on another fast break, centering the ball for Altobelli, the sub, who fired a left-footed shot past the keeper. West Germany scored at the eighty-third minute, but Italy's defense locked down, and Italy had its third championship—its first in forty-four years.

Starting with my near-zero understanding of soccer, I had made an assumption that Brazil could win any time with all that artistry. I had heard passionate condemnations of the *catenaccio*, but now I had seen defenders like Scirea and Gentile break downfield to lead the charge. Now I was watching the Italians, so unloved by their own fans at the start, cavorting on the field, being greeted by King Juan Carlos of Spain. I felt I was at the center of the universe.

Some readers of the *New York Times* might say they began paying attention to soccer from the time I showed up in Spain in 1982. I never thought of myself as an evangelist, never passed myself off as an expert. Millions of fans around the world knew more about the game than I ever could, as some would remind me in caustic e-mails. Maybe because I discovered soccer relatively late in life, I saw it with fresh eyes, a fresh heart. I loved the difficulty of it, the kaleidoscopic surprises, with a growing appreciation for the history and the strategy.

One fact of life I learned that summer: a fan can be a psychological bigamist, or worse. Love the one you're with. I still considered Brazil the warm and pulsing heart of the sport. I have great respect for the young men and women who represent my own country. I enjoy dozens of soccer nations when they are on a roll. I never hesitate to criticize Italy for its thuggish moments, its flamboyant *simulazione* (faking), its failure to finish the attacks. But whenever the Azzurri take the field and the loudspeakers play the anthem, I am reminded of first love, summer of '82.

4

NOT READY FOR
PRIME TIME

TORRANCE, CALIFORNIA, 1985

It was peaceful in the funky little football stadium.

Or, as they say in the old westerns, too peaceful.

The United States was about to play Costa Rica in a vital match before the 1986 World Cup. All the Yanks needed was a *result*, as it is called in soccer—just one point from a draw—and they would be moving into the final round of qualifying.

The match was at home. Theoretically. It was also being played in virtual secrecy, as if soccer were enrolled in the witness-protection program. An hour before game time, the crowd pretty much consisted of parents, girlfriends, little kids, college students, and a few soccer buffs wearing red regalia. On the day of this crucial qualifier, people in Southern California were vastly more excited about the victory by the Los Angeles Lakers in steamy Boston Garden two nights earlier to tie the NBA Finals at one game apiece.

That series had Magic and Kareem and Bird. This qualifier had Rick Davis and Paul Caligiuri.

In its wisdom, the United States Soccer Federation had placed this match in a drab little football stadium at El Camino College, south of Los Angeles, a few miles from the Pacific. It was pretty quiet on an obscure

Friday afternoon, when suddenly, over a distant hill, came the sounds of trumpets and drums and human voices, an army on the move: a couple of thousand Costa Ricans, brandishing flags and banners, chanting fight songs, honking and shouting and blaring.

Instantly, Costa Rica became the home team, no small advantage in this sport of emotion and pressure. Most of this marching army lived within hours of Torrance and observed the normal decencies of the territory—no flying batteries, no bags of urine lobbed onto the field, very few bilingual curses and insults.

They did, however, honk horns and cheer. The official attendance for that match is listed as 11,800, and maybe it was, which proved that a few thousand Costa Ricans could outroot four times as many Americans.

The United States was still trying to catch up with most of the world. Surely, all that dribbling around pink cones and trophies for Josh and Heather in the youth leagues of America would produce the long-awaited soccer boom?

"Respect my frankness, but the Americans are not World Cup material," Roderick Warner, the coach of Trinidad and Tobago, said politely after the United States defeated his squad, 1–0, a few weeks before the Costa Rica match.

FIFA seemed to agree. As expected, Colombia had defaulted as host for 1986, and the United States put in a bid that was generally regarded as amateurish. American soccer managed to offend the haughty president of FIFA, João Havelange of Brazil, who did not bother to send an inspection team to the United States, despite the dozens of huge stadiums and arenas, and the track record of being able to fill them for major events like the Super Bowl of American football and the Final Four of college basketball (and, later, in 1984, the hugely successful Summer Olympics in Los Angeles). The United States had a reputation for throwing big sporting parties, but FIFA seemed to have scorn for its soccer federation.

On May 20, 1983, FIFA chose Mexico as the replacement for Colombia for several sound reasons. First, Mexico had competently staged the

1970 World Cup and was more of a soccer power than the United States. Also, FIFA knew it could control the preparations for 1986 by using friendly companies to upgrade the security, the hotels, the roads, the electronics. Now the U.S. team would have to play its way into the 1986 World Cup instead of getting an automatic berth as host.

To prepare for qualifying, the United States Soccer Federation had created something called Team America, stocking it with supposedly the best players with U.S. passports and basing it in Washington, D.C., as a member of the dying North American Soccer League. Once flush with twenty-four teams, the NASL was down to nine, including Team America, coached by the courtly Alkis Panagoulias.

As American as gyro or spanakopita, Panagoulias loved his adopted country, where he had played and coached in some fast ethnic leagues. He had also coached the Greek national team for a while and served in the Greek parliament while his wife sold real estate in suburban Virginia. Now he was trying to improve America's status among the soccer-playing nations.

"It was very difficult," Panagoulias would recall years later. "I first had to sell the league people and owners on the idea that the national team has to be the No. 1 team in the country. We needed their players. I was almost crying when I talked about the national team. They looked at me like I was crazy. They didn't know from the national team."

Panagoulias had a theory of how to create interest in a national team: "All you had to do was bring in the Russian team and have the Americans lose, 10–0, to them," he said. "That would have gotten some action."

His problem was that many of the best American players refused to give up their security to relocate to Team America. Some wanted to go down with the ship with the Cosmos, and others could make a few more dollars playing indoor soccer. Hardly any Americans were wanted even by the lesser pro leagues of Europe.

In 1984, the NASL went the way of the Roman Empire, and all the players had to scuffle. Panagoulias recruited an assortment of young and old players, including Rick Davis, a twenty-six-year-old midfielder with the Cosmos, and Paul Caligiuri, a nineteen-year-old student who was taking final exams at UCLA.

In the spring of 1985, the United States was trying to qualify for the 1986 World Cup via a series of elimination rounds in the regional federation known as CONCACAF—the Confederation of North, Central America and Caribbean Association Football. In the second stage, the Americans were placed in a three-team group that would send one nation into the final qualifying round. The Yanks defeated Trinidad and Tobago twice and then tied in Costa Rica. Not bad. Going into the final game at home, the United States needed only a draw with Costa Rica to advance.

Panagoulias knew that his makeshift outfit did not have the cohesion to move the ball around for ninety minutes—no *catenaccio* here—so he had them play a full-field game, to keep Costa Rica occupied on defense, and for most of the match, the Americans did fine.

But soccer turns on mistakes, and in the thirty-fifth minute, the U.S. keeper, Arnie Mausser, called to punch away a free kick, and Kevin Crow—five times the Defender of the Year in indoor soccer—backed away slightly to give Mausser space. A Costa Rican player intervened and headed the ball toward the corner, where a teammate put it in the goal. After that point, the Costa Rica players knew how to protect a lead and held on for a 1–0 victory. For the ninth straight World Cup, the United States had failed to qualify.

I still remember Rick Davis sitting in the grungy little dressing room. He was the face of American soccer, an eager little brother to the *galácticos* on the late, lamented Cosmos, but now he was seeing the bleak future in the discarded tape and orange sections near his feet.

"I don't know where we go from there," Davis said, when he could finally utter words. "There was our best chance to make it to the World Cup. We won't have another chance until 1990. Who knows where soccer in America will be by then? I do know this: unless we develop a professional league for outdoors, we won't go anyplace. We can't do it with indoor soccer. We were playing for U.S. soccer—for its reputation and recognition in our country. It's another setback. We missed a golden opportunity."

It was a sad moment, something reporters never witness at the World Cup itself because journalists are not allowed in locker rooms. I was standing there when Gregg Thompson, a defender who earned his meager living in indoor soccer, plaintively asked the fatherly Panagoulias, "When are we ever going to play a home game?"

"Never," Panagoulias said.

Thompson then expounded on being road warriors in the state of California.

"We go down there and they've got twenty-five thousand screaming fans in the stadium at six thirty a.m. for an eleven o'clock game," he said, recalling the match the previous Sunday in Costa Rica. "Here, we schedule a game in California, where there are a lot of Costa Ricans. Why not play it in St. Louis or Tampa or Portland?"

"I'm not saying that cost us the game," Thompson quickly added. "But when the game starts, the crowd does get you into the game. Look how hard it is for the visiting team to win in Boston Garden. I'm just sick of seeing it, game after game, in our own country."

In the rubble of that disaster at El Camino College, the federation learned a lesson: do not schedule qualifying matches in Spanish-speaking regions where Costa Ricans (or Hondurans, Guatemalans, Panamanians, Salvadorans, or Mexicans) can march over the hill, honking their horns.

By the mid-1980s, the imbalance in the stands was hardly the main reason that the United States was not ready. The United States was hurtling past 300 million residents, with millions of children and adults registered as players, but it had not yet produced resourceful athletes who knew how to fire on goal and toss the odd elbow when the ref wasn't looking. American men were only starting to realize they had to duck the well-meaning college programs and seek out professional programs overseas.

The Costa Rican fans vanished back over the hill. The American players went their separate ways. The 1986 World Cup would go on, next door.

5

THE KID COMES BACK

MEXICO, 1986

Lunatics hear voices from God; so do geniuses. It is rarely a good thing when national leaders or generals attribute their actions to a celestial whisper or guiding nudge from on high. What about a stumpy forward with No. 10 on his back?

The 1986 World Cup is best remembered for Diego Maradona's punched goal, which he immediately attributed to the "Hand of God." In later years, he would deliver the phrase with a knowing smirk, meaning he did what he had to do—gangster talk, well within the norm of sport or life itself.

That overt piece of cheating overshadowed what Maradona did in the same match four minutes later—a ramble through the hedgerows of the English defense, one of the great runs in the history of the sport. But we remember the blatant heist in broad daylight.

El Pibe de Oro, the Golden Kid, came into 1986 carrying the memory of being pushed around by Gentile and the Italians in Spain in 1982, and of later being waved off the field in disgrace after kicking a Brazilian player in the groin. He had been shamed in the city where he was about to play, yet he suggested that the humiliation was God's plan. What is the difference between Joan of Arc and a self-involved goal scorer?

After assisting on all three goals in Argentina's opening victory in 1986 over South Korea, which fouled him eleven times, Maradona looked ahead to the next match. "God will want me to make a goal against Italy," he proclaimed. And then he did just that.

This was his position: his parents struggled to get from the backwater to a more promising slum of Buenos Aires. "I can talk about poverty because I lived it," he told Guillermo Blanco of *El Gráfico*, the major Argentine soccer magazine, in 1982. "Because my father worked much harder than I do and earned the bare necessity so that we wouldn't starve. That is why I can say that poverty is something ugly. One wants a whole lot of things and yet one can only dream about them."

He saw his success as a gift from on high because he was privileged.

"Sure, I am," he went on. "But only because God has wanted it to be so. Because God makes me play well. That is why I always make the sign of the cross when I walk out on the pitch. I feel I would be betraying him if I didn't do that."

The goat of 1982 had scored thirty-eight goals in fifty-eight matches in his first two seasons at Barcelona, but he was often injured and squabbled with management. His gross lifestyle, in one of Barcelona's most favored hillside neighborhoods, turned off the patrons of his club. In Buenos Aires he was considered one of the *cabecitas*, an outsider. In proud Barcelona he was labeled a *Sudaca*, somebody from South America. It was not a compliment.

In 1984, Barça unloaded him to Napoli for an estimated $12 million—the highest transfer price ever, at the time—and he found a psychological home in that tough old city with strains from Sicily and Greece and goodness knows where else.

Napoli, which had never won the championship, soon jumped in attendance from twelfth place to eighth and then to third. "More important, Maradona brought a great spirit that drives his teammates," said Corrado Ferlaino, the club owner at the time. "He always wants to win. A great actor is never afraid. That is what makes great theater."

Given his mixed roots in rural Argentina, Maradona was openly labeled a *terrone* in Italy, a word that means "hillbilly" or "redneck." That stigma fit his outsider attitude, in a city whose urban symbol was the *scugnizzo*, the bad boy who smokes and loiters and looks for his main chance. The *scugnizzi* of Naples walked through traffic, sold Marlboro cigarettes relabeled as Maradona brand, two for the price of one. When a Maradona associate inquired about perhaps being paid for the use of that golden name, he was told this was how it went down in Naples, home of the Camorra, the regional version of the Mafia. The suggestion was: Maradona should be proud of this tribute to him.

In return, Diego Armando got to indulge his impulses and appetites in Naples. Now he was back for another World Cup.

The World Cup almost did not take place in Mexico. On September 19, 1985, an 8.0 earthquake struck Mexico City, which is essentially built in the basin of the former Lake Texcoco. Aztecs once glided in canoes where their ancestors now travel in the thick, oily air of auto traffic, and the ground is unstable. An estimated ten thousand people died and another thirty thousand were left homeless, and for a time there was the question whether it was fair to expect this stricken region to hold the World Cup. However, by the spring of 1986, with rubble visible all over the sprawling city, Mexico was proudly displaying the slogan *Estamos Preparados*—We Are Prepared.

The World Cup offers a glimpse into the tortured soul of the host nation. I had a sense of that in 1982, when La Selección was eliminated. Sometimes, the home team has an edge because of familiar surroundings and time zones and language and friendly fans. Through the first nineteen World Cups, the host team has won six times, with England's victory in 1966 probably the most obvious home-nation advantage. Mexico had played in eight of the first twelve World Cups, with a rather mediocre record—three victories, four draws, seventeen losses, reaching the quarterfinals only as the host team in 1970.

Known as El Tri from its tricolored flag, the Mexican team was depending on Hugo Sánchez, the first Mexican to make it big in Europe. In the 1985–86 season, Sánchez had scored twenty-two goals for Real

Madrid, earning a reported $1 million salary, and was featured in a soft-drink commercial like one in the United States in which a boy offered a bottle of Coca-Cola to a dejected football player, "Mean Joe" Greene.

A few days before the opening match, I walked over to the National Museum of Anthropology, one of the great places in the world, to see an exhibit about pre-Columbian ball games, in which villages or tribes tried to toss a ball through a hoop, high above the ground. The Aztecs called it *tlachtli*, the Maya called it *pokyah*, the Zapotecs called it *taladzi*. Sometimes the winning captain was sacrificed, sometimes the losing captain. Tough crowd, the ancestors of the 110,000 fans in Azteca Stadium.

At the museum, a waitress was telling a few Brazilian visitors about her fond memories of the 1970 World Cup finals, when Pelé scored the first goal and Brazil beat Italy, 4–1, for the championship. Mexicans greeted Brazilians as if they themselves had played in that final; Brazilians bring that out in people.

Now Mexico was host again. I had been to the country four or five times, including when I covered the first trip of Pope John Paul II in 1979. I love Mexico's history, with Christianity thinly layered above the pre-Columbian culture, flavored by immigration from many parts of the world. While modern cars move along the Reforma, women squat on the side of the road making tortillas the way women did before Cortés. I was staying in the Polanco district, where streets are named for philosophers and playwrights—Boulevard Miguel de Cervantes, Calle Moliere, even Avenida Presidente Masaryk, after the first president of Czechoslovakia.

Mexico's international feel extended to its head coach, Bora Milutinović, a Serb who had played and coached all over the world and had married a Mexican woman, whom he charmingly called Pancho. With his mop of hair that made him resemble the Fifth Beatle, Bora called everybody "my friend" in five or six different languages.

Estamos preparados. Very young-looking soldiers with large automatic weapons patrolled the gates and barbed-wire fences around Azteca for the opening match, between the defending champion, Italy, and Bulgaria. The mood was bristling inside, too. When President Miguel de la Madrid was introduced, some spectators began whistling. In my hometown of New York, politicians are sometimes heckled when they show up at a ball game, but this reception sounded downright venomous. The *Times*' local bureau manager, sitting next to me, was aghast. "We never do that," she said.

Shades of the first round in 1982: Italy scored, then surrendered a goal in the eighty-fifth minute and drew with Bulgaria, 1–1.

"There is a big difference between sea level and here," Gaetano Scirea, the great Italian sweeper, said afterward.

The air was not only thin; it was polluted, particularly in the midday heat. FIFA had scheduled matches at noon and 4:00 p.m. for the benefit of European television seven time zones or more to the east. The rarefied air at 7,347 feet put pressure on human lungs and made the balls veer, leading to long-range goals.

"You cannot expect long running or long passing," said Enzo Bearzot, the Italian coach, who was back for another term. "You cannot expect the players to cover so much space, so we play with shorter passes. The Brazilians are good at it, but of course their players are better."

How to prepare for the thin air? Some teams had trained at high altitude before coming to Mexico. Other people just showed up, cold turkey, like me. I went jogging in Chapultepec Park immediately, just to show the bad air who was boss. Not a good move, as I later realized.

The Mexican players, theoretically acclimated to the thin, gritty air, beat Belgium, 2–1, on the fourth day of competition, with the help of a goal by Sánchez, who then kicked the ball into the stands to celebrate and was given a yellow card.

Azteca was rocking again for El Tri four days later against Paraguay, at least until Sánchez was given another yellow card in the seventy-fifth minute, meaning he would miss the third game. Then Julio César Romero, formerly of the defunct Cosmos, scored a tying goal for Paraguay in the eighty-fifth minute.

Still, there was a chance for Sánchez to win this match before he began his one-game suspension. In the final minute, he was jostled by a defender and took a histrionic tumble, convincing referee George Courtney of England that such misery must be compensated.

The setting was straight out of the classic American baseball poem,

"Casey at the Bat," as the pride of Mexico stepped up with the hopes of the nation upon him. He delivered a fairly soft kick to his left but the Paraguayan keeper, Roberto Fernández, lunged to his right and flicked the ball away. Mighty Sánchez had struck out, and Mexico had to settle for a 1–1 draw.

Afterward, Fernández said: "I have seen movies of Sánchez, and I have noticed that he always kicks to his left. I was lucky." Technology was making its mark.

As we left the stadium, Mexicans were packing the overpasses on the freeway, waving banners, but the mood seemed to have been cut in half by the miss by Sánchez, as well as his having to sit out the third match.

The absence of Sánchez turned out not to matter, as Mexico beat Iraq, 1–0. Sánchez was back for the round of 16 against Bulgaria—again in Azteca because the organizers wanted to fill the place whenever possible. Mexico triumphed, 2–0, to set up a quarterfinal against West Germany in Monterrey, a vastly higher level of opponent, a fact of life as any World Cup progresses.

The fans bustled when a West German player was sent off in the sixty-fifth minute and again in the sixty-ninth when Milutinović sent in the new national favorite, Francisco Javier Cruz, who was known as Abuelo—Grandpa—for his elderly appearance. Abuelo quickly plopped in a goal, only to have it annulled by an offside call. After 120 scoreless minutes, the game went to a shoot-out. Toni Schumacher stopped the second and third Mexican kicks, with Sánchez never getting to shoot. The party mood was over.

The debacle in California in 1985 meant that once again there was no American team to follow in the 1986 World Cup. That meant I could choose matches all over Mexico.

On June 2, I drove to Toluca with Sue Mott, a colleague from England, to interview the team from Iraq. It was the Muslim holy month of Ramadan, but the players were excused from fasting during the day in order to maintain their strength. We were introduced to Raad Hammoudi, a keeper who played for the Police Sport Club in the national amateur league. He quickly informed us he was not a police officer but rather owned a clothing factory employing nearly one hundred people.

Iraq had been at war with Iran for six years, and Hammoudi told us in excellent English that the team had no problem preparing: "We say, 'The war is on the border, it is far from Baghdad, and we are sportsmen, so we must play football.' We go to the hospitals and meet with the soldiers."

Hammoudi gave us souvenirs—keychains with the likeness of their leader, a bloke named Saddam Hussein. I often wonder what I did with mine.

The next day, I flew up to Monterrey on hooligan patrol. I had not come across English fans in 1982 because they were frolicking in distant corners of Spain, but I was well aware that England was considered—considered itself—the headwater of the world's great sport. (Never mind the ball games played by pre-Columbian people across this very land.)

The English had been playing soccer in leagues since the late nineteenth century, but there were traces of it going back centuries to the pastime of kicking a head or two from the local cemetery on Shrove Tuesday. Historians have recently determined that a young prince apparently took part in the ruffian's sport in the early sixteenth century and may have owned the first handmade soccer shoes with cleats. Henry VIII, the first footballer with traction, may have been the spiritual ancestor to such worthies as Vinnie Jones, the Wimbledon defender known for grabbing opponents' testicles; John Terry, bar brawler and cheap-shot artist; and Wayne Rooney, gambler and carouser.

English fans were justifiably proud of other parts of the patrimony, including the codification of the sport and its exportation by sailors and settlers to South America, where teams named Newell's Old Boys and Racing Club and Arsenal de Sarandí are all staples of the Argentine first division to this day.

But by 1986, English crowds were synonymous with mayhem and death. On May 11, 1985, a fire swept through the ancient stadium at Bradford City, killing fifty-six fans. Eighteen days later, fans of Juventus and Liverpool were caught in a ghastly crush before the finals of the European Cup in Heysel Stadium in Brussels, and thirty-nine fans, mostly from Juventus, were killed and hundreds were injured. After that, authorities belatedly began upgrading stadiums, and Interpol and other law agencies kept known hooligans from traveling.

Mexico was prepared. The newspaper *El Sol* ran a front-page headline: "Los Animales Atacan"—no translation needed—but many residents treated the visitors politely, even inviting a few of them home for a roast goat dinner. According to the newspapers, some teenaged girls found English fans rather cute. Some of the visitors took off their shirts and fried their pale skins—and a few even took off their pants, for which they were fined. Local authorities, as good hosts, offered guided tours of jails where they planned to stash troublemakers; after that, the lads cut down on extravagances.

On the day I went to see England play in Monterrey, their opponent was a distracted Portugal team. The Portuguese players had been threatening to strike over an alleged failure to pay their salaries or bonuses, which has been known to happen at the World Cup. The Portuguese seemed to be on a labor slowdown early in the match, ceding a goal to England, but rallied for a 1–1 draw.

On June 5, I drove out to Puebla de los Angeles, past the twin volcanoes Popocatépetl and Iztaccíhuatl, which loom over the main highway in the rugged area known as Paseo de Cortés. Awaiting me were a couple of volcanic teams—Italy and Argentina, two combatants in that classic Group of Death four years earlier. At a press conference at the Italian hotel, I spotted huge cartons of foodstuffs lined up in the hallways. "Pasta, a little spaghetti. Cheese, Parmesan. Olive oil, naturally. And mineral water. You can't do without that," said the gregarious Enzo Bearzot. The Italians also brought a cook. No wine? Actually, Signor Bearzot insisted, his players did not care for wine or beer.

Diego Maradona, who had said that God planned a goal for him against Italy, was marked on this day by Salvatore Bagni, a teammate of his at Napoli. Bagni did not kick Maradona the way Claudio Gentile had done four years earlier, but Bagni did keep one hand on his pal at all times—shirt, shorts, hair, whatever, just to keep him close. Maradona was now four years older and did not whine about the tactics. Undoubtedly, this was because he knew what heroics his maker had in store for him.

Italy took a lead on a penalty kick in the seventh minute, after the ref called a very marginal hand ball against Argentina.

In the thirty-fourth minute, Maradona dribbled past his buddy Bagni and was alertly picked up by Scirea, who forced Maradona far to the left, to an almost impossible angle. Maradona somehow pushed off on his right leg and shot with his left foot at almost a right angle, past Scirea and the keeper, Giovanni Galli, to tie the match.

After the match ended at 1–1, I watched Maradona hugging the Italian players, including Bagni; Bruno Conti, the modest-sized winger from Roma; and Scirea, who had hounded him so successfully for all but one split second. The affection was obvious. I was still learning that nasty club matches created a guild-member loyalty when players met after World Cup matches, exchanging sweaty jerseys on the field.

(I was later glad I observed Scirea as he marked Maradona; Scirea would die in an auto accident in Poland three years later while scouting for Juventus. His name still evokes sadness among Italian fans.)

Back in Mexico City, I arranged an interview with David Socha, a referee from Ludlow, Massachusetts, and the only Yank in uniform in Mexico. FIFA had decreed 1986 as "The Year of the Referee," whatever that meant. The referee "acts simultaneously as prosecutor, judge, and executor," said the general secretary of FIFA, a gent named Joseph S. Blatter. I was thinking, the last thing FIFA should want was for the referees to be noticed.

Socha had been working the line at the Brazil-Spain match when a Spanish volley hit the underside of the crossbar and bounced straight down near the goal line—very similar to the most notorious crossbar decision in World Cup history, the Geoff Hurst shot that was ruled a goal in the 1966 finals, helping England beat West Germany.

The goal-line call is virtually impossible for the human eye. So, according to eye specialists, is offside, which involves calibrating three separate moving objects at once. In the Brazil-Spain match, the referee, Christopher Bambridge of Australia, had to make a call on the spot, from one microsecond of "seeing" the ball hit on or near the line, and he signaled the teams to play on, as the Spanish players raged at him. But FIFA had no technology available to judge the geometric lines of the goal area, and the referee's call stood. And for emphasis, the English broadcaster noted, "David Socha from the United States kept his flag down." Brazil went on to win, 1–0, on a tap-in header by Sócrates.

A few days after the match, I met Socha at the hotel where many of the thirty-six referees were housed. If he was smarting over the publicity from the non-call against Spain, he did not show it. He told me he could not speak about specific instances but could talk about himself—a former player, briefly in England, a veteran of various ethnic leagues in America. At age forty-seven, Socha worked in a tavern when not officiating.

"I am the biggest unknown commodity in the U.S.," Socha told me. He had worked the line in the Italy-Poland semifinal in Barcelona in 1982 and had also worked a UNICEF all-star game in New Jersey that same year. "I looked around me and I saw Falcão and Sócrates and Zico, and I told the players, 'Just play,'" he recalled. "I am such a big admirer of Franz Beckenbauer. I was standing five yards from him watching him do things with his toe that I could not do with my hands."

I told him I hoped nobody would notice his work for the rest of this tournament. Some of his colleagues would not be so lucky.

My wife flew down, and we drove out to Querétaro to see the last match in the 1986 Group of Death, which included Uruguay, Scotland, West Germany, and Denmark. This city was an appropriate setting for the Group of Death, inasmuch as it is the home of La Corregidora, the heroine in the struggle for independence of 1810, and also the site where the Austrian puppet king, Maximilian, was executed in 1867.

The hotel reeked of cigarettes and beer, courtesy of the Danish and German reporters and fans. Corregidora Stadium was not filled, so officials allowed fans to filter down to the front rows, which ensured that their light hair and red-and-white painted faces would show up on international television.

The Danish fans, celebrating their nation's first World Cup appearance, were called *roligans*, a pun blending *rolig*, the Danish word for "calm," and "hooligans," and they were fun to be around—happy tourists, knowledgeable fans. They were even happier when Denmark beat West Germany, 2–0, to lock up first place in their group. However, West Germany managed to do collateral damage late in the match when Lothar Matthäus took a tumble near Denmark's Frank Arnesen, causing the referee to flash a yellow card that would make Arnesen ineligible for the next match. Matthäus promptly jumped up and hugged Arnesen as he left the field in distress. (Similar overacting by a Croatian player would cost France a player for the 1998 final. It's a bit late to console a dupe when you have caused him to be banned from the next match.)

On June 17, I was back in Mexico City, this time at Olympic Stadium, for France against Italy. Michel Platini, voted the best player in Europe in 1983, 1984, and 1985, scored one goal in the fifteenth minute and set up another in the fifty-eighth minute as France dismissed the defending champions, 2–0.

I was watching on television later that day as West Germany was awarded a free kick during a scoreless draw in the eighty-eighth minute against Morocco. Matthäus, aware that only two Moroccans were lined up on the right side of the wall, blasted a vicious right-footed ground shot with heavy topspin that curled back into the right corner of the goal. (A decade later, Matthäus would materialize in Major League Soccer, seeking, like many other aging European stars, the money and relative anonymity of America, like a paid luxury senior hostel trip. I introduced myself to him and said, "Monterrey—1986—free kick." He flashed his toothy warrior smile and said, "I will remember you.")

I was dragging—not the classic *turista* but rather, according to my self-diagnosis, a result of having gone out for a run in Chapultepec Park upon arriving. The problem was not so much the thin air—I was used to that from visits to Denver and other high locations—but rather the bad particles I had dragged deep into my lungs. I came to think of Mexicans as a superior race, evolved in a post-oxygen age.

On June 18, I watched England beat Paraguay, 3–0, at Azteca—another huge crowd, another hot afternoon, because of European television demands. After my day's work, I came back to the hotel room and felt the air-conditioning recycling the same bad air. My wife and I were having a great time seeing the country and visiting friends; she made sure I had fresh food and fluids, but still I was wearing down.

Plus, I was very much aware of having signed on for a trip to Moscow for Ted Turner's Goodwill Games, which started on July 5. I knew that if I stayed until the end of the World Cup, on June 29, I would have only a few days' turnaround in New York. My boss and friend, Joe Vecchione, told me to come home and rest up for Moscow. Alex Yannis, the *Times'* soccer writer, was in Mexico with a credential and could handle it by himself. (Soccer people were always asking me, "Where is Alex?" I knew my place.)

I hated to leave a country I love, an event I love. My wife said I looked better as soon as the air-conditioning started on the plane. My doctor checked me out at home—verdict: nothing wrong except exhaustion— and I wrote about the rest of the World Cup from New York.

It was strange to suddenly see this event through the filter of television. I always want to see the entire field—who is coming from where? what are the options for the player with the ball?—but the control room often calls for a close-up of one player. Plus, for American audiences, announcers yammer far too much about potential goals ("the U.S. would sure love to score by halftime") as if a baseball home-run derby were about to break out. Still, I was enjoying sea level and air-conditioning, family and friends.

In Guadalajara, France met Brazil in a quarterfinal that could have been a final. The two artistic teams played a 1–1 draw, and Sócrates was stopped early in the shoot-out, which enabled France to win on penalty kicks. Once again, Brazil would not win the World Cup.

Spain, after beating the rollicking Denmark team, 5–1, in the round of 16, added to its reputation for inconsistency by losing to Belgium in its quarterfinal, also on penalty kicks. Few people outside Spain and Belgium paid attention; this was the day the Hand of God appeared in the sky.

. . .

Diego Armando Maradona had come into the World Cup with a pack of troubles, most of them personal. While playing for Napoli, he had become involved with a woman who was now expecting a son. His longtime Argentine companion, Claudia Villafañe, was pregnant with a daughter. Some athletes thrive under chaos.

England and Argentina, the two combatants in the 1982 Malvinas/ Falklands war, collided in the quarterfinals at Azteca, with newspapers in both nations reviving the tensions. Before the match, John McDermott, the great soccer photographer, watched the two teams lining up side by side, making even less eye contact than usual. Then John noticed Peter Shilton, the English keeper and captain, reaching out his hand to Maradona, the Argentine captain. The gesture was clear: we are footballers, and this is not war. Maradona totally understood Shilton's gesture and shook his hand—a lovely moment, unfortunately hidden from the crowd, McDermott recalled.

In the ninth minute, playing the role of Claudio Gentile in this performance, Terry Fenwick hammered Maradona. The Tunisian referee, Ali Bennaceur (alternatively listed as Ali Bin Nasser) could easily have shown Fenwick a red card but instead displayed a yellow. In the Year of the Referee, FIFA had an official from Tunisia, not exactly a stronghold of the sport, working with line officials from Costa Rica and Bulgaria, in a quarterfinal with overtones of a territorial war. The officials may have graded out well for fitness, had knowledge of the rules, brushed their teeth, and said "yes, sir" to FIFA, but they were not necessarily up to the aggression and gamesmanship that this match would produce.

This is a fact of sports—the great players are often ahead of the officials sent out to monitor them. That was partially what drove John McEnroe mad; he could see the lines better than the official in the chair.

Later in the first half, Fenwick creamed Maradona with a straight arm. Perhaps the ref reasoned that Fenwick already had a yellow, and, what the heck, it was almost halftime, so why toss the bloke out? As a result, England still had a full formation in the fifty-first minute as Maradona made a quick foray toward the goal. Steve Hodge got his foot on the ball and squibbed it into the air. Shilton, eight inches taller than Maradona, came out to punch the ball away, as he had done thousands of times in his career. Maradona kept running and leaped toward the ball, somehow getting higher than Shilton. He elevated his left fist above his head, as if imitating the Statue of Liberty holding a torch. Watching on the tube back home, I could see the fist raised, could see the ball bounce into the goal, could see Maradona wheel away, jubilantly, trying to sell the goal to the official and the crowd. The broadcaster quickly said it looked like a handball. The Argentines flocked after Maradona to celebrate. And the referee went for it.

In this Year of the Referee, nobody from FIFA had sensitized the two sideline officials that they were also part of this operation. There was no electronic communication from the fourth official between the two benches or anybody else to tell the ref to hold a consultation before resuming play.

Instead, Maradona had heard his personalized will of God and made the instant calibration that it was worth a try—a red card for cheating versus a goal during a scoreless draw. The replay on television immediately confirmed that Maradona had punched it home. Everybody in the stadium knew he had, except Ali Bennaceur and his two assistants.

Play resumed, with the English probably still in shock from the blatant cheating and referee error. Then Maradona performed one of the greatest scoring romps ever seen in his sport. He received the ball near midfield, with Hodge and Peter Beardsley at his flanks. As Maradona took off, one broadcaster likened him to "a little eel."

Maradona wriggled onward, flicking the ball back and forth between his feet, as the defenders planted their own feet in the turf. He outraced Peter Reid, left Gary Stevens behind, and cut inside, leaving Terry Butcher with his back to Maradona, his right leg kicking backward in a vain attempt to slow Maradona down. Just outside the box, Fenwick seemed close enough to jostle Maradona, but, playing with a yellow card, Fenwick avoided contact, or maybe Maradona avoided him.

Now it was between Maradona and Shilton, the two pals from the pregame handshake. Shilton knew how to cut off angles, but he had never done it against Diego Maradona at the absolute peak of his career. Maradona shifted his weight, moved the ball from right foot to left foot, and slipped it past Shilton, so softly, so gently. The announcer shouted. We all shouted, even in my den, so far away.

Brian Glanville, the great chronicler of British sport, wrote that the goal was "so unusual, almost romantic, that it might have been scored by some schoolboy hero, or some remote Corinthian, from the days when dribbling was the vogue. It hardly belonged to so apparently rational and rationalized era as ours, to a period in football when the dribble seemed almost as extinct as the pterodactyl."

Years later, when he had time to understand what he had done, Maradona told an interviewer: "When I caught the ball towards the right and saw that Peter Reid couldn't catch me, I felt a very big urge to go on running with the ball. I seemed to be able to leave everyone behind."

Given Maradona's closeness with his creator, he no doubt had a sense of redemption. He had sinned and then sought absolution with the most developed part of his being—that is to say, his feet.

Later in the match, Terry Butcher was close enough to Maradona on the field to ask if he had indeed punched the ball into the goal. Maradona spoke just enough English to understand the question.

"He just smiled and pointed to his head," Butcher reported.

England scored late, and Argentina hung on for a 2–1 victory, followed by a worldwide dialogue about the border between gamesmanship and cheating. I normally absolve athletes who try to con the officials—it's part of the game—but Maradona's caper was so gross that I call it cheating.

Maradona seemed quite proud of himself. In the documentary of that World Cup, there is footage of him in the Argentina locker room, wearing only shorts and a smirk, pumping his left fist. His teammates all cheer.

In years to come, Maradona admitted he punched the ball because it was there. He would flash a childlike smile, like a boy caught stealing a cookie from his family pantry.

"This is something that happens," he told one interviewer.

Argentina then beat Belgium, 2–0, in the semifinal, with Maradona scoring both goals. Kinesiologists could still study films of his goals in this tournament—his low center of gravity, his ability to make ninety-degree turns in heavy traffic and somehow get power on his shot with the outside of his foot. Gravitational scientists could study the way he faked Eric Gerets of Belgium into a suicidal pirouette.

The other semifinal that day was between West Germany and France, a replay of the 1982 semifinal, the game of the *once tontos*. An hour before the match, the two aging lions, Karl-Heinz Rummenigge and Michel Platini, were chatting on the green lawn of Guadalajara. How did they communicate? In their common language, Italian. Platini was a fixture with Juventus of Turin and Rummenigge was playing for Internazionale of Milan. The Germans broke no jaws this time but scored a goal in each half to reach the final again.

In the final, Maradona was marked by Matthäus, one great offensive force trying to nullify another. Maradona did not score, but he did set up two goals early before Rummenigge and Rudi Völler tied the match. In the eighty-fourth minute, Maradona used an extra gear, swiveling past a defender and bursting toward the left corner, letting loose a left-footed parabola past Toni Schumacher, directly to the moving head of Jorge Burruchaga, who put it into the goal. Four years after his failure, Maradona had brought the World Cup back to Argentina.

· · · · 6 · · · ·

THE SWEETEST FANS

PORT OF SPAIN, TRINIDAD, 1989

After watching the pleasant little army of Costa Ricans march over the hill in 1985, I thought I had encountered the true passion of World Cup qualifying.

You haven't seen anything, people advised me. The atmosphere is far more volatile on the road, in nasty little corners of the Americas, where fans toss missiles and insults. Visiting players told me of being serenaded by horns—entire marching bands—outside their hotel windows in the middle of the night. Funny how fans always knew where the U.S. team was billeted. And distorted officiating on the road was legendary.

In November 1989, the Americans were again trying to get into the World Cup, which would be held in Italy in 1990. Going into their final qualifying match at Trinidad and Tobago, the United States had nine points and a goal differential of two while T&T had nine points and a goal differential of three. The Americans had to win to go to Italy.

The people of Port of Spain, a mix of black and white and Indian, were anticipating the first finals ever for the Soca Warriors (named after a form of Trinidadian music). When I wandered around downtown, people said hello. This did not seem like the kind of regional road match that had been described to me.

The fans had no idea what was about to come down. The secretary of the T&T federation, the highly entrepreneurial Jack Warner, had taken it upon himself to print more than 45,000 tickets.

The problem was, the National Stadium held only 28,500 fans. What was the sense of being a big man in FIFA if Warner could not print extra tickets?

The American team was staying in an upscale hotel behind strong gates, high on a hill. Most national teams, I was coming to understand, were essentially all-star aggregations, called together for periodic training and matches. When I got there, the players were enjoying table tennis and eating together in the training room, rekindling team camaraderie between workouts.

Only two starters were holdovers from the squad that had lost to Costa Rica four years earlier—Mike Windischmann, from the Queens neighborhood near Metropolitan Oval, and Paul Caligiuri, the UCLA player who had gone to West Germany to improve his game.

Caligiuri had tried to play for Hamburger SV but was lent to SV Meppen in the second division. The West German league, the Bundesliga, was a harsh Darwinian experience of practicing in the wintry sleet, on rock-hard fields, with desperate teammates trying to take each other out in a midweek scrimmage, just to impress the stoic coach and possibly earn a uniform on the weekend.

At the U.S. media sessions in Trinidad, Caligiuri told reporters that he and his countrymen were facing "the biggest game of our lives."

In the qualifying rounds, the United States had played in Kingston, Jamaica; St. Louis; San José, Costa Rica; St. Louis again; Torrance, California; New Britain, Connecticut; Tegucigalpa, Honduras; Guatemala City; and St. Louis a third time. (Costa Rica had already qualified, and Mexico was banned this time after being caught using overage players in a youth tournament.)

European clubs are not always happy to release players for the long trek across the ocean to play for their national teams; the United States federation had virtually no power in world soccer and sometimes had to rely on goodwill and begging to assemble its team. Caligiuri had managed to play only one qualifier in this sequence. Maybe it was to his advantage that he had toughened himself all season in that hard proving ground of the Bundesliga.

Caligiuri's roommate in Trinidad was Tony Meola, the new first-string goalkeeper. Twenty years old, playing for the University of Virginia and a coach named Bruce Arena, Meola was still an amateur, paid a small stipend from the federation, but he carried himself with a swagger.

Meola was a three-sport star from the soccer hotbed of Kearny, New Jersey, just across the Hudson River from Manhattan. His father, a barber from Italy, had encouraged him to play the sport of their culture. The son had seen Pelé and the Cosmos at Giants Stadium, which held a Kearny Day once a season. At Kearny High, he played soccer in the fall, often scoring a goal or two before switching to keeper to protect the lead. At six feet, one inch, he also played center in basketball. And in baseball he moved between catcher and center field and was projected as a selection in the first few rounds of the amateur draft. But Meola sent a message to the baseball scouts: Don't bother drafting me; I am a soccer player.

He seemed like a familiar movie character to me—young Sinatra or young De Niro or young Travolta, playing the cocky kid from Noo Yawk. (Or, in his case, Jersey.)

"The night before the game, Paul Caligiuri and I were in our room," Meola said later to the press. "I was on the bed and he was laying on the floor. He says, 'How's this for a headline: "Caligiuri Gets Goal; Meola Gets Shutout"?' He really did say that. I was laughing."

After a day around Meola, I was convinced he would not give up a goal against T&T, even if they played all week. My only question was whether the United States could score one, on the road.

The U.S. squad had two other talented players from Kearny—Tab Ramos, born in Uruguay, and John Harkes, born in America to two Scottish immigrants. In four years, the talent level on the American squad had increased.

The huge crowd was unaware that Jack Warner had sold extra tickets. People were surging toward the stadium, which was no joke, since 96 people had been crushed to death and another 750 or so injured in Shef-field, England, back in April. All it took was one panic toward a closed gate and people could be killed. The American reporters did not know this as we arrived in a team caravan, but some fans were fainting and others were cursing Jack Warner. But most remained in a good mood, and did not take out their anger on the visitors, moving aside when the U.S. bus arrived.

"We arrived in two little vans and walked right through the crowd," Caligiuri would recall years later.

At Azteca, experienced reporters told me, the fans would have been rocking the bus to make the players seasick. Here, people parted and smiled and wished the Americans good luck.

The United States started the match with the late-November sun at its back, shining in the T&T keeper's eyes. The players knew the glare would be worse for Meola in the second half. In the thirty-first minute, Tab Ramos chipped a sideways pass to Caligiuri, who was perhaps forty yards from the goal. Caligiuri deftly slid past one defender and advanced the ball to about twenty-five yards from the goal.

Those grim practices in Germany had toughened him up. He could not afford a novice's hesitation—"Gee, maybe I'd better not. What if Coach gets mad"—that seems to hinder American players. He let fly, with his left foot, the ball veering into the right corner, away from the keeper's lunge.

Looking back on the video, the shot is not a Matthäus cannonball or a David Beckham missile but more of a parabola that stunned the T&T keeper. There is no denying that Caligiuri's shot came out of the after-noon sun, but that is part of the game, too. "We knew we needed a shot," Caligiuri would tell reporters later. "I knew I had the space. You have to take what they give you."

The roommates did it: Caligiuri gave them a lead, and Meola held on during a taut second half. The United States was going to the World Cup for the first time in forty years. Many of the reporters in the press sec-tion realized the victory was also taking them to Italy, but we did not cheer, because of our professional code and also out of respect for the demoralized Trinidadians.

Then came one of the most touching displays of sportsmanship I have ever seen. As several dozen reporters made our way through the tight crowd toward the locker-room area, the fans parted and congratulated us. Kind faces turned to us, and people said, "Nice game," and some people shook our hands. We tried to say that we didn't do anything; it was the players. We are neutral. We just report. Some of that was a straight-faced lie, of course, but the code forbade us from any sign of chauvinistic joy.

Americans who have never been to a soccer match often make jokes about hooligans; they should have been there that afternoon in Port of Spain. The fans had been ripped off by their own federation head, were jammed together in dangerous circumstances, and had witnessed a goal that would haunt Trinidadians for sixteen years. Their hearts were broken, yet they treated us with respect as the Americans left in the same two flimsy vans, unmolested.

"I've played in Latin America and the Caribbean, where they throw rocks at you, the military police have to stop them from rocking your bus," Caligiuri continued. "Never, ever, did you hear people congratulate you the way people did in Trinidad. The guys started giving them paraphernalia—our shin guards, our headbands, anything. We appreciated it so much. Normally, you'd be ducking down in your seat."

When confronted later over the surplus tickets, Warner offered explanations, none of them accepted by his countrymen, who knew him best. Warner felt the heat and decided to give up his post as secretary of the T&T association since quite clearly a man who could print extra tickets and endanger thousands was meant for better things. In 1990, he became president of the CONCACAF regional federation, strengthening his power within FIFA. He was a big man.

Years later, the coach of T&T at the time, Gally Cummings, who had played for the early Cosmos, would claim that Warner had asked him not to say that the game was oversold. Cummings said he declined. "The place was packed like sardines," he said. "If we had had an emergency, a lot of people would have died." Soon Cummings was fired, and his coaching career was hampered in the Caribbean as long as Warner was in power.

At the end of 1989, T&T was awarded the FIFA Fair Play Award. As far as I was concerned, the fans could have won it for the entire century.

7

MARKING MARADONA

ITALY, 1990

In the 1980s, the best league in the world materialized on my television. Through the electronic snow of the UHF antenna, I could make out the *bianconeri* of Juventus, the *viola* of Fiorentina, the *rossoneri* of AC Milan, every Sunday morning.

I got to know the starters and subs on most of the teams in Italy's Serie A, I could recognize their playing style even without seeing their numbers, and I could second-guess the coaches' lineups the way I criticized the managers of the Mets and the Yankees.

Sometimes I saw amazing calls go the way of Juventus or other top teams in the eighty-ninth minute—offside, fouls, penalty kicks out of nowhere. I would not understand the officiating until 2006, when the power structure of the league was implicated in an influence-peddling scandal. Back then, strange calls were a Sunday-morning mystery on my wiggly television screen.

On Monday morning, I would rush out and buy *La Gazzetta dello Sport*, the pink broadsheet daily sports paper, which is widely distributed in the States, with its voluminous stories and statistics and diagrams of the goals. I could not read Dante or Calvino, but with my dictionary by my side, I began to get a feel for the language of *calcio—simulazione, polemiche, fuorigioco.*

I also came to understand that the highly regional nation known as Italy would unite for the national team, the Azzurri, as for nothing else. I was also getting a glimmer that powerful clubs like Juventus and AC Milan and Inter Milan were more cohesive (and possibly more talented) than the national team. The rivalries in the Italian league were ancient and deep. In the late '80s, the vast majority of players in Serie A was still Italian; players in gaudy uniforms marched onto the field like the Montagues and the Capulets colliding in the marketplace of Verona in the glorious Franco Zeffirelli film version of *Romeo and Juliet.* The intracity intrigue known as *il derby* reminded me of baseball in my childhood—my Brooklyn Dodgers and those New York Giants, who used to play twenty-two times a season and remain my model for ancient resentments. But Italy's rivalries went back centuries.

When southern teams traveled north to play Juventus in Turin or Sampdoria in Genoa, there were signs in the stands saying, *Benvenuto a l'Italia*—Welcome to Italy. This was close to racism. In most of those years, Sicily did not have a team in Serie A, so the southern outsider was upstart Napoli, with its imported instigator, Diego Armando Maradona.

Not quite thirty, he had run out of favor even in Naples, a city that values rough-cut individualists. After scoring the most notorious and perhaps the most artistic goals in World Cup history, Maradona had led Napoli to a championship—the *scudetto*—in 1986–87 and was on his way to a second in 1989–90, while making $3 million in salary and maybe triple that from endorsements. Sometimes he would fly to Japan in midweek to promote an account rather than practice with the team.

In the last match of the 1988–89 season, Maradona signaled to be replaced after only seventeen minutes, and the fans jeered him. "The Entire City Is Against Him," one Naples paper proclaimed, and Maradona asked to be transferred to another city. His manager, Guillermo Coppola—a flamboyant character in his own right—said the club was afraid to move him because the Camorra wanted him to stay in Naples due to the gambling he generated.

After another very public affair, he decided to marry his childhood sweetheart, Claudia Villafañe, because their older daughter, Dalma, "asked me to show her our wedding album." For the wedding in Buenos Aires, in the middle of the Italian season, Maradona stuffed himself into a tuxedo, looking like the figure atop a rococo wedding cake, and threw a reception for 1,500 of his closest friends, an orgy of bad taste in the amusement area Luna Park. The highlight of the reception, which lasted from 11:00 p.m. to 8:00 a.m., was Maradona punching a photographer in the nose. Later, there were allegations by Italian journalists that cocaine had been distributed in open bowls at the reception, but Maradona's accountant said they were bowls of sugar set out at each table.

With the United States taking part in the World Cup for the first time since 1950, the *New York Times* ratcheted up its interest in soccer, and I was asked to write a magazine article about Maradona, who proved to be as elusive in real life as he was skittering through the English defense.

I began by making contact with the multinational sponsors who paid fortunes for him to endorse their goods, but one sympathetic official said, "We have trouble getting him to appear for his promotions."

Somebody slipped me Maradona's home phone number in Naples. I dialed the number, and in my very modest Italian I explained my mission. A male voice at the other end immediately switched to a form of Spanish. All right. I switched to my limited Spanish. The man at the other end shifted back to Italian. He seemed to understand my message—I was a *New York Times* reporter, looking to interview Maradona—and he professed to take my number and promised to pass it along. I did not get a call back.

Club officials in Naples encouraged me to come over but guaranteed nothing. Maradona had already gotten away with swatting a goal with his paw, with the whole world watching; this seemed to indicate he did exactly what he wanted.

By reading the Italian papers in New York, I began collecting examples of Maradona's love life, his drug problems, his genius, his mood swings.

I flew to Italy during a cold snap in February and took the train down to Naples, with the *Times* bureau delegating a charming office assistant named Cristina to translate for me. On Saturday evening, Cristina located a restaurant where Maradona was known to hang out, but they said they hadn't seen him for a while.

On Sunday morning, the hard-core soccer fans, known as Ultras or Teste Matte (Crazy Heads), were assembled outside San Paolo Stadium, wearing leather jackets displaying the Confederate flag, a telling bit of self-image for the city definitely below Italy's Mason-Dixon Line. As I followed the other reporters toward the *tribuna stampa* (press box), I turned for a glimpse of the stadium, but an Italian reporter nudged me back under the overhang. Just then, a wad of wet paper towels, as big and nearly as hard as a baseball, whizzed past my head, landing with a nasty smack against the wall. *Benvenuto a Napoli.*

The match was brilliant—Napoli at its peak, with Maradona working in tandem with the Brazilian forward Careca, taking turns flitting through the Roma defenses like a pair of trout gliding along a creek bottom.

Roma took a lead in the fourth minute but suffered for its latter-day version of the Claudio Gentile defense. Stefano Pellegrini, a twenty-two-year-old defender, had told reporters during the week that "I am the man" to mark Maradona. Late in the first half, Pellegrini jostled Maradona, who took a learned flop, his body quivering in opera buffa fashion. It looked like just another yellow card to me, but the official went for Maradona's writhing and waved a red card. Rome would have to play the last forty-six minutes down a man, not a good plan with Maradona and Careca on the loose.

In the fifty-third minute, Maradona converted a penalty kick. In the sixty-second, Careca scored a goal. In the seventy-second minute, Napoli earned another penalty kick. Careca subtly nodded to the spot, twelve yards from the goal, and Maradona calmly iced the match.

Afterward, Napoli held a press conference in a room near the locker room. To my delight, Maradona himself materialized, his thick curls showing a touch of gray, an earring glittering from his left lobe.

After they lowered the microphone for him—geez, he was short—Maradona began answering questions.

That voice sounded familiar.

Son of a bitch. That was the voice on the other end of the phone, the guy who kept switching languages on me. Cristina said his guttural Italian, with an Argentine accent, was not bad at all.

Asked about the two penalty kicks, Maradona said: "You have to be cool; you cannot think about anything. When I shoot a penalty kick, I never look at the ball. I look at the goalie."

Asked about the rumors that he would be leaving Naples, he said, "No, gentlemen, I have decided not to leave. I don't want to move Dalmita to another city. She speaks Italian better than I do, and Claudia lives peacefully. I have a contract and I will remain in Naples."

He added that he wanted to break the club record for goals, saying, "I want to do something to leave my name in this city."

His responses were pretty tame for such a notorious figure, but at least I had a sighting, and a hearing. The more I thought about it, the more I respected the way he had goofed on me over the phone. After all, look what he had done with Peter Shilton.

On Monday, I had interviews with Napoli's owner and general manager, who clearly regarded Maradona as a difficult genius, worth all the aggravation as long as he won another *scudetto* and filled San Paolo. They asked a genial driver, Alfredo Sepe, to take me to Maradona's villa in Posillipo, an old Greek section on a hill, with high-rises and villas enjoying a stunning view of the bay.

The driver parked in front of a modern three-story mansion, with a gigantic television dish and high fences. "*Ecco*, Diego Armando," he said, pointing out a maid playing on a porch with Maradona's younger daughter, Giannina. By now I was becoming paranoid, apparently an occupational hazard for people in the wake of Maradona. I could imagine him lurking behind shuttered windows, peeping out at the sparkling bay, or maybe at us. (In 1994, he would fire a pellet gun at reporters who had intruded on his psychic space.)

"He sometimes takes a walk," Sepe said, "but he cannot take his children because too many people are looking for his autograph. It is a safe neighborhood because there is a man from NATO across the street, and he always has plenty of security."

The driver really tried; he called the house and left a message that a reporter for the *New York Times* was outside. I actually think Alfredo said I was a nice guy, harmless, a foreigner. But Maradona was not stirring. Eventually, a club representative drove up and apologized that they had not been able to produce Maradona. He suggested I try the next afternoon after practice.

On Tuesday, the players gathered for a short workout at the training base, on the edge of town. I did not spot the distinctive fireplug physique among the athletes in sweatsuits, jogging around the field.

"Maradona does not practice today," a friendly photographer told me. Apparently, he had a sore back. When practice was over, the coach emerged from his office, scuffing at the ground, looking more than a bit annoyed. Apparently, this was how it worked at Napoli. Diego Armando showed up when he felt like it. (At that same training base, a year or two later, a few goons infiltrated the practice field and shoved some Napoli players. Maradona told the press that management had cut a hole in the fence to allow the thugs to punish the players for their desultory performance—another glimpse into the fevered mind of Diego Armando.)

Club officials gave me their best Italianate shrug. What can you do? I went home to write my article, about the difficulty I had marking Maradona. On April 29, Naples clinched the league championship on a goal set up by an exquisite, lofting free kick by Maradona.

Then he and his Argentina squad prepared for the World Cup in Italy, with some of their matches scheduled in Naples.

Heading into my third World Cup, I was starting to get a glimmer of a sport millions of fans know from birth. People would tell me about some hero or incident from the past and realize I had no clue.

As New York baseball fans in the 1950s, my friends and I debated the merits of Willie Mays vs. Mickey Mantle vs. Duke Snider and tried to compare them to Ty Cobb or Wee Willie Keeler, who played in different eras.

For a soccer equivalent, I called the Professor.

"Every four years is another era," said Julio Mazzei, the former coach of the Cosmos, the friend of Pelé, who was always available for a private seminar on his sport, sometimes long-distance from Brazil. The Professor proudly believed that the one-touch beauty of the sport sprang from his homeland, from *jogo bonito*, the beautiful game. Old TV clips show Brazilian players in rudimentary gear booting mud-caked leather balls, apparently having the space to perform their art.

Because of my Hungarian surname, I became aware of Ferenc Puskás, with the thickest set of thighs in the history of humankind. People talked about the way Hungary had been the favorite for the 1954 World Cup, but Puskás was hacked so viciously in an early 8–3 victory over West Germany that he suffered a hairline fracture of his ankle. In the final, Puskás amazingly scored a goal on his cracked ankle, but the West Germans rallied from two goals down to win 3–2.

The Hungarians were legends, Brazil on the Danube, eight or nine of them swarming downfield, beating England, 6–3, at Wembley. The English could not believe it and came back for more, and Hungary won, 7–1. That first victory is memorialized by the 6–3 wine bar, still operative in Budapest.

In our long-distance chat, the Professor told me how teams had changed defensive formations to cope with teams like Hungary and Brazil. My high school had played with two defenders, five midfielders, and three forwards, a 2-5-3 lineup that may have helped all those opposing forwards to swarm past me. World-level teams had begun playing 4-4-2 or 4-3-2-1 or 3-5-2 to cope with Puskás or Pelé.

"For the next ten years, even in Brazil, when they looked at the kids, they didn't want the skinny ones, the artistic ones, anymore," the Professor told me.

The full-speed-ahead concept of the Hungarians morphed into the "Total Football" that Rinus Michels of Ajax Amsterdam expanded into the Dutch soul. Michels used to say he expected all ten of his field players to be able to play interchangeably, to move forward. But West Germany beat the Dutch in 1974, and Argentina beat them in 1978. Then

Michels, the coach, moved to Barcelona, followed by Johan Cruyff, the star player, and the concept of Total Football was integrated into another receptive culture.

In 1982, I had been prepared for the samba dancers from Brazil, but the Italians tripped them up. The same happened in 1986, when Argentina showed it could play nice or it could score on a handball, too. The Professor was not an admirer of Maradona—the old Brazil-Argentina rivalry. He called 1986 "the Maradona Cup," suggesting that sometimes chutzpah beat style.

After two previous World Cups, I had a new experience—an American team to cover. The United States knew nothing of national teams in any sport, except for the Olympic squads that popped up every four years. Now the United States was in the same position as real soccer nations. The few hard-core fans in America were debating who would make the twenty-two-player roster.

The coach was Bob Gansler, a product of the American ethnic leagues. He took the U.S. squad for a "friendly" (an exhibition match) in Budapest in March, part of the normal World Cup process, toughening up the candidates in foreign stadiums. My colleague Michael Janofsky caught up with Gansler on a hill overlooking the Danube, and this rather stoic man opened up about his European roots.

He was born in Hungary, and his father had been drafted and captured by the Russians during World War II. After the war, the Russians evicted all ethnic Germans to West Germany.

"It was not like a holocaust or anything," Gansler told Janofsky. "But we lost everything we had. I remember when they put us on a freight train. Everything was chaos. Then it took a couple of weeks for a trip that should have taken eight hours, because whenever the Russians needed an engine, they would take the one off our train and put it back a couple of days later."

When the family had trouble assimilating in what felt like a foreign land, Gansler's grandfather made a trip to Milwaukee and soon sent for his family. This was how Gansler became an American, gained a degree from Marquette University, played on two Olympic teams, earned five caps with the national team. He knew that if history had been different, he could have been a farmer in south-central Hungary.

"As I sit here, along with the river, some thoughts are floating by," Gansler said. "You wonder what might have been had you stayed here."

Gansler's reflections were touching. This is how Americans are made, with a trace of the Old World remaining. Unknown to most Americans, Gansler was charged with preparing the national squad for the World Cup in Italy.

The American squad of 1990 sometimes seemed to be a children's crusade, like the scene in *Doctor Zhivago*, when the military school sends fourteen-year-olds to die at the front. (A rather basic difference is that nobody died at that World Cup.) The American squad and the American federation had virtually no experience; everybody was doing this for the first time. The victory over England in 1950 was ancient history, although stalwarts like Walter Bahr, Frank Borghi, and Harry Keough were still around as gregarious totems to a victory nobody knew.

The country was vast, and interest in soccer localized. One corner of industrial New Jersey was doing more than its share, with Kearny contributing Tony Meola, Tab Ramos, and John Harkes to the squad. Paul Caligiuri was back, joined by Marcelo Balboa, whose Argentine-born father had played professionally, and Eric Wynalda, a brash forward of Dutch ancestry. Bruce Murray, an American-born striker, was capable of converting up front. As a Queens guy, I was thrilled to see Mike Windischmann, born in West Germany but raised in the German American community of Glendale.

As in real soccer nations, there was even some controversy over the selection of the squad. One of the most versatile offensive players in the U.S. pool was Hugo Pérez, born in El Salvador with a father and grandfather who had played at a high level. After moving to the United States, Pérez played in the closing months of the North American Soccer League and then dominated the indoor game in San Diego. Now an American citizen, Pérez had a great scoring touch, but injuries and work-visa issues in Europe kept him from playing enough outdoor games to show Gansler he could make it up and down the field for ninety minutes.

When Pérez was left off the final squad for Italy, some people saw this as an example that the federation did not want Latino players. To this day there is the alligator-in-the-sewers urban legend that Latino players with national-team potential are playing pickup games on weekends after working all week on gardening trucks. If that's the case, Bob Gansler, a sharp judge of talent, would have loved to have gotten their names and addresses, along with videos of their matches.

The U.S. team traveled to Switzerland for an exhibition, staying in the tiny mountain town of Bad Ragaz, home of thermal baths. "To say that it is quiet around here almost disturbs the calm," Janofsky reported. "Church bells ring at the appropriate times. Horses pulling wagons of tourists neigh now and again. Somewhere off in the distance, a dog barks and a rooster crows. But that's about it."

After an unpromising friendly, the U.S. team moved to a camp west of Florence, near the Ligurian Sea. My man Janofsky thought it best if he rented a flat overlooking the picturesque shops on the Ponte Vecchio. I can't say I blamed him.

It made sense to divide the territory, so I opted for a base in Rome. During my Maradona hunt in February, I had heard of an American writer willing to rent his flat for the entire World Cup while he and his companion escaped to the countryside. I committed without my wife seeing the flat and was somewhat insecure over whether she would love the old Roman building across from the Piazza Navona. When I covered the papal conclave in 1978, we had borrowed a flat at the Piazza Navona; it's hard not to love a neighborhood where you can gaze at a Bernini statue while eating a tartufo in an outdoor café. I should not have worried. When she arrived, Marianne looked at the opera albums, the architecture books, and the kitchen with its utensils and spices and decided she would enjoy it just fine.

We were living in the Piazza Sforza Cesarini, an ancient part of the city across from the Piazza Navona. As in many European buildings, the lights in the foyer were on a timer; when you came home at night you had to feel your way along the wall until you located the switch. The surface of the hallway was rough, pebbly—in one renovation, generations or centuries earlier, builders had used excess material dug out of the ground, including bits and pieces of ancient Roman pottery. As you groped for the light switch, you were putting your hands on shards of history.

Our sweet Roman summer included two trattorias directly below us; the smoke from their kitchens forced us to close the windows and shutters. The waiters in one trattoria had lived in England for a while and could chat in our language; sometimes we went to the other because we liked certain specialties. It took us weeks to discover that the "English" trattoria was rightist and the other trattoria was leftist, and the operators and clientele hated each other. In Italy there are so many layers.

Other times, Marianne went shopping in the narrow streets off Via Giulia and cooked lovely meals in the late afternoon. The media bus route conveniently began around the corner and went directly to the Olympic Stadium, with its lush gardens and statuary. In short order, I began to think of myself as a resident of Rome.

As the youngest of twenty-four teams in the field, with an average player age of twenty-three, the American team was not given any chance to advance beyond the first round of group play. In the first match in Florence, Czechoslovakia scored in the twenty-sixth minute, and then Mike Windischmann, the steady captain from Queens, got caught behind a Czech invader and decided he had no choice but to hack him down. FIFA had been instructing officials to call blatant fouls in the box, and the referee blew his whistle for a penalty kick. The Czechoslovaks did not squander the opportunity.

"Two goals down and back in the locker room, we were a bit disorganized," Gansler, said later, adding, "Michael was a bit unnerved. He knew that was a ball he should have cleared. Obviously, it weighed on his conscience."

In the second half, now down by three goals, Caligiuri, the hero of Port of Spain, found space on the right side and scored. But the United

States lost, 5–1, and reporters began to second-guess Gansler's strategy and personnel decisions—the normal reaction to a World Cup loss.

"The United States Soccer Federation and Bob Gansler have prepared us," Caligiuri insisted. "We don't have a professional outdoor league, and that makes a coach's job difficult," Caligiuri added. "The United States players have a lot of potential. This is where it begins."

Caligiuri was typical of the college-educated American players, who were comfortable talking with reporters. Many players from other countries did not have even a high-school education and could not express themselves comfortably in public, but the Czechoslovak players were worldly in other ways: the Soviet Union had pulled out of the country only a few months before, and the players were missing the first free elections in their country since 1946, with no provision for absentee ballots. Afterward, they dedicated their victory to the newly elected president, the playwright Václav Havel.

The United States moved down to Rome for its second match, against Italy. I wanted to write about the bonds between the two countries, so I called Tony Meola's parents, originally from the Avellino area, who were returning to watch their son play for their adopted country. Tony heard that his grandmother was walking around the town square near Avellino, just in case anybody wanted to chat about the American keeper.

When I reached him, Vincent Meola was laughing because a bank clerk had seen his American passport and praised him for speaking Italian so well. "Soccer was in my blood, my Italian blood," he said. "Like football is in the blood of most American kids." He did not mind admitting that he had tears in his eyes when his son walked onto the field against Czechoslovakia. (Tony did not tell anybody that he had not been able to sleep the night before that match.)

"There will be so many rooting for Italy, and just a few for us," Vincent said. "But you know what I say? I say, 'Viva, Stati Uniti,' and hope for the best."

"I find no changes," Maria Meola said of her first trip back since their honeymoon. "I love the fig trees and the pear trees and people's gardens. I like people saying: 'Buon giorno. Ciao.' In New Jersey, you walk into a store and nobody looks at you. But I love the U.S. It is my home."

Playing Italy in front of seventy-three thousand fans in Olympic Stadium, Gansler made three changes, which cut down on the Italian attack.
Still, there was one breakdown, with Gianluca Vialli flicking a back-heel
pass for Giuseppe Giannini, who had space to score.

The match stabilized after Italy missed a penalty kick, and the
Americans threatened in the seventieth minute. The players who were
there, on the field, still think about it. The Americans gained a free kick
from close range and discussed who was going to take it. Peter Vermes,
a defender, ceded to Bruce Murray, a striker, and Vermes positioned
himself at the right side of the Italian wall—just in case. Vermes had
survivor genes. His parents had escaped Hungary in the rebellion of
1956, settling in New Jersey, teaching their son to work hard, play hard.
Murray's shot rebounded to Vermes, who peppered a left-footed shot at
a sharp angle to Walter Zenga, perhaps the best keeper in the world that
year. Zenga was off balance; the ball did its best to ricochet between the
maze of Zenga's legs but was slowed down by Zenga's rear end and slowly
advanced toward the goal line, until an Italian defender cleared it, and
Italy held on for a 1–0 victory. In the never-ending polemic of agony,
some Italian fans and writers blamed the lack of goals on the importing
of foreign scorers into Serie A, claiming that homegrown forwards did
not develop as goal scorers. But the fans in Olympic Stadium did applaud
the United States for a brave showing.

Two decades later, as Vermes was inducted into the American Soccer
Hall of Fame, he declined to see the Zenga play as a lost opportunity for
fame. After a long playing career, he was the coach of a highly successful
franchise in Kansas City. "Everyone asks, 'If you would have scored that
goal, where would you be today?' I think it was the best thing that ever
happened to me, because I'm right where I want to be now."

Other Americans understood what it meant to take their stand in
Rome.

"We played Italy, one of the great teams in the world, and we showed
we could play a little," said Desmond Armstrong, a defender, an English
major from the University of Maryland. He admitted he had been thinking about a career change after the disaster against Czechoslovakia, but
the Italy match made him reconsider.

"I looked at my teammates; I saw Tab Ramos moving the ball, the best player on the field," Armstrong said afterward. "Before the game, I didn't know if there was a future in this. Now I think I could still be playing in four years when I'm twenty-nine. I see Bergomi playing, and he's twenty-nine," Armstrong said, referring to Giuseppe Bergomi, the smooth defender who had played in the 1982 final as an eighteen-year-old because of a teammate's injury and was now the captain of the Azzurri.

"The only difference between him and me is that he has a league to play in," Armstrong said. "We're playing for ourselves here," he added. "There is definitely a selfish aspect. We want to show we have serious players. We want to show America we should keep going. We've got to put our players somewhere else."

Gansler said, "The difference between our team in the first game and the second was psychological." He added, "Yes, the psychological drives the physical, but the difference this time was psychological."

The Americans went back to Florence for their third match and were thumped by Austria, 2–1. Their adventure was over, with three losses and only two goals. But they had played in the World Cup, and that was no small thing.

I met my first soccer hooligan in 1990. I had missed that pleasure in 1982 by virtue of being in Barcelona while the English fans were cavorting in other parts of Spain. In 1986, the Mexican organizers wisely greeted English fans with a mixture of hospitality and intimidation, so the boys mostly stayed under the radar.

Hooligans are serious business. As Bill Buford pointed out in his classic book, *Among the Thugs*, these are not casual troublemakers, out for a dustup on Saturday afternoon, but rather an antisocial element with jobs and the skills to stage military-like strikes against civilians.

England had a toxic image because of the stampede before the Juventus-Liverpool final for the European Cup in Brussels in 1985, which killed thirty-nine fans, and the panic in 1989, when nearly one hundred fans were crushed against unyielding gates in Sheffield. In 1990, Italy was taking no chances.

When England was drawn into a group with Egypt, the Netherlands, and Ireland, all three of its matches were placed in Cagliari, on the island of Sardinia, which made it easier to control fans arriving by ferry or plane.

For the first match against Ireland, I flew from Rome to Cagliari, and took my hooligan-watching position near the ferry landing. Hundreds of police were out, in full gear, arranging sturdy metal stanchions to keep the English confined to the street. If that treatment did not bring out antisocial tendencies, nothing would.

There they were! Chants and songs and horns and drums—not exactly the graceful samba legions of the Brazilian Torcida, to be sure, but not all hooligans, either. The dragnet had caught little old ladies in tennis sneakers, parents and small children, trudging along in this forced march.

I had always wanted to see real live hooligans up close, so I waved my press credential and slipped into the street, alongside a burly young bloke, with skin burned to a flaming crimson and belly extending over his shorts. Identifying myself as a reporter for the *New York Times*, I asked him how the ferry ride had gone and how the Italian authorities were treating him.

He regarded me with a baleful glare. Then in a thick accent he announced in a loud, cutting voice: "So you're from the effing You-nited States?"

Yes, I said.

He looked me up and down. Then in an even louder voice, he broadcast:

"Well, then, why don't you go write about your effing baseball?"

I got the feeling the interview was over. He did not want to enlighten me about the traveling fans, did not want to address stereotypes and injustices, the branding of all Brits as criminals. He just wanted me out of his way.

One fan did confide that he resented the police treating the English "like animals."

Later that night, Ireland drew with England, 1–1. Afterward, some British lads rioted in downtown Cagliari, before squads of police moved them out. Police arrested fourteen English fans and later deported them.

On the flight back to Rome the next morning, one Italian man praised an Irish fan for good deportment in the stadium the night before.

"We're not like them," the Irishman said softly.

The Irish, in their first World Cup, were the hit of Italy when Ireland beat Romania in the round of 16 and arrived in Rome to play the Azzurri in the quarterfinals. The Irish fans wandered around, wearing green shorts and green T-shirts but not carrying much green cash with them. The only place they were not welcome was inside St. Peter's, where priests and Swiss Guards pointed at their bare legs and shooed them away. Goodness knows where they stayed. But the Irish fans (and their surprising team) made such an impression that Italian tourism to Ireland swelled noticeably the next year, with some Italians staying to wander around or teach Italian or fall in love. A strange little sociological alliance, thanks to soccer.

Within a few days, my wife had become a regular in the neighborhood, an American who loved the city, who spent a few lire here and there.

"Signora," one shoplady said, after sussing out that I was a journalist, "you tell your husband that nobody spends money on this World Cup. They come for the match, and they go home."

It was true. Germans drove down the autobahn, maybe bought a beer or two, and then drove back at 150 kilometers per hour, to be at work the next day.

This exposed the great myth of World Cups and Olympics. Organizers always mooch government subsidies for stadiums and security and infrastructure on the premise that the events will be a boon for business. The fact is, sports fans are not good tourists. They do not bring money, or curiosity, or consumer tastes. They come to see a game, have some beers, cheer loudly, get sick in the street, and go home. Better to schedule a convention of accountants.

It is always pathetic to see shopkeepers stock up on artistic gifts or good food or merchandise for the normal tourist, only to see visiting fans stomp past their shop chanting "U-S-A." Most major events produce a dip in business, which is the reason I opposed New York's bid for the 2012 Olympics, which fortunately it did not get. When London held those Games, that city had a lower hotel occupancy rate than New York. Tourists avoided London as if the Great Fire and the plague were raging simultaneously.

No complaints from us about summer in Rome. My wife had the city to herself.

As per custom, the defending champions opened up the tournament, this time in Milan, the haughty center of business and fashion. Coach Carlos Bilardo, a medical doctor, had lobbied unsuccessfully for a shorter version of the Argentine anthem, which went on for nearly four minutes, as the hostile northern crowd (which hated Maradona as a Napoli player) whistled and jeered.

Maradona, in his own way, made the situation vastly better by visibly cursing during the opening ceremony, with the camera gaping inches away from his face.

Argentina's opening opponent was Cameroon, which had earned one of only two slots allotted to Africa, the continent often called "the future" by FIFA. Cameroon became the first surprise of 1990 when François Omam-Biyik stunned Argentina by outjumping Roberto Sensini and scoring on a wicked bouncing header in the sixty-seventh minute. The goal held up for a 1–0 upset victory.

Cameroon was bolstered by Roger Milla, its great star who had retired once, with fans taking up a collection to build a statue of him in Yaoundé, the capital. Just turned thirty-eight, the living icon was back in uniform, much to the surprise of Coach Valeri Nepomniachi, who hailed from Siberia and needed a French-Russian translator at his side.

The coach's strategy was to hold the old man out of the starting lineup and wait for the sun to go down over the lip of the stadium.

Milla came on in the eighty-first minute against Argentina. Then he arrived in the fifty-ninth minute against Romania and scored in the seventy-sixth and eighty-sixth minute in a 2–1 victory. Milla came on in the thirty-fourth minute as Cameroon was whacked by the Soviets, 4–0, in the third match, but Cameroon had already qualified for the knockout round.

In the round of 16, the shadows were two-thirds across San Paolo Stadium in Naples when Milla was sent on in the 54th minute of a scoreless match with Colombia. In the cool of the evening, he scored in the 106th minute. Then came one of the highlights of the tournament: Colombia's keeper, René Higuita, liked making offensive sorties downfield, which was why he was known as El Loco. Higuita tried to dribble his way out of trouble, but Milla stripped him and scored in the 108th minute. Colombia scored later, but Cameroon had a 2–1 victory, to become the first African team ever to reach the quarterfinals.

By now Cameroon was the darling of Naples, but the team's luck ran out in San Paolo in the quarterfinals against England. Gary Lineker scored a late-penalty goal to tie the match, and then in the 105th minute the Cameroon keeper, Thomas N'Kono, took down an English player, and Lineker made the penalty, and Cameroon was gone.

Maradona was conducting his personal home stand in Naples. At an early practice in San Paolo, he touched the grass with his right hand and made the sign of the cross.

"Now I'm the one who needs you, although you have given me so much already," he told the city's fans. "We must play well for ourselves and for the Neapolitans."

I used to wonder if Maradona enjoyed manipulating people with words and theories, but later I came to think he really believed the things he said.

"If you want to see me happy, root for me and Argentina," Maradona said.

Only Maradona could have the gall to commit another handball infraction four years after his infamous Hand of God performance. In Argentina's match with the Soviets in the first round, while helping out on defense, he swatted a soft shot away from the goalmouth, using his right hand this time. The official documentary for this World Cup made the observation that the Hand of God turned out to be ambidextrous.

Sometimes a round of 16 match can have the aura of a final. With this in mind, fans trekked to Turin, home of Fiat, the Agnelli family, and Juventus, to watch Argentina play Brazil in the round of 16, the countries' fourth World Cup meeting. Brazil was going through one of its periodic defensive upgrades, assigning a dozen or so defenders to mark Maradona at all times. While proclaiming himself the hero of Napoli, he was not popular in northern cities like Turin.

Unfortunately, the match had fallen into the 5 p.m. slot on a hot day. The teams slogged through a scoreless draw until the eighty-first minute, when Maradona escaped at least four defenders and released a gorgeous grass-skimmer pass to the left, to the fast-moving feet of Claudio Caniggia, who made a knowing wide swath to his left, drawing out the keeper, and then curling the shot past him. Argentina would live to play again.

The thing I remember most from that day is the overnight shutdown on a crowded train from Turin to Rome. *Sciopero! Sciopero!* (Strike! Strike!), they belatedly told us as we moldered on a siding outside Genoa. We were going zero miles per hour, and we were at the center of the universe, with fans from a dozen countries recalling Maradona's magnificent pass to Caniggia. Took us eighteen hours to get to Rome.

Branco, a defender with that Brazilian squad, had a different memory of that sultry evening. Fifteen years later, he began advancing the theory that he had been drugged by a water bottle tossed him from the Argentine sideline during an injury break. Would a team really reserve a water bottle containing a sleeping potion for the possible opportunity to toss it to an opponent? Maradona, who appears to love conspiracy theories more than anybody, has at times encouraged Branco's lament, perhaps to mess with Branco's mind. Or perhaps it happened just that way.

Maradona had his nervous moment in the quarterfinals against Yugoslavia, when his soft penalty kick was saved during the shootout. But his teammates rescued him, and Argentina moved on to the semifinals in Naples, against an invader from another country, that is to say, Italy.

Diego Armando upgraded his propaganda campaign for the Neapolitans to root for Argentina—against Italy—citing the city's history as an outsider, settled by Greeks who named the city Partenope; to this day the Italian sports pages refer to the Napoli club as the Partenopei.

It's a tough town, and this is not just some tourist's stereotype. When my wife and I traveled to Naples for the semifinal, she went out for a walk, and older ladies in black would stop her on the street and point to the modest gold chain around her neck and wag their index fingers in that very European gesture: *Scusi, signora*, but you need to hide that jewelry.

Maradona, the self-styled homeboy, tried to rally the Napolitani around Argentina. Most Neapolitans were street smart on their own and said, Hold on, Naples is still part of Italy, last time we looked.

Italy was going through its own dramatic relationship with the Azzurri—the fierce second-guessing and bickering of a clamorous family. Coach Azeglio Vicini had stunned the fans by selecting Salvatore Schillaci, an extremely late bloomer who had played seven full seasons for Messina in Serie B in his native Sicily before being purchased by Juventus—La Vecchia Signora, as the club is reverentially known. When Schillaci scored fifteen goals in his first season in Turin, Vicini put him on the national squad for the first time. If Maradona presented himself as an outsider, what did that make Totò Schillaci?

Vicini went to Schillaci in the seventy-fifth minute in the opener against Austria, and the Sicilian responded with a wise header for the goal. He was a late sub against the United States and then scored the first goal against Czechoslovakia, the first goal against Uruguay, and the only goal against Ireland. This romp by a reclamation project was looking like 1982, when Paolo Rossi led Italy to the championship, coming off his two-year suspension.

Schillaci's long years in Messina may have been a blessing to him and the Azzurri. Italians often moaned that the nation did not develop strikers because the rich teams were always signing some Dutch or German or French import to do the finishing. If Schillaci had been called to Serie

A earlier in his career, he might have been stuck on a glutted roster, subsidiary to the *stranieri* who were paid to score, and he might never have developed his instincts for open space. Instead, he came to Juve and the Azzurri as a striker who knew how to strike. Italy could never have enough of those.

Italy's coach must always be aware of the passionate fans with their strong opinions about the great talent pool in that country. Vicini had been successful juggling his roster, particularly Schillaci. Against Argentina in the semifinal, Vicini did not start Roberto Baggio, the creative young player about to move from Fiorentina to Juventus, or Aldo Serena, Nicola Berti, Andrea Carnevale, or Roberto Mancini, all offensive forces for their clubs. The greatest impediment to any Italian coach was that he could start only eleven players.

Against Argentina in the semifinals, Italy took the lead in the seventeenth minute, completing six touches before Schillaci banged in a rebound of Gianluca Vialli's shot. At this point, Argentina moved its defenders forward, often trapping Schillaci offside and forcing him to retreat.

Maradona was sometimes most dangerous when he lay in the weeds. In the sixty-seventh minute, he dished the ball forward to Julio Olarticoechea, who lofted it toward the goal, where Caniggia outjumped Riccardo Ferri and scored on a header, his two-tone tresses flailing. The goal was the first scored against Walter Zenga in six matches.

Now that the match was tied, Argentina went into ugly mode. The referee displayed six consecutive yellow cards to Argentina, two to Ricardo Giusti, forcing him out, and one to Caniggia, meaning he would miss the final, if Argentina could get there.

After hanging on for regulation time and overtime, Argentina made four straight goals in the shoot-out, including one by Maradona, who had missed against Yugoslavia. "I felt a great deal of fear," he admitted later, after converting on a soft ground shot to his left. Roberto Donadoni missed, and Serena was stopped by Sergio Goycochea as Argentina vaulted into the final, over the *stranieri* from Italy. Maradona's watchful deity was apparently still perched on his shoulder.

After the manic night in Naples, I did not have to make the trip to

Turin for the England–West Germany semifinal the next night. One thing I had learned from my first two World Cups was that the Germans were going to be around toward the end. They are professionals who almost never dog it, never get caught up in intramural squabbles, at least ones that the whole world could see.

I'm not the only one who thinks so. Gary Lineker scored four goals for England in 1990, including the clutch tying goal in the eightieth minute against West Germany, and he also delivered on the first penalty kick in the shoot-out. Only later did I appreciate Lineker as a true leader, who tried to calm his troubled teammate, Paul Gascoigne, after England lost to West Germany in the shoot-out.

Lineker delivered this epigram about his sport: "Football is a simple game; twenty-two men chase a ball for ninety minutes and at the end, the Germans always win."

Before the final between Argentina and West Germany, the third-place match between England and Italy was held in Bari on the same night as the Three Tenors concert in the Baths of Caracalla in Rome. I skipped both. I've never seen a third-place match, come to think of it. Instead, half a dozen American reporters went out for dinner, alfresco, on a gorgeous Roman evening.

With the Italy-England consolation match about to start, the staff served us wine and antipasti, took our orders, then vanished for forty-five minutes. They returned at halftime bearing our main course, steaming hot, al dente; I don't know how they did it. Then they vanished again for forty-five minutes as Italy beat England, 2–1, for third place. We could hear cheering in the kitchen as they brought us the *dolci*. What a wonderful country. Perhaps I have said that already.

Caniggia was out for the final, so Maradona had no fast-moving target up front. He also had no hustler's edge, and he seemed to know it. He knew many of the Germans from Serie A. What kind of mind game could he attempt on these guys?

For the final, Dr. Bilardo prescribed one of the most cynical game plans I would ever see. The Mexican referee, Edgardo Codesal, started waving yellow cards and red cards, tossing Pedro Monzón in the sixty-fifth minute. West Germany finally earned a penalty kick in the eighti-eth minute, and Andreas Brehme, a left back who used his right foot for penalty kicks, iced the soft shot. Argentina was down two players by the end of ninety minutes, and, mercifully, the final was over, with West Germany winning, 1–0.

After a month of Milla and Totò and the Irish and other charming faces, this stinker of a final gave more ammunition to Americans who are spooked by soccer. Plenty of diving. The championship decided by a penalty kick. My attitude was, this is soccer; get over it. But still, the final stunk.

What else do I remember about that evening? Franz Beckenbauer, who had just become the first man to be both captain and coach of a World Cup champion, arrived for his press conference. As he stood in front of a live mike, waiting for the media swarm to assemble, Becken-bauer spotted my colleague Lawrie Mifflin, who had covered the Cos-mos back in the day and was now a deputy sports editor at the *Times*. Speaking into the open mike, Beckenbauer said, "Ah! Lawrie! How are you! How is New York?"

Beckenbauer had been cool while earning his nickname Der Kaiser in the Bundesliga. Now he had coached the World Cup champs, and he was still cool.

The next day my wife and I went downstairs for our last meal in Rome and discovered both trattorias, the leftist and the rightist, jammed with Italians sitting territorially at their favorite tables. The air was thick with smoke from the kitchens and tobacco from the patrons. It was the live-liest Rome had been since we arrived.

The waiters explained: Instead of waiting for the annual monthlong holiday in August, Romans had gone away for June—to the shore, to the mountains, to ancestral homes, to California, to New York, anywhere there was no soccer, and no cheapskate tourists honking and wearing shorts and waving banners. Now the Romans were back. They had reclaimed their city.

We flew home. I have not been back to that piazza since, but once in a while, I turn on the satellite world view on the Internet and zero in on Piazza Sforza Cesarini, "our" piazza. I can smell the delicious smoke from the two kitchens. I wonder if the two staffs speak to each other.

8

MR. BLATTER COMES
TO AMERICA

NEW YORK AND LAS VEGAS, 1993

Sepp Blatter was worried. He was visiting the United States in 1993, terribly concerned that the 1994 World Cup could be a disaster.

What if nobody came? This country did not even have a soccer league, and only a few of its players were good enough to play in Europe.

Blatter, the second-highest-ranking official of FIFA, was taking an inspection tour of the New World. Like many Swiss citizens, he could speak French, German, and Italian, and his English was coming along. His press aide, Guido Tognoni, was there to help with the nuances during his interviews with the American press. When my turn came, I chose to meet at a Belgian restaurant on the East Side of Manhattan as a European touch, to make him feel more comfortable.

He seemed particularly boggled that a great city like New York did not have a world-level stadium near the center, as other great cities do. I told him that, however strange it sounded, industrial New Jersey directly across the Hudson River was considered part of the New York region, at least for sports purposes. People often drove from New York to Giants Stadium in the polluted marshlands. It could be done. But Blatter kept shaking his head.

By now, Joseph S. Blatter is known around the world for having presided over a laissez-faire epoch of arcane politics and unexplained decisions, with a growing list of scandals that saw many of his closest associates disgraced and banished.

He is also known for a litany of comments that ranged from impractical to inappropriate—the World Cup should be held every two years rather than four (which would dilute the event and disturb the entire soccer calendar), and female players should wear tight shorts so men will watch, and gay fans should refrain from sexual activity if they attend the 2022 World Cup in Qatar (a nation with considerable money but not much soccer and which was awarded the tournament under Blatter's watch).

Back in 1993, Blatter and FIFA still seemed to me like a cute little operation that conducted soccer matches, but I was not totally fooled by his effusive bonhomie. I had seen FIFA up close, as the 1994 World Cup approached, and its disdainful attitude toward the leadership of the United States Soccer Federation seemed uncomfortably like a powerful nation seeking a regime change in a puppet state.

Every World Cup is a traveling circus, temporarily leased out to a host country by the home office in Zurich. In 1988, FIFA had made the calculated risk to award the 1994 World Cup to an emerging soccer nation with stadiums and corporate sponsors and wealthy television networks—but also with government and corporate oversight unthinkable in most of the world. FIFA was always uneasy with its new partnership with the United States Soccer Federation.

After the weak showing by the U.S. team in Italy in 1990, FIFA clearly regarded the U.S. federation as a mom-and-pop operation, once run out of a cluttered office in the Empire State Building by dedicated lifers from the old ethnic leagues. Attention must be paid to these earnest people with roots in Europe who nurtured the sport in rickety stadiums in the old cities, mostly along the East Coast. Some games drew thousands of fans on weekend afternoons, rooting for clubs like Brookhattan-Galicia, New York Hakoah, Newark Portuguese, Brooklyn Italians, Philadelphia Ukrainians, New Brunswick Hungarian Americans, Newark Ukrainians, Warsaw Falcons, Galicia-Honduras, Brooklyn Hispano, Baltimore Pompeii, or Kearny Celtic.

Soccer was not exactly born with the arrival of the Cosmos in New York. The grand old soccer city of St. Louis, home to German and Irish and Italian immigrants, produced generations of players at midcentury. "Every Catholic parish had a team," recalled Colonel James Hackett, a former chief of detectives in St. Louis, once a star forward for Chaminade High School. Hackett recalled thousands of fans paying to see a scholastic match at Fairground Park, followed by a semipro match involving teams like Simpkins-Ford and Mike Breheny Furniture. The St. Louis system produced several members of the 1950 World Cup team, including Harry Keough. "He was my postman," Hackett said, marveling that a man who helped beat England had delivered his mail.

The ethnic clubs were the heart of the sport in the United States, but by 1990, they were as archaic as the fedoras and ties and topcoats on the male fans in the wrinkled old photographs. In the age of multinationals and multimedia and big money, FIFA was ready for new friends.

Nearly four years away from the 1994 American World Cup, FIFA made the decision that it was time for the U.S. federation to modernize. Colombia had given up the 1986 World Cup for financial reasons, and Mexico had done fine. Did the United States want to suffer the same fate as Colombia? FIFA's motto seemed to be: We can make you, we can break you.

With FIFA's overt encouragement, the voting members of the U.S. federation abandoned the president, Werner Fricker, a Yugoslavian-born businessman and former player who had lost the confidence of FIFA. The U.S. federation installed in his place Alan Rothenberg, an American-born lawyer who had started in sports by doing legal work for the Los Angeles Lakers and later ran the soccer competition for the 1984 Olympics—a huge success, even though the organizers had to deal with ABC's squeamishness about showing live soccer games. (No time-outs! No hands!)

Ten years later, Rothenberg was again expected to fill the gigantic stadiums of America. He had learned from Peter Ueberroth, the highly capable chief executive of the 1984 Summer Games, who had made a huge profit by using existing facilities rather than leaning on taxpayers to build pools or gyms or fields. All Ueberroth needed, he insisted, was security and decor—pastel banners and chain-link fences. That was the role model for Rothenberg.

"We are very happy with this result," Tognoni, Blatter's press aide, told the *New York Times* after Rothenberg's election in August 1990. "Now, we can make a new start with a credible person."

FIFA did not mess around. Blatter was the point man for the cold and autocratic president, João Havelange, a tall and haughty Brazilian who resembled Charles de Gaulle. It would not have surprised me if Havelange kept a de Gaulle uniform and trademark kepi in his closet and wore it around his office, looking at himself in the mirror and reciting the words of Louis XIV: *L'état, c'est moi.* He was a former Olympic swimmer and water polo competitor, who rose in the Brazilian swimming federation and moved to FIFA because that seemed like a more proper calling for a Charles de Gaulle lookalike. Or maybe there was more money in soccer.

Havelange had a way of looking down his nose at people. He spoke only French at official FIFA functions, and once seemed stunned when Phil Hersh of the *Chicago Tribune* told him he was full of it, in fluent French.

In 1993, Blatter was the heir apparent to Havelange. He seemed quite approachable and sensible, as the former head of public relations of tourism for the Valais region and later the general secretary of the Swiss Ice Hockey Federation and director of sports timing and relations for Longines, which was how he made his move into soccer.

In 1993, Blatter was under pressure from UEFA, the Union of European Football Associations, which had just formed the Champions League, with the top clubs playing a separate midweek competition for gigantic television income—the hamster wheel of soccer. UEFA's president, Lennart Johansson, from Sweden, had a reputation for honesty and was a logical alternative to run FIFA. Blatter seemed quite nervous that a total bust in the New World could hurt his candidacy when Havelange finally retired.

I am hardly a chamber-of-commerce booster type, nor am I a businessman. As a sports columnist, I have huge misgivings about spending public money in the name of circuses for the people. But in 1993, I could justify holding the World Cup in the United States, which already had dozens of football stadiums, just waiting to be filled for a month of soccer.

One thing I knew about America was that our entrepreneurs, our leagues, our sponsors, our television networks, our hotel chains, our national and local governments, all knew how to throw a party. I told Blatter: If you build a World Cup, they will come.

By the time we had espresso, Blatter seemed reassured. Then I did something he may never have seen before. I grabbed the check. The *Times* insists on paying, I said. Blatter seemed intrigued by the concept of journalistic independence. As he left the restaurant, he had regained his peppy demeanor. I had discovered a new sideline of my job— reassuring FIFA executives about the wisdom of their decisions.

On December 19, 1993, FIFA held its quadrennial draw ceremony for the upcoming World Cup, this time in Las Vegas, the sordid personification of the new American dream. Barbara Eden, the blond star of *I Dream of Jeannie*, was serving as hostess for the international television show.

The secretary general of FIFA beamed when the comedian Robin Williams burst onto the stage, obviously fascinated by the name Blatter.

"It is nice to meet you after feeling you all these years," Williams said.

I'm not sure Blatter understood the shtick, but Williams continued his journey into matters urological.

"Mr. Blatter!" Williams said with a thick German accent. "May I call you Mr. Blatter?"

As part of the draw, Blatter dug out a plastic ball from a bowl and was about to call out the name of a team.

Leering at the plastic ball, Williams asked, "Panty hose?"

Then Williams pulled out a rubber glove and told Blatter: "Turn your head and cough."

That night in Las Vegas was the beginning of the public phase of Sepp Blatter. He looked at Robin Williams sporting with him and seemed to be thinking, "Hey, I am not just some officious Swiss bureaucrat cutting deals with obscure third-world federations. I am a fun guy."

Blame Robin Williams. Ever since that draw in Las Vegas in 1993, I have never been able to think of the head of FIFA as anything but Mr. Blatter.

We had one other glimpse of the inner FIFA during that schlocky outing in Las Vegas. Pelé, merely the most famous soccer personality in the world, was involved in a legal dispute with Ricardo Teixeira, the president of the Brazilian federation, who was the son-in-law of João Havelange. Because of the feud, Pelé was banned by FIFA from appearing on the worldwide draw show, clearly a loss of publicity and identity for the American organizers. FIFA did not care. Pelé, sitting in the audience, laughed off his exclusion when interviewed by reporters. He said a World Cup in his second home was "my dream come true," and he added, "My life doesn't change" because of the snub. This is the essence of Pelé. He keeps his balance. He smiles. He goes for the goal.

The thought occurred to me that night: perhaps Blatter was not just a dippy bureaucrat who put on tournaments out of love for the game, who enjoyed a night out in Las Vegas in the presence of Barbara Eden and Robin Williams.

Ban Pelé from the World Cup draw show in America? What wouldn't these people do?

9

THE BIG EVENT

UNITED STATES, 1994

We all knew the American World Cup would be different—spread across a huge country, with loyal ethnic fans following the teams, with indoor matches for the first time.

But nobody could have predicted the tournament would be accompanied by a film-noir double murder or the killing of a player who had been on the field days earlier.

Five days before the opening match, Nicole Brown Simpson and Ron Goldman, a casual acquaintance, were found murdered in Los Angeles. Her husband, the retired football star O. J. Simpson, was the obvious suspect. The nation, and much of the world, was somewhat preoccupied by this gruesome spectacle as the tournament opened in Chicago's Soldier Field.

By tradition, the defending champions played the first match, but West Germany had merged with the German Democratic Republic just months after the World Cup victory in Rome. The unified nation was now simply Germany, Deutschland, but most of the players were from the nation that had won in 1990.

A fleet striker, Jürgen Klinsmann, put Germany ahead in the sixty-first minute against Bolivia, and the Bolivian coach sent in his aging star, Marco Etcheverry, to try for the equalizer. Etcheverry, known as El Diablo, was whacked by Lothar Matthäus and responded with a kick, earning himself a red card and expulsion. Total minutes played, three.

Immediately after the match, I rushed to O'Hare for a flight to Detroit, for the Americans' first game against Switzerland at 11:30 a.m. the next day.

That evening, while driving my rental car toward Pontiac, I turned on the radio to find WFAN, the clear-channel New York all-sports station that could be heard after sundown in more than a dozen states. Madison Square Garden was shimmering with excitement that month: the Rangers of ice hockey had just won their first Stanley Cup in fifty-four years, while the Knicks of basketball were in the National Basketball Association (NBA) Finals against Houston.

It was one of the craziest sports months we have ever had in New York. I'll admit it. I was resentful that the hometown finals had erupted in the same month as the World Cup, and I could not be everywhere.

Now the games were overshadowed by the hideous drama in California.

With WFAN coming in loud and clear, I discovered that O. J. Simpson was involved in an ominous low-speed car chase on the freeways of Southern California, with television helicopters displaying the scene live, to the world. Basketball fans in the Garden were rushing into the corridors to watch the chase on television, as the Knicks took a 3–2 lead in the series; Simpson surrendered at 8:50 p.m. Los Angeles time—everything was connected.

At 11:30 a.m. on Saturday, the United States played Switzerland in the Pontiac Silverdome. Americans had been playing baseball and football in stadiums with domes or retractable roofs since the mid-1960s, on artificial grass placed over hard layers, which increased injuries to athletes. FIFA had rightfully insisted on grass fields for its major tournaments.

In 1983, the Italian national team visited New Jersey to play a friendly on the rock-hard carpet in Giants Stadium. Claudio Gentile and his mates watched the soccer ball veer like a bowling ball down a polished lane and decided they would not be making any sliding tackles that day.

A decade later, scientists from Michigan State University had concocted a system of trays of grass that could be nurtured in the sun and rain outdoors, then hauled indoors before a match—around two thousand segments of hardy grass, each weighing three thousand pounds.

The first indoor match in the Silverdome had been held on June 6, 1993, between Germany and England as part of a three-team tournament called the U.S. Cup. Julie Cart of the *Los Angeles Times* described the "steamy, stultifying" air, noting the lack of air-conditioning for players or fans. But FIFA went ahead with its plans for four first-round World Cup matches indoors.

The Silverdome was part of the objective to sell tickets, lots of tickets. The original conservative plan for 1994 had been to use midsize stadiums, but the nation had dozens of huge stadiums sitting empty in June and July. FIFA did not award the World Cup to the United States because of its soccer prowess. This was America. Think big.

The organizing committee was run by Rothenberg and Scott Parks LeTellier, a lawyer from Los Angeles, and they recruited talented people, many with soccer backgrounds, to run the ambitious project. This was not amateur hour.

The stadiums selected were: Stanford (capacity 80,906), the Rose Bowl in Pasadena, California (91,794), the Citrus Bowl in Orlando, Florida (61,219), Soldier Field in Chicago (63,117), the Cotton Bowl in Dallas (63,998), Foxboro Stadium in Foxborough, Massachusetts (53,644), Robert F. Kennedy Stadium in Washington, D.C. (53,142), the Silverdome in Pontiac, Michigan (77,557), and Giants Stadium in East Rutherford, New Jersey (75,338). The Giants played on nasty artificial turf, but for the World Cup officials trucked in trays of real grass.

With a minimum of rejiggering, these football stadiums were converted into soccer stadiums, with slightly wider and longer fields, although sometimes dodgy sightlines for the lowest rows and precious little room for corner kicks or warmups. But they could surely pack in the fans.

All the 1994 stadiums had one thing in common: the organizers did not feel the need to spend money for extra lavatories for temporary facilities like media centers and hospitality tents. Instead, at every stadium, they installed dozens of Porta Potties, which sat there for a month in summer weather. Charming.

Just in time for the 1994 World Cup, FIFA changed a major rule: keepers were no longer allowed to pick up the ball when it was kicked back by a defender under pressure. Opposing fans would whistle derisively at such timidity, as the keeper would cradle the ball like a babe in arms, coo softly to it, waste many seconds to let the danger pass, and eventually deliver the ball upfield. Under the new rule, if a defender kicked the ball backward, the keeper could not touch it with his hands but had to kick it. He had to be a footballer.

Over the winter, I had seen Franco Baresi of AC Milan screw up an exchange with his keeper. If the great Baresi had to adjust to the new rule, how would other defenders do under increased pressure?

Sepp Blatter, who often spouted off as informal interpreter of rule changes and general societal trends, issued this pronunciamento just before the World Cup: "When in doubt, keep the flag down." That was easy for him to say. Woe to the player who botched a play near the goal-mouth.

The rules for group play had also been changed, allotting three points for a victory, thereby encouraging more aggressive play. And sixteen of the twenty-four teams would advance to the knockout round, which meant four squads would advance after finishing third in their group. The consensus seemed to be that Italy, Mexico, Ireland, and Norway formed the Group of Death because there was no obvious weak team.

England had failed to qualify, thrilling local police who did not have to monitor hooligans. The usual contenders were back—Brazil, Italy, Argentina, and the unified Germany.

Considering that the United States was not seeded among the top teams, its group of Switzerland, Colombia, and Romania was not terrifying. The United States' first opponent, Switzerland, was considered the least of the three, which meant that if the United States got a victory in its first match, it would have a good chance of advancing.

The American team was a huge upgrade from 1990. There was still no major professional league, and many players were still coming out of college programs, subsidized by the federation, but more of them were finding employment in Europe.

The three players from Kearny, New Jersey, with overseas roots were the core of the team—John Harkes, Tony Meola, and Tab Ramos. Other talented players included Eric Wynalda, who had scored twenty-one goals in sixty-one games for Saarbrücken in Germany; Marcelo Balboa, the solid defender whose father had played in Argentina before migrating to the United States; Alexi Lalas, a fast-talking defender who had spent part of his childhood in Greece, his father's homeland; Hugo Pérez, with his roots in El Salvador, who had been left off the 1990 squad but was picked for 1994; and Roy Wegerle, born in South Africa, who had moved to Florida for college and then played for clubs in England.

The U.S. federation, always on the lookout for players with claims to American citizenship, found Earnie Stewart, the son of an American airman who married a Dutch woman and stayed. Stewart was a regular in the Dutch league but had never played for the Dutch national team at the international level, so he was eligible to join the U.S. team.

The scouts found another prospect in Germany—a steady midfielder named Thomas Dooley, whose father had been an American soldier. Dooley could not speak English when he was recruited for the U.S. team. I remember seeing him in the gift shop of a Washington hotel the day of his first friendly with his new nation; he was having trouble buying postcards and stamps. A born leader and communicator, Dooley was chatting in English within weeks.

Then there was Fernando Clavijo, who had come to America from Uruguay to support his family and play in the semipro leagues in his spare time. While waiting for his papers to be sorted out, Clavijo had been working at a restaurant in the eastern reaches of New York City, down on his hands and knees, cleaning a carpet, when he spotted the plain black shoes and cuffed slacks of law-enforcement agents. To Clavijo's great fortune, his boss escorted him to a table, whisked off his white apron, and handed him a bottle of wine, making him look like a customer. While the feds chased other aliens out the back door or through bathroom windows, Clavijo sipped away, in the affluent glow of suburbia.

When the feds left, his knees were not functioning perfectly, but he was otherwise safe. His boss helped him get a green card, and Clavijo was later discovered by the federation.

By 1994, Clavijo was the conduit for the new American coach—the peripatetic Bora Milutinović, the Serb who had coached Mexico in 1986 and Costa Rica in 1990. In hotel lobbies or airport corridors, Bora was the center of the cluster of fans and reporters, calling everybody "my friend."

Bora was inscrutable in many languages. I sometimes charted his sentences as they veered from one language to another: *My good friend, vamos a ver what kind of giocatori we have here because je suis un étrangère, you know?*

The players did not claim to understand Bora and looked to Clavijo to decipher the linguistic peregrinations.

In the first indoor match ever held in the World Cup, the Americans got into trouble when a free kick handcuffed Meola for a Swiss goal in the thirty-ninth minute. But soon the upgraded level of professionalism kicked in. By now, many of the American players had been in tough games in the better leagues in Europe and could react under pressure the way Paul Caligiuri (still starting for the United States) had done in Trinidad in 1989.

Rather than let the half run out and head for the locker room, John Harkes made something happen. He had scored vital goals in three seasons for Sheffield Wednesday, acquiring a swagger as well as reigniting the latent Scottish accent he had inherited from his parents. Harkes made a run upfield, eluding defenders until a Swiss player decided to dump him rather than let him advance. The tactical foul earned a free kick.

Tab Ramos, who played for Real Betis in Spain, and Harkes both hovered near the dead ball. In the group-dynamics negotiations that often take place before free kicks, they acknowledged that Eric Wynalda, the scorer for Saarbrücken, should take the kick.

"Too far for me," Ramos said later.

Wynalda, using the experience from playing overseas, spotted the Swiss keeper shading slightly toward his own left. Wynalda put the ball into the far opposite corner, nudging the underside of the crossbar, tying the match in the forty-fourth minute. Later, the Swiss players would admit that the goal just before halftime deflated them. The 1–1 draw held up for the first point by the United States in the World Cup since the great victory over England in 1950. But Harkes and some of the others were upset that they had missed a chance to score again and perhaps dominate their group.

After Wynalda scored, the stale air in the dome combined with his allergies to make him sick to his stomach, and he had to come out in the fifty-eighth minute. The segments of grass held up, but there was a torpor to the indoor atmosphere.

Back home in New York, the magical spring in Madison Square Garden was lasting much too long for me. The *Times* needed me to fly to Houston the next morning to cover the conclusion of the NBA Finals— the Knicks against the Rockets. A columnist always wants to be told, Big guy, we need you at the big event, but I would have preferred not to have this intrusion on the World Cup.

I was quietly hoping the Knicks would close out the series in game six so I could cover the U.S.-Colombia match at the Rose Bowl three days later. Instead, Hakeem Olajuwon blocked John Starks's final shot to preserve a two-point victory for Houston. Now I was mad at the Knicks for making me miss the soccer match.

On June 22, Chris Brienza, a Knicks PR staff member and soccer buff, and I found a spare TV set in the labyrinth of the Houston arena, and we watched the first fifteen or twenty minutes of the match, until the basketball game started. Then we went to work and watched Starks shoot two-for-eighteen as the Knicks lost the game and the series. I thereby missed all the scoring in the 2–1 U.S. victory, including an own goal by a Colombian defender, Andrés Escobar, in the thirty-fifth minute.

I caught up with the own goal later, on television replay. The mistake could not be blamed on the new rule banning back passes to the keeper. Harkes made the goal happen by crossing the ball toward Earnie Stewart, who was coming in from the right. The keeper (no longer René Higuita of the happy feet but Oscar Cordoba) had wandered out to his left to combat Stewart, leaving the goalmouth open, and Escobar, the solid captain, desperately slid to intercept the ball but arrived a fraction of a second late, shunting it into the goal. Stewart scored in the fifty-second minute, and Colombia scored late.

Colombia had been the overwhelming favorite in this match; now it was out of contention because of the loss. But something worse would happen. Two weeks later, on July 2, Escobar was shot dead outside a night-club back home in Medellín. There were rumors that major drug dealers had bet heavily on the national team and were angry at their losses. A driver for one syndicate was convicted and sentenced to forty-three years in prison but was released after eleven. To this day, fans carry photos of Andrés Escobar to matches of his former team.

With the Knicks gone, I caught up with the third U.S. match, a 1–0 loss to Romania in the Rose Bowl. With four points, the United States qualified for the knockout round, but Harkes was given a yellow card for yapping at officials during the usual scuffling before a free kick. Because he already had a yellow card, Harkes was ineligible for the next match, in the round of 16.

Sixteen years later, while broadcasting from the World Cup in South Africa, Harkes would refer to dumb yellow cards incurred by a Uruguayan (Luis Suárez) and German (Thomas Müller), forcing them to miss semifinal games. He knew the feeling.

The United States had eight days before their round of 16 match. This gave me a chance to catch up on everything else that had happened in the first round.

Some sites were within commuting distance in the northeast corridor, but others were scattered around this huge country, cutting down on the feeling of community I had felt in Spain and Italy. For years afterward, people raved about the orange glow of Dutch fans and other zealots who congregated in downtown Orlando. I never got there.

Just as in Mexico in 1986, many matches were scheduled at midday in the blazing heat, sacrificing the health and durability of the players for the convenience of fans in Europe.

The match between Germany and South Korea on June 27 at the Cotton Bowl in Dallas began at 4 p.m. with the temperature at 100 degrees. Germany took a 3–0 lead after thirty-seven minutes, with two goals from Klinsmann. On one of the longest days of the year, the sun was not going anywhere, and neither were the Koreans, who are known for their tenacity and combativeness. They scored twice in the second half as Germany threw in two substitutes and managed to hang on for a 3–2 victory.

Germany then staggered through a 3–2 victory over Belgium in the round of 16 but succumbed to Bulgaria, 2–1, in a noon match in New Jersey in the quarterfinals, on a goal in the seventy-eighth minute. In my opinion, they never recovered from the heat and the Koreans.

I never caught up with Greece, coached by the former U.S. national coach Alkis Panagoulias, who had led the American team in that fatal qualifying match against Costa Rica in 1985. Nine years later, Panagoulias finally got to coach in the World Cup.

Months before the World Cup, Panagoulias had invited me to lunch in the old Greek neighborhood of Astoria, Queens—at the landmark Uncle George's Greek Taverna, open twenty-four hours. When he showed up, the place went nuts. *Panagoulias is here! Panagoulias is here!* People flocked to his table, chattering about the old days, chattering about Greece's chances. Once again I could feel the strength of soccer in New York's ethnic outposts. But in the tournament, Greece never scored against Nigeria or Bulgaria or Argentina and was eliminated.

Diego Maradona was back for his fourth World Cup, having worn out his welcome with Napoli and other enablers, having tested positive for cocaine in 1991 and been banned for fifteen months, but each time he was allowed to stumble back into the limelight. FIFA wanted Maradona to play in the 1994 World Cup because it believed that Americans needed his celebrity to be induced to buy tickets to this strange event. In 1992, Blatter had brokered a chance for Maradona to join Sevilla, so he could get back into shape for the World Cup.

"That night I explain that Maradona is like a member of a family,"

Blatter later told the journalist Jimmy Burns, adding, "He has failed his family and been punished for it. But he has served his punishment. The same family must now do everything possible to bring him back into the fold." Blatter also put out a public statement that he expected the prodigal son to "stop making insulting comments against football leaders whether at club, federation or international level." Presumably, Blatter was referring to himself.

Maradona came to the United States with his weight down, but he was still a mess. Having been introduced to body-building drugs as a prodigy in Argentina, he had taken to so-called recreational drugs at an early age. His appetites knew no limit. He played eighty-three minutes and scored a goal in beating Greece, 4–0, and played ninety minutes in Argentina's 2–1 victory over Nigeria. But on June 29, while preparing for Argentina's match against Bulgaria, he was told that he had tested positive for a "cocktail" of five illegal drugs, including ephedrine, and was out of the tournament.

When he heard the news, Maradona broke down in tears, wailing that he had worked so hard to get his body in shape, and now somebody must have made a terrible mistake. Then he was gone, his life a whirlwind of heart problems, medical treatment, and drug rehabilitation in Cuba, a friendship with Fidel Castro, inflammatory statements about the United States, tangled relationships with his wife, girlfriends, and children in and out of marriage.

The World Cup went on without him, quite easily. On July 3, I flew back to the West Coast and covered a racehorse match between Romania and Argentina in the heat of the midday sun at the Rose Bowl. Showtime! Argentina won, 3–2, without its seedy star.

It was hard to feel at one with the World Cup while trekking through airports and hotels in this vast land. However, some days were memorable. The next morning I flew to the Bay Area for U.S.-Brazil on the Fourth of July, my fifty-fifth birthday. The match was at Stanford University's football stadium on the idyllic campus, a festive celebration of the holiday as well as the Yanks and Brazilians. The Stanford rowing club was selling souvenir T-shirts, white with red lettering. Nearly twenty years later, mine is a bit frayed around the collar, but then again so am I.

The lettering says:

STANFORD

WORLD SOCCER

BRASIL vs. U.S.A.

Below that is a soccer ball and crossed flag poles bearing the American stars and stripes and the mystical Brazilian globe and the words:

ORDEM E PROGESSO

July 4th, 1994

Stanford Stadium

Stanford, California

USA

The one word it does not contain is FIFA, which suggests that Sepp Blatter could still sue somebody for royalties, maybe even me for wearing it.

I love the Brazilian flag. Everybody loves the Brazilians. At least they did until Leonardo of Brazil coldcocked Tab Ramos.

In the forty-third minute, Ramos grabbed Leonardo's jersey as they tangled near the sideline, just another skirmish in a sport full of them. Perhaps frustrated by the Americans' early aggression, Leonardo drove his right elbow into Ramos's face, putting him out of the match with a broken bone in the eye socket.

The vicious shot earned Leonardo a red card. (Ramos was also given a yellow card for grabbing Leonardo's shirt.) Leonardo, who had a fine reputation, went to the hospital that evening to tell Ramos he did not intend to hurt him, and Ramos accepted the gesture. A heady, inventive two-way player, probably the best on the American squad, Ramos was never quite the same after that.

In the second half, playing a man down, Brazil remembered its roots in ball movement, widening the field, keeping possession. The twin engines, Romário and Bebeto, began coming at the U.S. goal until in the seventy-second minute Bebeto gained a few inches on Alexi Lalas and drilled a goal from a wide angle. Brazil hung on for a 1–0 victory, and the U.S. players knew they had missed an opportunity to do better in front of a supportive crowd of 84,147 fans.

That night I headed to the San Francisco airport for the flight to Boston. In the airport, I spotted Bob Ryan of the *Boston Globe*, one of the few major American sports columnists to take the World Cup seriously. I don't think Ryan was a soccer buff, but as a curious journalist he knew a good story in his homeland and put himself on the red-eye to cover it from coast to coast.

A few hours later we reconvened in Foxboro Stadium, the home of the New England Patriots, for a match between the latest great African hope, Nigeria, and the diva of any World Cup opera, Italy.

The Azzurri were doing what they do best. They were suffering.

The coach this time around was Arrigo Sacchi, who had once been a shoe salesman and had never played professional soccer. Because Sacchi had worked his way up from the lowest leagues, his every move was suspect in the Italian mind, which only added to his introverted manner. He was proud of hailing from the same region, Emilia-Romagna, as the director Federico Fellini and maintained a distracting half smile, as if he knew some inner truth that nobody else did—the odd captain of a listing ship that may or may not reach shore.

"I am never afraid of being unpopular or else I wouldn't have done ninety-nine percent of everything I have done," Sacchi once said.

The Italian ball handler, Roberto Baggio, was also introverted. He had played on the 1990 national squad and then moved from Fiorentina to Juventus. Born in the northeast region of Veneto, the slender, ascetic-looking Baggio wore a ponytail that earned him the nickname Il Codino—the Ponytail. Sometimes he was even called Il Divin Codino.

Baggio was a convert to Buddhism, and his mother once said she prayed for his conversion back to Catholicism. He tended to keep to himself. On the field he was capable of sudden acts of genius, popping up in open spaces, controlling the ball, changing the course of a match.

After my first few World Cups, I had come to believe that coaches—whether former stars or outsiders like Sacchi—tend to be wary of shifty little artists like Baggio, even though they are capable of creating goals from nowhere. The reason is simple: geniuses render their teachers slightly less relevant.

This odd couple, Sacchi and Baggio, had been yoked together in a desperate moment in November 1993. Italy, with all that talent, went into the final qualifying match needing at least a draw against Portugal to qualify for the Stati Uniti.

Having experienced American anxiety about qualifying for the two previous World Cups, I wanted to witness the process in a major soccer country—*la paura di sbagliare*, as Andrea Bocelli sings in a ballad, the fear of screwing up. I convinced my editors to approve the trip by arguing that the Meadowlands, the stadium in New Jersey that had spooked Sepp Blatter, was projected to be the home for Italy because of the three million Italian Americans in the New York metropolitan region.

When I arrived in Milan, *La Gazzetta* and the other papers were stirring memories of 1958, when Italy came down to the final qualifier against Northern Ireland, in Belfast, and was upset, 2–1. The Azzurri had not missed a World Cup since, but you never knew.

All week long, Sacchi had been insisting that Italy would not play defensively, but the fans would have been fine with pulling the sturdy *catenaccio* across the portals and getting out of there with a draw.

With anxiety hanging over marshy northern Italy like late-autumn clouds, I took the trolley from the Duomo, gliding through curving Renaissance streets toward the stadium on the edge of town. A few older chichi ladies on the tram took on a pained expression as they regarded the fans, boisterous from nerves. One mistake could ruin four years.

On my way into the stadium known as San Siro, I ran into Alan Rothenberg, the president of the American federation.

"No country is more important than Italy," Rothenberg said. "To me, it's a matter of the excitement the fans will bring." He did not mention the tickets he was hoping to sell in New Jersey. Rothenberg had been given a blue Forza Italia scarf that he discreetly tucked in his pocket—you always want to appear neutral—but he confided that he would keep his hand on the scarf for the entire match, like a Greek clutching worry beads on a bumpy flight.

The great majority of the 71,513 fans normally booed Baggio when he came in with Fiorentina or Juventus, but now he was the great pony-tailed hope.

In the first half, Baggio kept Portugal occupied with his dribbling and passing and a few shots near the goal. There was a terrible moment of fear as the goalkeeper Gianluca Pagliuca overran a ball as it skittered near the goalmouth, but the ball did not want to go in.

"We were afraid late in the first half," Sacchi would say later. "Fear blocks you."

At halftime, the press box provided espresso—the real stuff, from an ornate espresso machine, just like the ones in the city's elegant cafés and arcades, with real cups and real spoons.

The match was still scoreless, disaster lurking, with ten minutes to go, when Sacchi sent in Roberto Mancini, the dapper forward with wavy hair from Sampdoria, who twenty-two years later would coach Manchester City to a Premiership title. Three minutes later, Mancini fed Roberto Baggio, who passed to Dino Baggio (no relation), who kicked the ball past the Portuguese keeper. Italy's celebration consisted mainly of breathing again.

"Now we go to the U.S. as the first team in our group," Sacchi said later.

And Alan Rothenberg let loose the Forza Italia scarf in his pocket.

While I was in Italy, it just happened that AC Milan was home against Napoli the following Sunday. I took the tram out to San Siro again, noticing a much rougher crowd for a club match, security all over the place, as if the city-states were still at war.

On the gelid field, Paolo Di Canio of Napoli collided with my favorite defender, Franco Baresi, the captain of the Azzurri. I was partial to the earnest Baresi, unemotional and modest-sized, because he reminded me of a few fathers in my old neighborhood, who worked on the docks in Brooklyn. Now, as medics attended to Baresi, I figured he was done for the day, but he trudged back onto the field, blood staining the wide swatch of bandage, making him look like the piper in the famous Archibald MacNeal Willard painting, *The Spirit of '76*.

Still groggy, Baresi shuffled in place while the graceful Paolo Maldini covered the zone for both of them. Just before halftime, Napoli exploited Baresi's sector for a goal, but he revived in the second half, and Christian Panucci and Demetrio Albertini both connected on long-range shots for a 2–1 victory for AC Milan.

After the match, I spotted Baresi slipping through the mixed zone; good grief, he was no more than five feet nine, even smaller than I had thought.

The next day the papers said there had been only one or two stabbings and beatings at the match—a relatively calm night at San Siro.

After a five-hour *sciopero* at the airport, I went home. Mission accomplished. All that talent, all that angst was coming to America.

The *ansia* did not disappoint the following June. Having been seeded into the Meadowlands, as everybody knew would happen, Italy was now disappointing its constituency. In New Jersey, the sociological reality was that the next generation of Italian Americans had moved out to the suburbs and gotten Americanized; somewhere along the line the love of soccer had been bleached out of them. The team was encamped at a private school in a leafy suburb in New Jersey, attracting a cast of journalists and roaming *tifosi* and other Felliniesque characters.

Instead of the usual first-round draw, Italy was stunned by Ireland, 1–0, in its first match.

American sportscasters fell in love with the name of the Italian keeper Gianluca Pagliuca, pronouncing it over and over again when Pagliuca fouled a Norwegian attacker, incurring an automatic ejection. Sacchi was forced to remove a player to make room for his substitute keeper. To his horror, Roberto Baggio, theoretically the centerpiece of the Italian offense, saw his No. 10 illuminated on the portable signboard held by the fourth official. His eyes and mouth narrowing into tight little lines, Baggio trudged off the field.

Much of the entire Italian diaspora went mad: take out your most imaginative player so early in a scoreless tie? The fans said they always knew that they should not have faith in the shoe salesman.

"Baggio on the bench? It's something that I will never understand in my lifetime."

This comment was attributed to another country's star who would dominate the next World Cup, and who essentially would replace Baggio at Juventus in 1996. They were kindred souls, Baggio and Zinedine Zidane.

Sacchi did not become coach of the national squad without a ration of good fortune. Dino Baggio saved the second match, scoring while the team was shorthanded in the sixty-ninth minute, thereby keeping Italy alive. For all his spiritual journeys, Il Codino was a pure competitor, who hated it that Sacchi took him out; very un-Zenlike, he glared out at the world.

The horrors continued: Baresi, the stoic defender, underwent arthroscopic knee surgery after the second match.

Sacchi's moves paid off again in the third match against Mexico in Washington, D.C. At halftime, he sent in his supersub, Daniele Massaro, who had played for him at AC Milan, and two minutes later Massaro scored. Mexico countered for a draw, and all four teams in the group finished with four points and were even on goal differential. However, Norway was punished for its defensive posture, having scored and allowed the fewest goals; once again, Italy barely survived the first round.

Now things really got crazy: after Roberto Baggio's tepid performance against Mexico, Gianni Agnelli, *il padrone* of Fiat and Juventus, who had just spent millions for Baggio, labeled him "a wet rabbit."

Before the tournament, Baggio had said: "I am hoping to be the Paolo Rossi of this World Cup," but he was not exactly following the path of Rossi in 1982 or Totò Schillaci in 1990. Some supporters were now calling for him to be benched, but he was in the starting lineup for Nigeria in Massachusetts.

Disaster was closing in as Nigeria took a lead in the twenty-fifth minute, and Gianfranco Zola was tossed out in the seventy-fifth minute for not very much.

In the front row of the open press tribune, the head of the Italian federation was pacing. It looked to me that he was edging closer to tossing himself over the railing. Keep an eye on that man.

Il Codino cut it close, waiting until the eighty-eighth minute before leading a furious swarm toward the Nigerian goal and taking a sideways pass and from fourteen yards out rolling a low shot between the moving legs of a teammate and a Nigerian defender. Peter Rufai, the Nigerian keeper, sprawled but could not stop the shot out of the forest of legs—the first goal for Baggio in this World Cup. The harried head of the Italian federation backed away from the railing. Maybe he wouldn't jump, after all.

Now that the match was drawn, in the 102nd minute, Italy's Antonio Benarrivo went sprawling near the goal while settling under a lobbed pass from Dino Baggio. The sprawl was at least 50 percent theatrics, but the referee went for it. Italy would have a penalty kick. Il Codino calmly arranged the ball on the scruffy disk area and calmly scored the penalty kick—low, off the left post. Italy had endured into the quarterfinals.

Four days later, Italy was back in the same stadium in Massachusetts, this time against Spain, the classic underachiever of the World Cup. With its great domestic league and obvious talent, Spain always found a way to self-destruct. Did Italy count on that? Dino Baggio scored in the twenty-fifth minute, Spain scored in the fifty-eighth, and Il Codino waited until his time, now established as the eighty-eighth minute.

Baggio received a looping pass from Giuseppe Signori in the penalty area, as the Spanish keeper rushed toward Baggio to intimidate him. With feline grace, Baggio flitted to his right and flicked the ball into the goal for the 2–1 lead.

With a lead, Italy transformed from quivering wreck to swaggering bully, straight out of the classic American movie *Breaking Away*, in which a seasoned Italian cyclist sticks an air pump into the spokes of the admiring kid from Indiana. In this version, Mauro Tassotti ascertained the official was not looking and hammered Spain's Luis Enrique to the ground. Blood dripping onto his shirt, an enraged Luis Enrique tried to get through to Tassotti, but Spain was done, again.

When FIFA caught up with the films, weeks later, it banned Tassotti for eight matches, which became academic since Italy never again chose him for the national team. (Seventeen years later, on the sideline before a Serie A match, Tassotti and Luis Enrique, both long retired, happened to meet, and Tassotti mumbled something that may or may not have been an apology.)

Now Italy was heading for the semifinals, again in New Jersey. Tickets were going fast.

As I traveled across America, I had the melancholic impression, more than usual, that I was missing half the World Cup. Bulgaria and Sweden had both advanced to the semifinals, with players who earned good livings in the better leagues of Europe. The reward for both nations was that these players gained experience against other top players and were not in awe of anybody.

Bulgaria's powerful striker, Hristo Stoichkov, now playing in Barcelona, carried his nation to the semifinals with his wiles and free kicks. Then in the Meadowlands on July 13, Roberto Baggio scored two goals before Stoichkov scored one, for a 2–1 victory that sent Italy to the finals. Baggio hobbled off late with a tender hamstring.

Sweden had won its quarterfinal in a shoot-out over Romania in the midday sun at Stanford on Sunday and had one less day of rest than Brazil for the semifinal. In the Rose Bowl, Sweden had to play the final twenty-seven minutes after an ejection, and Romário put in a header past Thomas Ravelli in the eightieth minute for a 1–0 victory for Brazil.

Everyone arrived at the Rose Bowl early in the morning for the final, which began at the ungodly hour of 12:30 p.m.—nine hours later in central Europe. Pelé, no longer shunned by the thought police from FIFA, was looking spry and handsome in a white suit as he jogged across the field, escorting Whitney Houston, who was quite gorgeous in a billowing outfit, along with white socks and sneakers, as she sang a little pregame concert.

The Brazilian and Italian players looked weary as they marched out.

Baresi was back in the lineup for the Azzurri, after arthroscopic surgery on his knee just twenty-four days earlier.

"I decided to play," Baresi said later. "I haven't been playing for a month, but this game for the national team will be my last game." He was the captain; that was his code.

Italy had other problems. Two players had been suspended for yellow cards, Donadoni's hamstring had tightened on the six-hour flight west, and Roberto Baggio's hamstring was still twanging. He advised Sacchi that he might be more valuable coming off the bench but the coach said he would start—or not suit up at all.

This is the cruelty of soccer, with its quickie summer vacations. Most of the finalists were playing from memory after a long club season in Europe. They were the best footballers in the world, but they were gassed. The strikers shot and the defenders blocked and the keepers dove, and nobody could score.

In the thirty-sixth minute, Baresi, squat and postsurgical, spotted an opening and went forward with Il Codino on a two-on-one break, my two favorite players on that squad, the lame leading the lame. That sortie was broken up, and after that, Baresi stayed closer to home, admirably keeping track of Bebeto and Romário. The ninety minutes ended without a goal, and in the final minute of added time—120 minutes on his feet—Baresi went down on the field with cramps. Two teammates tried to stretch his legs, and the trainer took him off the field on a motor cart.

When the game ended with no goals, some American fans booed when it was announced that a shoot-out would decide the championship.

Boo FIFA for a killer schedule, I wanted to say. Just don't demand that these players run anymore. American fans, many just discovering this sport, dream up all kinds of gimmicks to decide a match, but soccer already has a method—the shoot-out, the only humane ending after the players have run eight or ten miles.

The teams casually saluted each other on the sideline, acknowledging that whatever happened afterward was a fluke, "a lottery," as Baresi would say. In the moments before the shoot-out, Baresi lay on his back as the trainer massaged and flexed his legs. He opened his mouth in pain, like somebody being bombed in Picasso's *Guernica*.

This man was not some *zeppole*, some creampuff, all soft and sweet on the inside. When you saw Franco Baresi's teeth bared, it was time to stop the running.

The two coaches, Carlos Alberto Parreira and Arrigo Sacchi, turned in their lineups for the shoot-out. I would guess that everybody in the Rose Bowl was shocked to see that the first man out was Baresi. Then somebody looked it up: in the fatal semifinal against Argentina in 1990, in steamy Naples, Baresi had also been the first Azzurri shooter. And he had converted. That's what captains did. They went first.

"It was a great game, but Italy doesn't have a history of doing well in shoot-outs," Baresi said later. "I was asked if I was willing to kick first, so I did." Of course, Sacchi never should have asked the brave captain to shoot first.

Flexing his legs, facing the ball on the ground, Baresi skied his shot above the crossbar, to land in the twentieth row. Brazil also missed its first, but then made three straight. Italy made two straight, but Massaro was stopped. Italy was trailing, 3–2, after four kicks. To stay alive, Italy sent out Il Codino.

Many great scorers hate penalty kicks. They will take their chances freelancing on the field, but they detest the rigidity of kicking from the twelve-yard spot with the entire stadium, the entire world, watching.

Baggio did not look comfortable. He bent over the ball, as if humming some Zen koan, but there was no peace in his tight visage. He used his artistic hands to eliminate any mole hills, any seismic eruptions, in the grit on the Rose Bowl floor. Then he trudged back a few steps, bad karma evident in his askew jersey. He took a few steps, and after a mild approach he dispatched the ball over the crossbar, almost exactly where Baresi had put his.

The World Cup was over. Baggio stood in place for a long time, more Schillaci than Rossi, no shame in that. Everybody cried on the Italian bench, even the public-relations man. Franco Baresi cried. It's Italy. The opera was over.

Brazil, the champion everybody loves, had won its fourth World

Cup, the first I had seen. But after the shoot-out, it did not feel like a championship. Where were Sócrates and Falcão from Barcelona in 1982? Everybody staggered to the exits, looking to get out of the sun.

As the organizers trucked away the Porta Potties and took down the fences, FIFA counted its swag from this excursion into the strange new world of O. J. Simpson and enclosed stadiums and surging happy crowds.

The legacy of Alan Rothenberg and his staff was a total attendance of 3,587,538 for fifty-two matches, a full million ahead of Italy in 1990 for the same number of matches. The average per match was 68,991.

Four World Cups later, the United States still holds the record for attendance and profit. Sepp Blatter knew it all along.

10

AMERICA'S FIRST
SOCCER CHAMPION

ATHENS, GEORGIA, 1996

Loyal fans of the University of Georgia know the expression "between the hedges," a reference to the thick privet hedges that ring the hallowed field.

Not much is allowed between those hedges except football, American-style.

In 1996, the hedges were removed for the first time since being planted in 1929, to accommodate a strange activity—soccer.

After Atlanta was awarded the Summer Olympics, a World Cup–style tournament was planned around the eastern United States. The semi-finals and finals for men and women would be played at the state university—but only if Sanford Stadium could accommodate a soccer field, which at 115 yards by 74 yards is larger than a football field. That meant the hedges would have to come down.

Some officials were a tad uncomfortable telling Georgians that the hedges were being removed to accommodate this rather suspicious foreign sport, so the public was informed that the hedges were imperiled by nematodes, a minute but dangerous parasite. Citizens were reassured that a healthy crop of hedge would be planted a few days after the Olympics ended.

As a result, one of the great moments for women and soccer and the Olympics took place in Athens, seventy miles from Atlanta.

To its credit, the International Olympic Committee, under Juan Antonio Samaranch, had added more sports for women in time for the 1996 Summer Games. Women had been kicking the round ball in Europe, just like men, since the nineteenth century, and there were even leagues for women early in the twentieth century.

The Title IX legislation of 1972 helped women play organized sports, with college scholarships now available to female athletes. By 1982, the National Collegiate Athletic Association held its first official women's Division I championship, won by the University of North Carolina, which has dominated the event ever since. But the American federation maintained only a "paper team," in the words of Mia Hamm, a North Carolina player who became one of the icons of female soccer. She meant that female players were only occasionally called together for international play.

In the United States and elsewhere, women encountered stereotypes about female athletes, but the women persisted. FIFA began organizing competitions for women and by 1991 counted 65 national women's teams, compared to 165 men's teams. FIFA authorized the first Women's World Cup in late November of that year in China, even though that country did not yet have a powerful soccer team.

"There is still a lot of condescension when it comes to women's soccer, even in Europe," Andreas Herren, a FIFA spokesman, told the *New York Times*. "We were afraid that if the games were held in Europe, the crowds would be very small, the stadiums not the best. It would be embarrassing and not the best way to promote the sport."

Chinese officials made sure that large stadiums were packed, even in the late November chill. "The Chinese fans didn't have a team in the finals, so they would cheer for good soccer," recalled Carla Overbeck, an American defender. "If we made a good play, they cheered us. If the Norwegians made a good play, they cheered the Norwegians. It was a very healthy atmosphere."

In the championship match in front of sixty-five thousand fans in Guangzhou, Michelle Akers (then married and known as Akers-Stahl) scored both goals, one with three minutes left, in a 2–1 victory over Norway.

"I think we feel we are on a mission now and no one will get in our way, no matter what," Akers told the *Times*. Off the field, Akers was a gentle soul, but on the field she could track down any opponent and divest her of the ball—Big Bird with a mop of curls and an attitude. She and Carin Jennings and April Heinrichs, the other forwards, were labeled "the triple-edged sword" by Chinese reporters, and Akers was the best player in that tournament. For that matter, she remains the best female player of all time.

That first national team was coached by Anson Dorrance, who had won eight of the first nine national tournaments for North Carolina. The team was blessed with skill and personality, including the three youngest players: Julie Foudy, twenty years old, an activist Stanford midfielder known to her teammates as Loudy Foudy; Kristine Lilly, age nineteen, who could score and defend, a true footballer; and Mia Hamm, also nineteen, a highly skilled and competitive forward with the aura of a Jackie Kennedy or a Greta Garbo, a superstar who seemed to shun attention and therefore received more of it.

When the American women returned home, they were greeted at the White House by President George H. W. Bush and lauded in an editorial in the *New York Times*, but the championship did not attract much attention. America's soccer self-esteem was still quite low after the men's poor performance in Italy in 1990.

That championship in China created a heritage, which included a rivalry between the U.S. women's team and Norway. Linda Medalen, now an Oslo police officer, hounded the American forwards as if they were alleged perpetrators, as law-enforcement officers say. One of the best things that ever happened to women's soccer took place in the 1995 Women's World Cup final in Sweden, when Medalen and the Norwegians knocked off the Americans, 1–0. That was a signal to other countries that they could compete with the Yanks. Then the Norwegian players chose to celebrate on their hands and knees in an elaborate ritual known as the Train. The American players stood at the edge of the field and watched the Norwegians cavort, and implanted the scene in collective memory.

Many male soccer buffs scorned women's soccer because, they said, the women's speed and power and technical skill were far below that of men. Yet others—and I was one of them—loved women's soccer because they played with teamwork and heart and brains at a pace anybody could follow.

Another interesting thing about female players: they had much better balance than their male counterparts. That is to say, they did not flop nearly as much.

"Our front-runners want to keep standing up," Carla Overbeck said in 1995. "The instinct is to stay on your feet. But our coaches have been reminding us that one Norwegian player got five penalty kicks from diving. That's a huge amount of penalties. Our coaches are saying, 'If you get hacked, go down.' The other teams are so successful at it."

In 1996, the Olympic tournaments consisted of separate male and female groups in Orlando; Miami; Washington, D.C.; and Birmingham, Alabama, with the semifinals and finals moving to Athens, Georgia—after the hedges were removed to eradicate the dreaded if perhaps nonexistent nematodes and coincidentally provide space for the wider field.

In the semifinals, the American women met their chums from Norway. Medalen scored in the eighteenth minute, but Akers scored in the seventy-sixth minute—two great players coming through for their teams. In the ninety-sixth minute, U.S. coach Tony DiCicco sent in Shannon MacMillan for the weary Tiffeny Milbrett, and MacMillan scored four minutes later to put the Americans into the finals. China moved past Brazil, 3–2, in the other semifinal.

Great things were happening in Athens, but somehow the excitement had not reached NBC, which was televising the Olympics. American television executives were still fearful of soccer because it did not have time-outs for commercials, and Americans were said to dislike the sport, so the network gave minimal coverage to some of the most charismatic athletes performing in those games. (Television still prefers to show hours of Olympic women's beach volleyball, butts in bikinis, than more traditional sports.)

In the final, the Americans beat China, 2–1, as Mia Hamm centered the ball on a fast break to Joy Fawcett, who fed Milbrett racing in from the left for the decisive goal in the sixty-eighth minute. The attendance was 76,481, the largest crowd ever to watch a women's game anywhere in the world.

Now that the actual game was over and the Americans were champions, a network official tried to arrange a live shot of the women celebrating. That touched off the fury of Hank Steinbrecher, the executive director of the U.S. federation, who told the official, "NBC must think the world is full of divers," a reference to television's affinity for women in swimsuits jumping into pools. Steinbrecher was standing up for his athletes, but he was no fool. He then made the women available for the cameras.

Within days, the University of Georgia regained its privet hedge in time for football season. Years later, it came out that a few Georgia officials had made up the part about the nematodes. The fib helped the nation, the world, discover a charismatic band of champions.

11

ALLONS, ENFANTS

FRANCE, 1998

The French public had extreme reservations about Les Bleus. The new coach, Aimé Etienne Jacquet, did not have much international experience, having played only two matches for the French team during his career, and he stressed fundamentals more than fans wanted to hear.

When Jacquet cut the eighteen-year-old star Nicolas Anelka—much the way César Luis Menotti had dropped Diego Maradona before the 1978 World Cup—there were calls for the coach to resign. He did not. Instead, he talked about the Michel Platini era, when the French were "the Brazilians of Europe"—silky style and skill.

There was one major difference. Brazil had won four World Cups and France had won none. Now France was about to be the host in 1998.

Another burning question about Les Bleus was raised by Jean-Marie Le Pen, the leader of France's far-right political party the National Front.

"It's a bit artificial to bring players from abroad and call it the French team," LePen said.

Many of the players had roots in French-speaking countries in Africa or far-flung departments of France and were eligible for French passports. Many other federations, including the United States, recruit players for their national team, but Le Pen was uneasy with the new face of France, known as the Rainbow Warriors.

"Our team gives you a sense of the socio-cultural mix that is France today," responded goalkeeper Bernard Lama, who was born in Guiana and arrived in France when he was eighteen.

It was true that many of the key players had roots outside metropolitan France, but they had legitimate rights to a French passport. Marcel Desailly, the defender with AC Milan, was born in Ghana; Christian Karembeu in New Caledonia; Lilian Thuram in Pointe-à-Pitre in the French Caribbean island of Guadeloupe; Patrick Vieira in Dakar, Senegal. Thierry Henry, the fleet young striker, was born in a Paris suburb of a father from La Désirade, an island of Guadeloupe, and a mother from Martinique. Robert Pirès was born in Reims but grew up alternately wearing gear from Portugal and Real Madrid, the roots of his parents. David Trezeguet's parents were from Argentina, where he had lived as a child; Bixente Lizarazu's heritage was Basque; Youri Djorkaeff's mother was Armenian and his father, Jean, who played for France in the 1966 World Cup, was of Polish and Kalmuck descent; Alain Boghossian was born in France but proudly referred to his roots in Armenia.

Then there was Zinedine Yazid Zidane, the elegant playmaker and scorer who was born in Marseilles to parents from the Kabyle ethnic group in Algeria, who had emigrated nineteen years earlier. Zidane had played for Cannes and Bordeaux and Real Madrid and was now at Juventus. He was a native son of France, but Le Pen's remarks raised the question, Who, exactly, is French?

In 1993, the French national team had stunningly lost its final qualifying match to Bulgaria in the ninetieth minute.

The next morning, *Libération* ran the headline: "France Qualifies! For 1998!"

That was cold, inasmuch as the host team automatically qualifies.

Coughing up the ball to Bulgaria, rather than killing the clock in the corner, was probably a worse moment than the *once tontos* semifinal in

1982, when France kept attacking West Germany with a 3–1 lead, drawing sarcasm from the bartender in Barcelona.

At least the 1982 team got to the semifinals. The only Frenchman seen at the 1994 World Cup was Michel Platini, hosting a cocktail party at the Beverly Hills city hall, to promote the 1998 World Cup.

France had achieved some glory in *le foot*, including a dashing championship in the 1984 European tournament—when it was the host—but some teams peak for the Euros and regress two years later. The World Cup is a different animal.

After four World Cups, I still had not seen the host country win, or even reach the championship game. Quite frankly, I did not pay much attention to the French team going into 1998, partially because past French squads had seemed a trifle soft but also because my colleague Chris Clarey, of the *International Herald Tribune*, who had married a French woman, lived in France, and spoke the language, was keeping an eye on Les Bleus.

I was going to focus on Our Lads during group play and commute to other matches from Paris. My wife and I had lived in France for a month here or there; we have French friends and consider it one of the most beautiful countries in the world. We rented a flat from an American editor in a quiet neighborhood on the Right Bank, arrived one tranquil holiday morning, chatted with the Portuguese concierge, and immediately felt at home.

After the vastness of the American World Cup, this tournament was the right size. My credential got me on all trains, plus any metro or bus in any host city, which was handy, since the American team was based outside Lyon. Far outside Lyon.

After their somewhat accidental foray into the round of 16 in 1994, the Yanks were starting over. The peripatetic Bora Milutinović had moved on to coach Nigeria, and the United States had promoted his assistant, Steve Sampson, a Californian with an open smile who had learned to speak Spanish quite admirably. Whether Sampson could coach soccer at the World Cup level was another question.

There were already signs of dysfunction as the Yanks revealed their training camp—a château deep in the Burgundy countryside. Sampson said he chose the retreat in the name of togetherness, but it turned out to be a rural version of the asylum in *One Flew Over the Cuckoo's Nest*, with Sampson playing the role of Nurse Ratched.

This was the first U.S. team in the World Cup since Major League Soccer had gone into operation in 1996 under Commissioner Doug Logan. The new league had a mutual-ownership plan that kept salaries low while young Americans learned from international ancients like Jorge Campos of Mexico, Carlos Valderrama of Colombia, and Roberto Donadoni of Italy. The ten teams in MLS drew an average of 17,406 fans per game to see homegrown stars like Tony Meola, Tab Ramos, and Brian McBride.

Other Americans found the competition and salaries were much better overseas. Kasey Keller was tending goal in England. Claudio Reyna, who had been injured in 1994, resumed his career in Germany.

Another stalwart was John Harkes, who was under the impression that Sampson expected him to lead the team into the future. His was the handsome face of America; he was a border collie yapping at his mates on the field, who had scored vital goals in the English league and led the Yanks onto hostile fields during qualifiers.

Days before the trip to France, Harkes was stunned to discover that he had been dropped from the squad. Just like that. There were whispers that Harkes had been breaking curfew and questioning Sampson on the field. Others suggested that Sampson had to make room for Reyna's talent in the midfield, which made no sense because Reyna's subtle style did not demand favoritism. Harkes's disappearance touched off discontent as the Yanks were dropped into the vineyards of Burgundy.

Ever since 1998, I have been describing the Château de Pizay as a rustic survivalist hideaway for a reality show about athletes who need to bond. That was the impression I retained, perhaps because of the stir-crazy athletes I encountered within. However, in 2012 I looked up the château on the Web and discovered this:

Château de Pizay, 45 minutes from Lyon and 30 from Mâcon, in the heart of Beaujolais country, was built between the 11th and 15th centuries and is the ideal spot for a truly peaceful stay.

Château de Pizay Hotel - Meetings - Vineyard & Spa Resort is located between Brouilly and Morgon, in the middle of 80 hectares of its own vineyards, and is one of the great wine estates in the region.

The Estate brings together the finest wines in the region: Beaujolais Rouge, Morgon, Régnié, Beaujolais Blanc, Brouilly Château de Saint Lager.

The entire production is made into wine, aged and bottled at the Château. It is aged in cellars which can be visited on appointment.

Winner
Certificate of Excellence
2012
Château de Pizay

On the Web, the resort is obviously a classic château, like Versailles or dozens in the Loire Valley, with crisscrossing walkways and topiary and handsome gates keeping out the riffraff—perfect for a romantic getaway for a couple slipping out of Paris for *le weekend*. This is not some humble *gîte*, a few feet from rumbling trucks on a national highway. Sampson had seen the château the year before during an inspection trip and loved its elegance and seclusion. But I missed the charm of the château because of the paranoia and ineptitude of that failed mission in 1998.

The château was so remote that Sampson could mostly keep his lads away from the hordes of American journalists who had wangled the assignment to France. We were led to feel that if we tried to visit we would be bombarded by boiling oil, but one fine day in early June, the team held Media Day. When the ramp was lowered over the moat (I made that part up), Our Lads were skulking in the handsome courtyard, the look in their eyes saying, "Get me out of here!"

Brian Maisonneuve, a midfielder from the American Midwest, was sitting outside the team wing of the château, both feet stuck in a bucket of ice, which, as I noted, "under better circumstances might have chilled a new bottle of Georges DeBoeuf."

Despite his very French name, Maisonneuve did not speak a word of the language. He said he had been reading an epic thriller called *Les Pages Jaunes,* not much of a plot but a huge cast. "I'm looking at the pictures," Maisonneuve told us.

Sampson held a news conference in the courtyard, explaining his reasoning for putting the team in a rural château. "We have to prepare for Germany," he said. "I don't want them on their feet all day shopping." Sampson quickly added that he had planned an outing to Lyon, forty-five minutes away, and held a golf outing, at which Alexi Lalas had taken twenty-four strokes on the first two holes. (Perhaps his ineptitude at golf explained why Lalas was low man on the defensive depth chart.) Plus, Sampson quickly added, the team had first-round matches in Paris, Lyon, and Nantes, three lovely corners of this diverse country. "After they are finished with this World Cup, they will not say they did not have a World Cup experience," he promised.

What were the players complaining about? They had a dart board, a television with English soccer news, plus a VCR equipped with tapes of *Hoosiers, JFK,* and *Jerry Springer Too Hot for TV.* They were allowed one beer with dinner and could play cards as long as they wanted, as long as the game ended by 10:30 p.m.

"We just came from New York, where the horns honk twenty-four hours a day," Tab Ramos told us. "Here there are no horns."

At the château, the biggest excitement was watching geese waddle around the grounds. For a cohesive team, the château would have worked. For a team with issues, it encouraged problems to fester.

Sampson was enforcing the old sporting tradition of monasticism based on the theory that enforced celibacy produces more energy and combativeness. Wives and girlfriends were forbidden except on an occasional daytime pass, but it was difficult to, shall we say, conduct a conjugal visit when the players were grouped two to a room. The Italian media boycott in 1982 had begun when some journalist wrote that teammates were sharing rooms—as man and wife. For the Americans, crankiness kicked in early.

Sampson clearly had no plans for Lalas, who had parlayed his good run in 1994 and his flamboyant persona into being the first Yank to play in Serie A, with Padova. Ramos, who had declined after being crow-barred by Leonardo of Brazil in 1994, was stewing as a spare part. And the ghost of John Harkes hovered over the squad.

Then there was *l'Affaire Régis*. The U.S. federation had discovered a defender named David Régis, a French citizen, born in Martinique, play-ing in the Bundesliga, with an American wife. The American bureau-cracy has never moved so fast to get somebody his citizenship. But first, Régis had to pass a written test, which posed a problem inasmuch as he did not speak, read, or write English.

Pas de problème. Sampson asked Jeff Agoos to tutor Régis. Agoos had his own frustrations. He had been the last player cut by Bora in 1994 and had burned his uniform in the fireplace at the team lodge. Now, four years later, in the name of team unity, Agoos was being asked to tutor the new left back—which just happened to be Agoos's position.

With Agoos's help, M. Régis now carried a certificate that he was eligible to play for the Yanks. What would Jean-Marie Le Pen think of that?

The United States had a nasty draw, playing two rugged European teams, Germany first and Yugoslavia third. Although the nation of Yugoslavia was being dismantled, it had plenty of talent left for its last blast. The middle opponent was Iran, with its tense political history with the United States, including the hostage crisis of 1979. Iran figured to be the easiest of the three opponents, but the intrigue only complicated matters.

The Germany match was in Parc des Princes in Paris. Once the play-ers took a look at the City of Light, "We were thinking of barricading our-selves in our rooms and not going back," Kasey Keller, the starting keeper, said years later.

The American players had great respect for the German team. Thomas Dooley, who had barely been able to speak English when he joined the U.S. team in 1994, was now an articulate and positive leader. "When I came over here, I don't want to say they weren't organized, but they had more freedom," Dooley said of his colleagues on the American team. "The Germans like more control. If the coach says you have to stay somewhere, the players do not say anything." He seemed to be suggesting that the 1998 players had complained themselves into a bad attitude because of the château and other issues.

Among the Americans, Claudio Reyna spoke admiringly of his fifty-eight matches for Bayer Leverkusen and Wolfsburg, including the brutal midweek practices when scrubs tried to earn a uniform for the weekend games by tackling their own teammates viciously. And in the fifth minute against Germany, Reyna received a reminder of past practices—a vicious elbow to the kidney area, thrown by Jens Jeremies and unacknowledged by the referee. Reyna was far too professional to be elbowed into submission, but he was not much of a factor in the match after that.

Sampson mandated a 3-6-1 alignment for the match, leaving Eric Wynalda pretty much alone up front, easily nullified by the German defense. Sampson's strategy seemed to be borrowed from the film *Dances with Wolves*, in which Kevin Costner plays a lone soldier posted out on the prairie. Germany won, 2–0, as the fleet striker Jürgen Klinsmann scored a goal, as if to introduce himself to the nation where he would one day live—and coach.

The Americans moved south and east to Lyon to play Iran. Twenty minutes before the match, the morose Ramos sat on the team bench and chatted on a cell phone with his buddy Harkes back in the States. Wish you were here, Ramos said. Harkes felt the same way.

The Iranian players had their own distraction: thousands of Iranian émigrés had purchased tickets, and although political demonstrations were banned on the grounds, they uncovered T-shirts that indicated their opposition to the ayatollahs. The Iranian and American players linked arms in a gesture of friendship beforehand, a nice touch.

This time, Sampson put two strikers, Brian McBride and Roy Wegerle, up front, with Wynalda never stirring from the bench. McBride scored late on a header, but Iran stunned the United States, 2–1, pretty much eliminating the Yanks.

After the Iran loss, I called Harkes at his home in Virginia; he was as combative in absentia as he was on the field. "We went through so much hard work, and now the World Cup is over so fast," Harkes said, conceding that the Yanks were not going to score a ton of goals against Yugo-slavia. "I feel for the players. I'm part of it," he added.

"I know I should be there," Harkes continued. "I thought I could con-tribute something with leadership. We had such good chemistry."

Harkes did not hide his hope that Sampson would be gone soon, and he ripped the coach for sticking Wynalda up front all alone against Ger-many. "He didn't have a chance," Harkes said. "He was out there playing against four backs, like he was a defender."

I asked about Sampson's suggestion that Harkes could not move well on defense any more, and Harkes said, "I've been known to play more than one position." When I mentioned Sampson's comment that Harkes was showing a bad attitude during practices, Harkes replied, "I don't buy that body-language stuff. I was the captain. I was leading in my way, keeping the team together. We beat Brazil." He was referring to a 1–0 victory in a friendly four months earlier.

"We had some great games," Harkes continued. "Steve is the only one who ever questioned my leadership. I think it was evident they lacked leadership. Where was the fighting spirit?"

Harkes did not let up about the way Sampson cut him after a friendly in Portland on May 24. "He hugged me after the Portland game and said, 'You're going to your third World Cup,'" Harkes said. "Then he cut me. The way it was handled was so unprofessional."

For the third match, against Yugoslavia in Nantes, Sampson stuck McBride out there in Costner-land and did not use Wynalda until des-peration time in a 1–0 loss. When asked where Wynalda had been, Samp-son said it was nobody's business.

Dissidence was Sampson's legacy. With three losses and only one goal, the United States was ranked thirty-second out of thirty-two teams in that World Cup.

Régis, the instant American, wound up playing all 270 minutes, thor-oughly invisible. Jeff Agoos never got in a game, but he did prove his talents as a tutor.

A year later, Harkes published a book, *Captain for Life: And Other Temporary Assignments*, with the help of Denise Kiernan, who had cov-ered that World Cup for the *Village Voice*. In it, he ripped Sampson for lacking "credibility to a group of guys who had hundreds and hundreds of caps among them" and "putting a huge amount of pressure on young, internationally inexperienced players." He added, "I can't think of one thing that Steve did right in the months leading up to the World Cup."

The rumors and bad vibrations lingered twelve years later, when John Terry, the English captain, was revealed to have had an affair with the former girlfriend of a national teammate. By now, Harkes and Wynalda were working as television commentators for separate television networks. In discussing Terry, Wynalda referred on the air to an "inappropriate relationship" between Wynalda's former wife and Harkes in 1998. Harkes, who was still married, declined to comment, saying only that 1998 had been a bad time in his life.

Sampson, now also a commentator, claimed he had discovered just before the 1998 World Cup that Harkes had had an affair with Amy Wynalda. Sampson also repeated the old scuttlebutt that Harkes had been setting a bad example, breaking curfew, questioning authority, and potentially getting in the way of Reyna. Was Sampson ignoring the bad attitude by his captain until he heard about a possible affair? Or was he looking for a rationale to get rid of Harkes?

Whatever the truth was, my sense is that Harkes and Wynalda were both important players, and the team could have functioned better with both of them on the field for all three matches, rather than using, say, Citizen Régis. The players were more pragmatic than their coach.

While the legion of the lost was going down in three straight, I found time to bustle around the country. For Brazil's opening victory over Scotland, I took the No. 13 metro line to Saint-Denis, the train packed with Scots in kilts singing a scurrilous ode to Ronaldo, to the tune of "Winter Wonderland."

One drizzly French morning I took the high-speed train, the TGV— Train à Grande Vitesse—from Paris to Bordeaux for the Italy-Chile match. The cultivated countryside flashed by in the rain, and I arrived early enough that I could enjoy a proper meal right in the train station. How civilized.

Roberto Baggio was back for his third World Cup. In the past four years, he had been dropped from the national squad and had left Juventus and the owner who had labeled him a "wet rabbit," moving to AC Milan and then to Bologna, where he had the liberty to show his stuff. The new national coach, Cesare Maldini, once a fine defender himself— and also the father of the smooth defensive star Paolo Maldini—was secure enough to invite Baggio back into the fold. When Alessandro Del Piero was hurt in the spring, Maldini the Elder installed Baggio as the engine of the Azzurri.

In the tenth minute against Chile, Maldini the Younger lofted a long knowing ball that caught Baggio in full stride down the left side (the two had played together briefly at AC Milan), and Baggio then flicked a right-footed pass to Christian Vieri, who scored, as any striker should.

Remember, Italy never does things easily. The Azzurri fell behind, 2–1, but in the eighty-fourth minute, Baggio dribbled up the right side and chipped the ball at the right arm of the defender, and the referee ruled it a handball. At first, I was convinced Baggio aimed that ball at the defender's arm to earn a penalty kick, but then I remembered how he had botched the final *rigore* against Brazil in 1994, and how his teammates had to escort him off the field. Otherwise, Baggio might still have been standing in the arroyo in Pasadena.

I was just starting to have a memory like a true soccer fan. I've been watching baseball since 1946 (Dixie Walker hit a home run for the Dodgers that day), and when something strange happens in a current baseball game, I may remember something similar in Brooklyn from when I was a kid. As I watched Il Codino shuffle toward the disk in the humidity of Bordeaux, I was remembering the heat of Pasadena, four years earlier.

Baggio stood in a submissive position for many long seconds, his head hanging down. Surely he knew his duty was to take the penalty, but he could not seem to summon the audacity, until a teammate patted him on the back. His face blank, Baggio went to the disk. A Chilean player, a few yards behind him, was yapping as if to remind him of his public failure four years earlier. Baggio kept his head down, easily made the kick, and Italy survived with its normal opening-match draw.

Two days later, I took a train to Nantes, out west in Brittany, with a glimpse of salt marshes and a whiff of sea air, for the highlight of Bora Milutinović's coaching career, a 3–2 victory for his new team, Nigeria, over Spain. Once again, Spain had come in with players of great reputation but found ways to self-destruct.

Our apartment in Paris was on the top floor—several maids' rooms turned into a roomy flat. One evening we noticed televisions flickering in just about every apartment below us, as our neighbors watched France defeat Saudi Arabia. Not known as rabid fans, the French were getting into the swing, starting to appreciate the coach they had wanted fired.

In the spring of 1998, Aimé Jacquet had told *France Football* magazine: "The Frenchman is always critical, so critical that he criticizes himself." And he added, "The Frenchman is often negative, too, seeing beauty elsewhere but not at home. However, when a big event comes along, when national pride is at stake, he is there. That's what assures me. It will be up to us on the field to deserve that support."

Most national coaches don't have the time or the mandate to delve into cosmic issues like this. They take over what are essentially all-star teams and try to get the players to work with one another. "We can win and be spectacular," Jacquet said in May. "I now have more offensive weapons at my disposal. I just can't afford to misuse them; otherwise I will get buried by the press."

Paris, like most great cities, is a cluster of neighborhoods. I would go out for newspapers in the morning—the *International Herald Tribune*, for sure, and maybe *Libération* (I liked its politics), and for soccer results, either *L'Equipe* or *Gazzetta*. After a day or three, the Arab vendor inside the kiosk would hold out a sporting paper, to let me know he recognized me. I was a regular.

The second time we patronized the café on our block, the manager greeted us in that lovely French singsong way: *"Bon-JOUR Ma-dame. Bon-JOUR Mon-sieur,"* like bells ringing. We were regulars.

One day I didn't realize I had lost my World Cup credential until the *Times* bureau called to say that a street cleaner had found it and was in a bar a few blocks from my flat. I rushed over and gave some francs to two French African workers to thank them for being so thoughtful.

All these moments informed my writing about the World Cup and the country that was hosting it. We were regulars.

As the American team vanished, unlamented, the only Yank left was Esse Baharmast. And for a few days he was more visible than referees ever want to be.

Baharmast attracted attention around the world during the Norway-Brazil first-round match by awarding a penalty kick after detecting Junior Baiano of Brazil tugging at a Norwegian jersey in the closing minutes. The penalty was converted, and Norway advanced ahead of Morocco, which had celebrated, prematurely. Television replays did not immediately detect the jersey being pulled, so Baharmast took a great deal of criticism, particularly in the United States, with its understandable low sense of soccer self-esteem.

Look, our refs can't even get a penalty right.

A full news cycle later, Baharmast was vindicated. A Swedish television station was able to isolate a frame that clearly showed the Norwegian jersey being pulled in the box. Baharmast could have said (but did not) that officials were only following orders from Sepp Blatter, the newly elected president of FIFA, who had urged the refs to get tough on defenders taking down offensive players near the goal. I thought back to my first World Cup, in 1982, and wondered what would have happened if the referees had been similarly warned before Claudio Gentile of Italy whacked Diego Armando Maradona into a bloody stump.

The refs understood their Wild West status. They had to monitor an entire prairie full of outlaws and gunslingers, all by themselves, in a never-ending rerun of *High Noon*. One hard-shell ref, Javier Castrilli of Argentina, was even nicknamed El Sheriff.

FIFA was a full generation behind the times and technology. In 1998, it had not yet gotten around to instructing the two sideline officials to take a proactive stance in advising their lone colleague out on the field.

The assistants waved their flags in calling offside and possession, but they mostly suspended vision and judgment on everything else.

In 1998, Blatter wanted everybody to enforce the rules. I've seen that happen in pro basketball at the start of the season when the home office sends out a missive that too many players are palming the ball or traveling. In the opening game, the refs will call palming on LeBron James or Kobe Bryant, evoking a cynical grimace from the superstar. Then it all blows over.

The middle of a World Cup, a low-scoring sport, with the whole world watching, is a tricky time for refs to adjust to mandates from the home office in Zurich.

At the end of group play, FIFA issued statistics showing that the officials had given out sixteen red cards and 195 yellow cards in the first thirty-six matches. Blatter was pleased. Argentina's players had flopped and writhed their way into receiving seventy-four fouls in three matches and somehow the United States was tied for third with sixty fouls suffered. I interpreted that to mean that Our Lads could not get out of the way of the other teams' boots.

In the normal process of elimination of a World Cup, referees who were perceived to make bad calls were soon sent home, but Baharmast—vindicated by Swedish television—was assigned as fourth official in the France-Paraguay match in the second round. El Sheriff survived the cutdown to be assigned to work Croatia-Romania, tumblers and actors as well as footballers. Perhaps the conservative law enforcer from Argentina was put off by the punk-rock blond dye job on Romania's Gabriel Popescu, but El Sheriff went for a dive by a Croatian player. Davor Šuker converted the penalty for the only goal of the day. The Time Study Man from Zurich was watching. By the next round, El Sheriff had been disappeared.

On Tuesday, June 30, I took the train to Lyon and switched to a funky clattering old rail line to Saint-Étienne for Argentina-England. That match could have been remembered for the stirring romp by eighteen-year-old Michael Owen, who scored between two savvy defenders. Instead, this match is remembered—certainly in England—for David Beckham's petulant kick at Diego Simeone while Beckham was lying on the ground, visible to the world, not even surrounded by a scrum of players.

Beckham was tossed out, putting England at a disadvantage, and he was not available for the shoot-out, which, of course, England lost. From the moment he trudged off the field, and for four full years, Beckham would be vilified in England and elsewhere for his loss of poise—not to mention his glam haircuts and posh lifestyle. Nobody that night could have imagined he would persevere through the scorn of a nation to become one of the great sporting brands in the world. Give him credit; he survived.

Beckham and I both had a bad night in Saint-Étienne. After writing, I squeezed through the crowd at the station and found an air-conditioned special train and zipped back to Paris in a few hours. The next day, I could not find my passport, a horrifying feeling. Through the efficiency of the American consulate in Paris, I received a replacement passport in one day, but for the next fourteen years, whenever I returned to the States, polite immigration agents always needed ten or twenty minutes to sort things out. Finally, in 2013, I was notified I was off the stop list.

My colleague Chris Clarey advised me not to stay in Marseille for the quarterfinal and semifinal to be played there, but rather in Aix-en-Provence. Chris not only knew of a renovated monastery in the center of town; he knew the best room in the hotel—as I recall, *chambre* 32, with a terrace and back view of a churchyard and a steeple. Every day my wife and I had breakfast in our room and raised a cup of café au lait to M. Christophe.

Ensconced in Aix, I prepared to go to a local café to watch the France-Italy quarterfinal, being played back in Saint-Denis. France had romped over South Africa and Saudi Arabia but lost Zidane for two matches because he foolishly stomped on a fallen opponent and dragged his cleats along the man's hip—a gratuitous piece of violence that infuriated his coach.

"You can't let a gesture like that go unpunished," Jacquet said.

Zidane had been brilliant in the first two matches, admittedly against inferior teams, and missed the victory over Denmark, won by Emmanuel Petit in the 56th minute, and the round-of-16 win over Paraguay, on a goal by Laurent Blanc in the 114th minute. Now he was back to meet Italy, whose players he knew because he had played for Juventus.

At the Belle Epoque café in Aix, the waiter said, *"Boissons!"* Drinks only. The staff was not about to cook and serve, not with Les Bleus in action. I looked around the café. The patrons were not wearing tricolor jerseys or waving banners or chanting. They were too French for all that. However, they did exhibit a tone of intensity as they dug elbows into the tables and stared up at the television.

"Don't root; they'll kill you," Marianne warned, knowing my affinity for the Azzurri. Was it that obvious? I was controlling my arms and facial gestures, but my legs were twitching under the table.

Kill me? They were already doing a good job, what with their cigarettes—including the press rooms of the World Cup. I could never understand how a nation that cares so much about good food and elegant clothing could stink up the air. I did not pursue that dialogue with the patrons, however.

I studied the faces and physiques of the French players during warmups, particularly Zidane, so cool, so graceful, so lethal. And on the Italian bench was the Zizou of Italy, Roberto Baggio, man of a thousand soap opera episodes. Many of the starting twenty-two players were from Serie A in Italy and seemed so respectful of one another's talents that they were afraid to make a mistake.

In the sixty-seventh minute, Cesare Maldini sent in Baggio.

"Watch the game change," I whispered to Marianne.

For the first time all day, the ball swung from side to side with purpose, five or six touches in a row. The French patrons grew quiet, feeling that the balance had shifted, but the match was still scoreless after ninety minutes.

With thirty minutes of overtime ahead, I owed it to Marianne to get her out of this smoky pit, so we rushed back to *chambre* 32 with the view of a church tower and a functional television set.

Early in overtime, Baggio made a run down the right side and caught a pass on the outside of his right foot. Turning to his left, in full stride, he unloaded a moderately hard shot that whistled just wide to the left. My legs kicked into the air; had I performed this act in that smoky café, I would have been dispatched to the guillotine. I could not help myself. This was not a rejection of our wonderful host country; it was a feeling for one club over another. Can a fan love two teams? Or more?

With a minute to go, Gianluca Pagliuca stopped a crafty shot by Youri Djorkaeff, the Kalmyk-Polish-Armenian-French artist who played for Inter of Milan. The 120 minutes had produced no goals. I was exhausted.

Having covered Italy's losses in shoot-outs in 1990 in Naples and 1994 in the Rose Bowl, I knew what was coming next. Baggio and Zidane both made their shots, with Baggio putting his index finger to his lips in some obscure little salute while jogging off the field. In the fifth round, the steady French defender Blanc made his shot, and the match was over. The home team had won.

In the streets of Aix, *les citoyens* were honking horns and cheering, the way the borough of Brooklyn had done on that October afternoon in 1955 when the Dodgers finally won a World Series.

I looked it up: five of the first fifteen home teams had won the World Cup—Uruguay in 1930, Italy in 1934, England in 1966, West Germany in 1974, and Argentina in 1978. I think it used to be easier in a more rudimentary age because the host teams benefited from familiar surroundings and time zones and also because there was not as much depth in world soccer. Despite the ambiguity of Jean-Marie Le Pen, this diverse team was going to the semifinal.

I drove down to Marseille for the Netherlands-Argentina quarterfinal, on July 4, my birthday. I've been in Europe often on my birthday, but I made it a practice never to tell anybody. It's always a sweet day in England, with pubs serving hamburgers and hot dogs, and at Wimbledon, the military band plays American favorites. There was no trace of Independence Day in Marseille, the origin of the French national anthem, which would be heard on its national day ten days later.

I'd like to tell you about the goal Patrick Kluivert scored for the Netherlands in the twelfth minute, but I missed it. We reporters were seated low in the stands, near the VIP section, which was great, except that some rich patrons sneaked their chauffeurs into the aisle next to us. As the

Dutch surged forward, one idiot driver stepped directly in front of me, and I saw only his loutish shoulders as the stadium erupted.

Argentina tied the match in the seventeenth minute and went up a man in the seventy-sixth because of a red card, but they gave back their advantage in the eighty-seventh minute when Ariel Ortega, one of the more accomplished Argentine floppers, hooked his foot onto the leg of Jaap Stam, the burly Dutch defender, and writhed on the ground, trying to work the ref. After Edwin van der Sar, the tall Dutch goalie, ran over to warn the ref not to fall for the histrionics, Ortega jumped up and butted the jaw of van der Sar, who went sprawling. Who would not? The Mexican referee, Arturo Brizio Carter, got it right, waving a red card at Ortega—another No. 10 leaving a World Cup in shame.

That expulsion opened the match for the opportunistic Dutch. In the ninetieth minute, Frank de Boer lofted a parabolic pass to fleet Dennis Bergkamp, fifteen yards from the goal, and Bergkamp faked the goalie into the Mediterranean for the goal that sent the Dutch through to the semifinals. The Argentines trudged off, presumably to enroll in better acting classes.

On July 7, I drove back to Marseille for the semifinal, Brazil against the Netherlands. Ever since I started covering the World Cup, I had been waiting for Total Football to triumph once again. Kluivert tied the score at 1–1 in the ninetieth minute, but Taffarel—Brazil's keepers are never highly regarded—saved two penalty kicks in the shoot-out, and the Brazilians were into the final.

We flew home—that is to say, Paris—the next day, in time to watch the France-Croatia semifinal from Saint-Denis. This was Croatia's first appearance in the World Cup since the nation broke away from the disintegrating Yugoslavia. I had seen Croatian fans early in the tournament, tough guys wearing red-and-white checkerboard T-shirts, eyeing the airy decadence on the Métro. The Croatian team was tough, also, having pulverized Germany, 3–0, in a nasty quarterfinal, one of the rare times a German team seemed to lose heart late in a match. Now Croatia was taking on the host team.

France's Lilian Thuram, one of those players who seemed somewhat less French in the eyes of M. Le Pen, was not used to playing at outside back, and allowed Davor Šuker to slip past him for a goal in the forty-sixth minute.

Thuram, who rarely shot, much less scored, then scored twice, once in the forty-seventh minute and once in the seventieth minute—the only two international goals of his long career, as it turned out—and France still had the lead with only fourteen minutes remaining.

Lining up for a free kick, Slava Bilić, a wily Croatian who played in the English league, grappled with Laurent Blanc, the French defender. Blanc waved a handful of knuckles in the general vicinity of Bilić, who immediately staggered backward, as if punched by an invisible Maradona-esque hand from the sky. Bilić, who played in a band in England when he was not playing defense, had a highly developed stage presence. He clutched his chest, his eyes, his throat, searching for the source of his inner pain, and José María García-Aranda, the fascinated Spanish referee, was taken in by the histrionics and waved a red card at Blanc.

Where exactly did Bilić get hit? "He hit me somewhere around here," Bilić told interviewers, gesturing in the general direction of his chin. "It's hard to remember," he added. He could not come up with any welts or cuts or gashes or bruises, but Bilić insisted, "He hit me; I reacted. That's part of the game, to react."

Once waved, the red card automatically put Blanc out for the next match, too.

When the match was over, Bilić sidled up to Blanc and said he was sorry the ref had shown a red card; he had not intended things to go that far.

"I guess I should have hit him right there," Blanc said.

Too late. France was going to the final, courtesy of its 2–1 victory, but Blanc would have to sit it out. FIFA had no process to review Bilić's writh-ing, and the sideline officials were useless. Bilić pretty much admitted he had faked the injury. Sepp Blatter said he was sorry, but what could he do?

For the first time since 1978, the home team was in the final. French fans were abandoning the Gallic shrug, halfway to the ecstatic state of

American college football fans on a Saturday morning in Tuscaloosa, Lincoln, or South Bend.

My guess was that M. Le Pen was liking Zidane better each match. After missing two matches for attacking the Saudi player, Zidane had elevated the French squad by distributing the ball, always a threat to score, although he had not yet done so.

"A genius," Aimé Jacquet had said of Zidane earlier. "Since going to Italy, he's had to be at his best every weekend and has taken on a new dimension. He's well aware now of what he's capable of, and we're hoping that he can give back to our team what our team has invested in him. With him, we can win the World Cup."

Going into the final, Jacquet reaffirmed his earlier promise: "On July 13, I will say good-bye after having done a victory lap the night before in the Stade de France; after the French team has been crowned champion."

The World Cup had a glamorous final—the defending champions from Brazil against France, the first time a home team had reached the final since Argentina won in 1978. The final had two stars from Serie A, the best league in the world: Ronaldo from Inter Milan against Zidane from Juventus.

The final turned out to have more suspense before the match than during it. When the lineups were distributed an hour or so before kick-off, Ronaldo was not starting.

Ronaldo—pronounced "Honaldo" in the Brazilian version of Portuguese—was merely the leading star in the world, still only twenty-one years old, a large and nimble striker who could pounce with the quickness of a smaller man. When his name was listed among the reserves, the huge open-air press box began to quiver.

If this were the Super Bowl, and a star quarterback was not in the starting lineup, the NFL would surely offer some minimal explanation, perhaps even vaguely truthful. In the States, good reporters can gain the trust of executives or coaches or players or public-relations officials to provide some inside information, but as far as I could see, soccer did not have those avenues. We began hearing rumors of Ronaldo having some kind of seizure or reaction to medication, but there was no way to trace it back to any source.

Shortly before game time, a flurry of paper produced a new lineup—Ronaldo was starting, after all. No explanation from FIFA.

From the time I was a child, I had heard the stirring anthem "La Marseillaise," with its lyrics exhorting sacrifice and victory. Now I was standing in a stadium, with many people in the crowd singing lustily:

Aux armes, citoyens!
Formez vos bataillons!

Sometimes a reporter should look around and think, "Wow, look where I am." That was one of those times.

Ronaldo was not nearly so energized. The whippet of the first six matches, with his gap-toothed smile, was gone. He was on the field but not necessarily on this planet. He floated ethereally, as mysterious as the globe on the Brazilian flag, a distant object, devoid of life.

Instead, all the energy in the stadium was in the feet of France's No. 10, Zidane, as he glided purposefully from space to space, his balding head a target, a player at the peak of his career, at precisely the right time.

In these electronic times, there is a YouTube video called "Zidane * All in the Touch," which enhances the memory of what Zidane did that day—improv ballet, on grass, in public. Don't look at the ball, look at the feet. Zidane performs the *adage*, the *arabesque*, the *avant*, and the *pirouette*, controlling the ball against world-level defenders like Aldair and Roberto Carlos. This is an artist playing the most virtuoso final we may ever see.

At twenty-seven minutes, Emmanuel Petit's perfect corner kick soared toward Zidane, who outleaped Leonardo for the soft header to put France ahead—his first goal of the tournament.

Still in the first half, Ronaldo low-bridged Fabien Barthez, the keeper, and both went down. Barthez was surprisingly solicitous of Ronaldo, who expended all his energy on one questionable sortie.

In the first minute of injury time in the first half, Zidane found another pocket to guide another header into the net.

The entire Brazilian team seemed to be sleepwalking. Mario Zagallo, the combative forward on two World Cup champions, who had coached the champions of 1970 and was an assistant on the 1994 champions, was back coaching. Zagallo later said that he had been thinking of taking out Ronaldo, but he did not, even when down, 2–0, at halftime. Ronaldo made one or two runs and had one shot on goal, but suffered a mental whiteout and pushed the ball directly to the French keeper rather than at Didier Deschamps, the midfielder guarding the corner.

It was the only chance of the afternoon for Ronaldo, who played the entire game, even when Brazil had a one-man advantage for the final twenty-two minutes after Marcel Desailly went out with his second yellow card. In the closing seconds, France made a leisurely counterattack, with Petit running down a lovely through ball to make it 3–0, tying the record for the largest margin in a final.

The French fans celebrated in most un-French delirium, waving flags, chanting, cheering, with tricolors painted on their faces, but *très chic.*

Underneath the stands, reporters screamed at Zagallo for details about Ronaldo, accusing Brazil and FIFA of a cover-up. Left on his own by FIFA and his own federation, the old coach bolted from the room. This was the true face of FIFA, then and now. The money was in the till. Why explain?

The two billion viewers finished that day with no idea what had befallen the best scorer of the time. Did Ronaldo have a psychic or medical breakdown? Was there a concern he would test positive for something?

The next day, the Brazilian team doctor, Lidio Toledo, said that Ronaldo had suffered a stress-related episode, whatever that meant. And a few days after that, members of the medical team that had treated Ronaldo at the hospital earlier on Sunday told *Le Monde* that the player seemed to be suffering from severe fatigue, weariness, and stress. One doctor said that it was possible Ronaldo had had an epileptic fit, but the staff did not have enough time to diagnose his problem because he left the hospital to play in the final.

Officials of Inter, who had a huge amount of money invested in Ronaldo, criticized the Brazilian team for allowing Ronaldo to play under such conditions.

Six weeks later, on August 21, quotes attributed to Ronaldo were issued. "What happened was that before the game, I went to eat, then I went back to my room because I was feeling tired and wanted to rest and I went to sleep," he said. "When I woke up, I felt pain in my body. I felt really bad. Then I went back to eat, and the doctors told me that I had had this problem."

What kind of problem? It was not hard for Brazilian fans to work up a conspiracy theory that the player had been slipped something dangerous by gambling or rooting interests.

Eleven years later, Ronaldo apparently spoke at greater length in an unsigned interview posted on the Web site ronaldohome.com.

Ronaldo said that on the morning of the match, in the team hotel, he had a "seizure," lasting thirty to forty seconds. When he woke up, ten friends were around him. Team officials told him he was out of the match, but he went to the hospital, "which was all OK." Then, he said he went directly to the stadium bearing results of the medical exam and told Zagallo, his coach, that he wanted to play and he claimed Zagallo told him, "You will play."

He claimed he played "reasonably well" but said he was "labeled as a villain"—even by some teammates—because Brazil lost. "This was rubbish as if there was any risk, I would be the first to jump out," he said, adding that he has a checkup every year and has never had those symptoms again. Ronaldo said he takes Voltaren because of tendinitis in his knee, but said that the drug was not the reason for his "seizure."

Interesting story, but not necessarily medically true, according to one doctor I know who obviously had no contact with Ronaldo, but who said that Voltaren is not likely to produce convulsions or seizures. More likely, somebody had given Ronaldo lidocaine, an anesthetic used to dull pain before a big game. If the lidocaine hit the wrong spot near a big muscle, it could produce convulsions or a seizure, he said.

Why would team doctors do that? Team doctors are paid to get a player back on the field. That's their job.

Could France have mounted such a disciplined attack if it had to worry about the big feller being awake on offense? We will never know.

The way France looked that day, perhaps nobody could have beaten them. The French squad peaked at the right time. The nation cheered, and Jacquet followed his promise and resigned. He went out a champion.

After the match, we wrote our stories of French perfection and Brazilian sleepwalking, and it was time to get back to Paris.

Five reporters commandeered a taxi outside the stadium. The driver was old and calm, apparently Arab, smiling proudly as he negotiated his taxi through the Quartier Arabe, where thousands of jubilant people of Algerian and other North African ancestries chanted "Zee-dahn! Zee-dahn!" and rocked the cab back and forth. We opened the windows and applauded and gave high-fives and chanted "Zee-dahn!" and the driver edged his way past the shimmering presence of Sacré Coeur, and glided downhill into central Paris.

Back at our flat, Marianne described her perfect vantage point, ten rows high, near Zidane's two graceful headers, the ticket courtesy of a friend. We opened the windows and listened to the chants and thousands of footsteps as Parisians instinctively took the path of ancient French crowds. In the past, they had flocked to riot and throw paving stones (*aux barricades!*) or watch the executions by guillotine in the Place de la Concorde, at the base of the Champs-Élysées. Now they congregated on the ancient streets, chanting "Zee-dahn! Zee-dahn!" to honor the superstar, born in Marseille, who had won a championship for France.

Ben Queensborough/isiphotos.com

After Landon Donovan scored in the ninety-first minute against Algeria in the 2010 World Cup in South Africa, he, Edson Buddle (left), and Benny Feilhaber (right) race to the "dog pile" in the corner. The dramatic goal sent the United States into the knockout stage.

AP Images

Joe Gaetjens, a Haitian with claims to American citizenship, scored on a well-timed deflection for a 1–0 victory by the United States over England in the 1950 World Cup, the biggest upset in U.S. soccer history. He was lofted by fans in Belo Horizonte, Brazil, after the match.

Great players brought the aura of the World Cup to the New York Cosmos during the short, flamboyant life of the North American Soccer League in the 1970s and '80s. Here the Brazilian superstar Pelé celebrated a goal in Giants Stadium in New Jersey.

Giorgio Chinaglia (9) showed his burning drive to score during his run with the Cosmos. After growing up in Wales, he played for Italy—rough on his coaches, worse on rival defenders.

Carlos Alberto (5) was running on empty during his final games with the Cosmos, but the Brazilian still demonstrated the finesse of a World Cup defender.

Paolo Rossi was suspended in a gambling scandal but returned in time to lead Italy to the 1982 World Cup championship in Spain. In this 3–2 victory over Brazil in Barcelona, he dodges Falcão (15) and Júnior.

Dino Zoff, age forty, was the oldest player in the 1982 World Cup. The keeper for Juventus lofted the trophy for Italy after the final victory over West Germany.

Before the game between their squads at the 1986 World Cup in Mexico, Argentina's Diego Maradona accepted a handshake from England's Peter Shilton, but in the match he outleaped Shilton and punched the ball with his left fist for the goal he attributed to the "Hand of God."

After blasting a goal in the thirty-first minute of the United States' qualifying match against Trinidad in 1989, Paul Caligiuri (second from left) joins the celebration with John Harkes, Bruce Murray (arms in air), Tab Ramos, and Peter Vermes. The 1–0 victory put the United States in its first World Cup in forty years.

At the 1990 World Cup in Italy, the Cameroon coach kept Roger Milla, thirty-eight years old and already retired once, on the bench until the sun went down. Then Milla emerged and helped Cameroon become the first African team to reach the World Cup quarterfinals.

Vilified by the owner of Juventus, his club in Italy, Roberto Baggio rebounded from a slow start to score twice against Bulgaria in the 1994 World Cup semifinal in New Jersey. But his hamstring would slow him down in the final.

Fans celebrated on West 46th Street, the Brazilian center in midtown Manhattan, shortly after Brazil's shoot-out victory at the 1994 World Cup final in Pasadena. This was the fourth title for Brazil but, hard to believe, the first since 1970.

Criticized as not being "French" enough, Les Bleus—with roots in corners of the French-speaking world—nonetheless enchanted their nation's fans at the 1998 World Cup in France. Zinedine Zidane (10) scored two gorgeous headers in the final victory over Brazil.

Brandi Chastain coolly switched to her left foot to score the deciding penalty kick in the U.S. team's victory over China at the 1999 Women's World Cup final at the Rose Bowl in Pasadena, California. Known to her teammates as Hollywood, she shed her jersey to celebrate, just like the men.

Francesco Totti of Italy (10) pleaded for a penalty kick after hitting the ground in a match against South Korea in 2002. Instead, the referee gave him a yellow card for diving, which led to his expulsion, and Italy would lose, 2–1, to the home-nation Reds.

In his last World Cup match before reaching maximum age, the great referee Pierluigi Collina wielded two early yellow cards, one to Miroslav Klose of Germany (center), in the first nine minutes of the 2002 final and then presided over an orderly 2–0 victory for Brazil.

Pino DiBartolo operated L'Angolo, a café in New York's Greenwich Village, attracting Italians and other fans. Its closing in 2008 left a giant hole in many a social life. *Siamo molto tristi, ancora.*

At the 2006 World Cup final in Berlin, France's Zinedine Zidane turned and head-butted Marco Materazzi after the Italian made vicious personal comments during the match. With Zidane banished with a red card, France lost the final in a penalty-kick shoot-out.

Nelson Mandela celebrated in Zurich on May 15, 2004, as South Africa was awarded the 2010 World Cup. Archbishop Desmond Tutu bows before (left to right) an unidentified official, former South African president F. W. de Klerk, Mandela, FIFA president Sepp Blatter, and South African president Thabo Mbeki.

Plastic horns, called vuvuzelas, allowed South Africans to demonstrate their joy at hosting the World Cup—and for fans to rattle eardrums in stadiums and in front of televisions all over the world.

Chuck Blazer of the United States and Jack Warner of Trinidad were allies in the CONCACAF regional federation, which oversees the sport in North America, Central America, and the Caribbean. Later they would turn against each other, and both would be banished from soccer, accused of financial impropriety.

Demonstrations across Brazil in 2013 claimed a link between domestic inefficiency and corruption and preparations for the 2014 World Cup. This was the first time the World Cup had ever been criticized so openly by people of the host nation.

Playing in a surprising snowfall outside Denver in March 2013, the United States' Clint Dempsey (8) scored the only goal and celebrated with Michael Bradley (4) during a vital qualifying victory over Costa Rica.

12

AMERICANS WIN
WORLD CUP—AGAIN

UNITED STATES, 1999

The world was back in the Rose Bowl. But instead of Dunga and Baggio taking the final penalty shots, it was Sun Wen and Brandi Chastain.

Those charismatic Olympic champions of 1996 were mostly back in 1999, with a sense of teamwork that came from within. That team had leaders everywhere, including Joy Fawcett, the great defender who was now the mother of two young daughters.

"It's like a second family," Kristine Lilly said a few weeks before the tournament. "Female sports are different. You do a lot better when you care about each other. We are nurturing people, caring people. I'm glad to have my friends out there. It goes a little bit deeper than just sports. We all want to see each other happy."

This is the kind of team, the kind of family, it was: after a dispute with her parents, Shannon MacMillan had left home during college; between semesters, MacMillan lived with Joy Fawcett and her husband, Walter, helping care for the children.

Coach Tony DiCicco understood that leadership on this team came from the strong personalities of the players, from their sense of unity. He acknowledged that his coaching techniques changed the more he was around the women. Female athletes cannot be coached the same way as male athletes. Women internalize criticism, he said, and often need to fix things on their own, which these players did.

He worked with a soccer-savvy sports psychologist, Colleen Hacker, particularly when a former player filed a harassment suit against Anson Dorrance, the previous coach who was still producing championships at North Carolina. The tangled loyalties could have split the team, but everybody agreed to work together. (The case was ultimately settled.)

DiCicco did make one big change, welcoming back Brandi Chastain, an extroverted veteran from the 1991 champions who had been given an unrequested sabbatical by Dorrance. Perhaps Chastain needed a break; or perhaps the coach felt he could not mold her into his image of the team. Chastain was talented and irrepressible, traits that tend to make coaches nervous.

After her time away from the national team, Chastain was in the best shape of her life. She was proud of her physique—and was known to display it, as a tribute to her hard work. Her nickname among the players was Hollywood. When Julie Foudy filled out a team questionnaire that requested her favorite actress, she wrote: Brandi Chastain.

The women competed for playing time, and for space during scrimmages. Mia Hamm was as tenacious in practice as she was in games, but she came into the 1999 World Cup in a scoring slump, and her confidence was down. Michelle Akers suffered from chronic fatigue syndrome and needed constant medical attention but was still a force.

The third Women's World Cup was run by Marla Messing, a lawyer in Los Angeles who had worked with Alan Rothenberg and his team in 1994. She followed the same template from the 1984 Olympics and 1994 World Cup. Think big. Think Rose Bowl. By committing to large stadiums, Messing sent a message to the world—female athletes are not second best.

In the opening round, the United States outscored its opponents, 13–1, in three group matches in New York, Chicago, and Foxborough, Massachusetts. In the quarterfinals against Germany outside Washington, D.C., Chastain scored an own goal in the fifth minute, misdirecting a back pass around keeper Briana Scurry. Captain Carla Overbeck and the others told Chastain, Hey, Brandi, we'll get it back. Mistress of drama that she was, Chastain scored in the forty-ninth minute to tie the match. In the sixty-sixth minute, Fawcett scored for a 3–2 victory.

Afterward, a fan named Bill Clinton tied up the entire stadium by deciding to greet the players, as the Secret Service held everybody in place. The national bandwagon was forming, and the president was right on it.

In the semifinals at Stanford University, Cindy Parlow scored in the fifth minute, and Akers stepped up and converted a penalty kick in the eightieth minute for a 2–0 victory over Brazil.

Just before the final against China in the Rose Bowl on July 10, President Clinton once again disrupted traffic outside the stadium by arriving near game time, causing many fans to miss the start. Politicians never seem to know they are inconveniencing tens of thousands of people by choosing to attend a sports event.

The match teetered into extra time with no goals, just like the men's final between Brazil and Italy nearly five years earlier. Akers, who was wearing down, was not sure she could last on the brutally hot afternoon. In the ninetieth minute, she and the very solid keeper Scurry went for the ball, and Scurry punched Akers as well as the ball. Akers was done. The doctor and trainer had to revive her in the locker room while the game veered into extra time.

After being a gracious host for the first Women's World Cup, the Chinese government had upgraded the program, overcoming old prejudices against women playing sports. Out of this drive came a new and talented generation, including Sun Wen, a rebel who used to dribble a ball and bang it against the nearest wall as neighbors called her a pseudo-boy. The Chinese program, emphasizing rote drills, produced a player like Sun, who was on a level with the best Americans.

China was good enough to hold off the Americans for ninety minutes in the heat. In the tenth minute of overtime came the most desperate moment, when Liu Ying's corner kick soared across the goalmouth, past Scurry. Fan Yunjie was in perfect position and headed the ball diagonally past Scurry toward the goal line, and many of the American players saw the tournament ending in front of their eyes.

But Kristine Lilly, the modest veteran, was protecting the near post, as she had been taught to do, and she gracefully slid sideways and leaped, her head and neck braced, deflecting the ball from the line. Then Chastain went horizontal, balancing on her left hand and blasting the ball away from the area with her right foot. An act of poise by Lilly, a sheer reaction by Chastain, both fighting off exhaustion, stemmed from their long experience as admirable old pros.

Once again, a World Cup final went into penalty kicks in the Rose Bowl. Everybody hates the shoot-out, which often produces knee-shaking yips in the richest stars.

DiCicco's assistant, Lauren Gregg, was in charge of the lineup for penalty kicks. Gregg knew that Hamm hated penalty kicks, and had been shooting them poorly in practice, but she told Hamm that as one of the top scorers she had to go in the top five. Then Gregg asked Chastain if she wanted to shoot, and when Chastain said yes, Gregg said she had to shoot left-footed because she had become too predictable with the right. Growing up, Chastain had listened to her father's preaching a fundamental of this sport—how many goals go unscored because a player is not flexible enough to propel a ball with either foot?

The first four players made their shots, but Liu Ying's shot was deflected by Scurry, who appeared to be moving forward before the kick, but the referee did not call a violation. Lilly, Zhang Ouying, Hamm, and Sun Wen all made their shots. A goal now would win the World Cup. The tenth shooter was Chastain, who calmly hooked her left-footed shot into her right corner to win the championship. Then Hollywood celebrated by doing exactly what men do in great moments on the field: she yanked off her jersey. Her black industrial-strength sports bra was noticeable for a second or two before she was engulfed by teammates. Some people still remember her flamboyant but hardly provocative gesture more than the endurance and heart of the two teams.

After the celebration, Lilly was holding five-year-old Katelyn Rose Fawcett, the daughter of Joy and Walter Fawcett. She shrugged off praise for her goal-line stop. "We practice this on all corner kicks," Lilly said in that noisy room. "I shift with the ball. That's exactly what I was doing."

That was the point. The nation and many fans around the world were captivated by the strong personalities and skill of the women, including the Chinese, the Brazilians, and the Norwegians. These athletes had everything—personality, talent, technique, experience.

In the days after the final, people debated Scurry's save on Liu Ying. Some insisted that Scurry's forward break from the goal line had intimidated Liu, certainly cut down on the angle, and was a violation of the rules.

Was this the action of a competitor with impatient feet—or the practiced device of somebody defying the rules? The referee, Nicole Petignat of Switzerland, did not detect a violation. Soccer players flop, sometimes they deserve a yellow card—it's a fine line. Baseball batters pretend to be hit by an inside pitch. Basketball players reel backward from imagined contact. My own opinion then and now was that even if Scurry consciously decided to go after this one player, it was "cheating" only in the narrow sports definition. Others, whose opinion I admire, thought a player demeaned the sport by deliberately breaking the rule. Later, DiCicco, himself a former keeper, admitted that he had prodded Scurry to be more aggressive in moving forward, and let the referee sort it out afterward.

The attendance of 90,185 in the Rose Bowl remains the world record for a women's match. The attendance for that tournament was 1,194,221, an average of 37,319 per match, still the best figures for the event.

More important, fans around the world had a new event in their consciousness—the WWC. And Americans, who revered men's Olympic champions like the 1960 and 1980 ice hockey teams and the 1992 basketball Dream Team, now had a World Cup champion to celebrate—as Jeré Longman would call them in his knowing book, *The Girls of Summer*.

It would be a mistake to say that women's soccer took off from there. Within days, the federation and players were quarreling over a national tour planned by the players without permission by the federation. During the infighting, DiCicco resigned as head coach, and the federation was exposed for double standards toward the men's and women's programs.

Three other World Cups have followed the epic 1999 tournament. In 2003, a SARS scare forced China to postpone its turn as host. The United States stepped in on short notice, with somewhat less excitement, and

Germany won. In 2007, China nearly beat the Americans' attendance record from 1999, falling four thousand spectators short, and once again Germany won. In 2011, Germany was the host, as Japan, still reeling from the horrendous damage from a tsunami and nuclear-plant meltdown, defeated the United States in an emotional final. The 2015 WWC is scheduled for Canada, which had a gallant run to the semifinals in 2011, losing to the United States after several controversial officiating calls, not yet forgotten.

Since the exciting debut in 1996, women's soccer has become a staple in the Olympic Games, including an epic final in 2012 with the United States outlasting Japan.

In its way, women's soccer has set an example for the world. The United States won the 2012 Olympic gold medal with a Swedish coach, Pia Sundhage, a former World Cup player in her own right, who delivered her opinions fearlessly and kept her players loose by singing "The Times They Are A-Changing" and other anthems of the counterculture. She was right about that: it was quite known and accepted that Sundhage was gay.

One of the best American players on that squad was Megan Rapinoe, a blond sprite who roamed the field and came up with gigantic passes and goals and became something of a national favorite and also let it be known that she was gay. After generations of athletes and coaches, male and female, had agonized over coming out, the separate examples of Sundhage and Rapinoe broke down some of the mysteries. In 2013, Robbie Rogers, who had played for the national men's team, came out as gay and temporarily retired before joining the Los Angeles Galaxy. And the world did not end. Nor did it end in 2013, when Abby Wambach, the powerful striker who had surpassed Mia Hamm's world record of 158 goals, announced that she and her longtime partner, Sarah Huffman, also a player, had been married in Hawaii.

Despite the popularity of the women's team, the United States has been unable to build a successful league. The Women's United Soccer Association began in April 2001, backed in part by John S. Hendricks, a founder of the Discovery Channel. The players called him "St. John" because of his generous patronage to women's soccer, but even a saint has limits. The league featured many of the stars from 1996 and 1999 but was top-heavy with salaries and short on fans and sponsors. It lasted three years, and another league came and went.

In 2013, the National Women's Soccer League began, with eight teams scattered around the country, with backing from the national federation. The future of women's soccer is still murky, but Hamm and her teammates remain among the greatest national teams in American history—the '99ers.

···· 13 ····

THE YEAR OF
THE OUTSIDERS

SOUTH KOREA AND JAPAN, 2002

In 2002, for the first time, the World Cup was held in two neighboring countries.

The two-headed World Cup was either a feat of diplomacy worthy of a Nobel Peace Prize for Sepp Blatter or a cynical and lucrative compromise.

Japan and South Korea, with their tangled history, had been competing to be the World Cup's first Asian host. Representatives of the two nations had courted FIFA delegates, who can be quite sentimental about token gifts like ties and souvenir photo books, and they did not want to offend either suitor. So FIFA voted to accept Japan and South Korea as cohosts.

This decision caused a huge outlay of energy and cost, since both Japan and South Korea felt the need to spend billions of dollars to build or upgrade twenty stadiums that might never house the promised games, concerts, and conventions.

How do you say "double white elephant" in Japanese and Korean?

In the same year that FIFA produced unprecedented twin hosts for the World Cup, the organization underwent rare public exposure. FIFA had traditionally done its business in private, with very little controversy from within or scrutiny from the press. However, in 2002, a few of FIFA's secrets and divisions went public.

Sepp Blatter, who was up for reelection, came under rare criticism because of the collapse of FIFA's marketing organization, International Sport and Leisure (ISL), in 2001, with a disappearance of money, eventually estimated at $300 million. ISL, founded in 1982 by the Dassler sporting-goods company and a Japanese advertising company, had negotiated the television rights for the Mexico World Cup in 1986 and subsequent Olympic and FIFA events. Up to the bankruptcy of ISL, Blatter had mostly come off as an official who said loopy things; now he was being accused by soccer insiders of presiding over a careless and perhaps even corrupt organization.

At a meeting of FIFA in Zurich in early May 2002, Michel Zen-Ruffinen, the general secretary, and also a lawyer and former referee, issued a thirty-page report charging Blatter with financial mismanagement. Five of FIFA's seven vice presidents urged Blatter to resign immediately, but he denied the charges and insisted that insurance would limit FIFA's losses from the ISL debacle to $32 million.

As delegates arrived at the hilltop Seoul Hilton later that month, Zen-Ruffinen was claiming that Blatter had paid FIFA members to support him in the coming elections. "I have again and again asked for the necessary information," Zen-Ruffinen said. "Neither the audit committee or myself got access . . . and I am supposed to be in charge of the administration and accounts of FIFA."

Blatter forbade Zen-Ruffinen from presiding over the meeting and said, "He is in big trouble." Blatter said the finances of FIFA were in good order and he added, "Wait awhile till I come up with ideas to restore the credibility of FIFA."

Blatter was challenged for reelection by Issa Hayatou of Cameroon, who was trying to assemble a third-world bloc in the upcoming FIFA elections. FIFA now had 205 participating nations, and Hayatou, as president of the African confederation, had some influence over 52 of them. Now Blatter had to work hard to demolish Hayatou. Under rare public exposure, Blatter refused to allow debate before the vote, even though delegates from England, the Netherlands, Somalia, Tunisia, and eleven other nations had requested time to speak. Blatter's solid victory, by a 139–56 margin, was turned sour by his refusal to discuss criticism.

David Will, the head of the suspended internal-audit committee and a FIFA vice president, was not allowed to address the congress. "I want the congress to know that the finances are in a serious situation," Will said after the meeting. "Nobody seems to take this seriously. If we were a company, we would have to declare insolvency."

As usual, the United States seemed comfortable with the status quo in FIFA. As delegates rushed out for fresh air following Blatter's banana-republic reelection, Dan Flynn, the longtime chief executive of the United States Soccer Federation, who had cast America's vote for Blatter, stopped for an interview. Flynn said it was "fair to ask questions," but added, "Sepp has had twenty years of running FIFA. The last four years may have had some difficulties, but we are committed to Sepp because he has always been committed to us." Flynn then praised Blatter for having placed the 1999 Women's World Cup in the United States. He also put in a bid for future major events to be held in America. And that's the way it works.

For many Americans, soccer was perceived mostly in simplistic terms of hooligan riots and scoreless draws—or a cute little recreation for children. The public (and sponsors and networks and newspapers) generally did not appear to know or care much about FIFA politics. A lot of good American support for Blatter would do eight years later, when the United States competed with Qatar to be the World Cup host in 2022.

When compared to FIFA, the International Olympic Committee was a model of Athenian democracy. When some IOC delegates were caught accepting favors before the 2002 Winter Games in Salt Lake City, David D'Alessandro, the head of the John Hancock insurance company, warned the IOC to clean up its act if it wanted his company's sponsorship dollars. There was no evidence of a single David D'Alessandro in the orbit of FIFA.

Some delegates booed and whistled as Blatter shamelessly triumphed over Hayatou. A few left the meeting openly criticizing Blatter. When questioned about the election and the state of FIFA, Blatter said, "The result of the election is that there are no questions." He added, "The people cannot lie. The people love the truth." It was a stunning exposure of a leader who was being accused of mismanagement by many officials close to him, and who would not tolerate public dialogue.

FIFA's money machine did more than collaborate with rogue outfits like ISL and engender charges of bribery of voting members. FIFA also devoured its greatest asset, its players. This was clearly evident as the defending champions from France arrived in Seoul for a friendly with the indefatigable Reds of South Korea.

The television camera in the tunnel under the stadium showed the French players slogging off the team bus, with headsets on, ball caps or knitted wool caps scrunched down over their heads, wraparound sunglasses to ward off the outside world.

This is standard mode for world-weary athletes getting off a team bus, but what was not standard was the immense fatigue, physical and mental, that showed on the players. As they stepped gingerly off the bus, they all seemed to buckle, as if a knee or two, perhaps a spinal column, maybe the pedal extremities, were not working properly.

"These guys are screwed," I said to my wife as we watched the scene on television. We were ensconced in a gorgeous Marriott on the south side of the Han River, with a great south view of green hills and an arts center. We would have a sensational month. The French would not.

The best players in the world were running on the hamster wheel of soccer. In 1992–93, the European association had upgraded an old cup competition into a made-for-television midweek extravaganza, the Champions League. In the days off from expanded club schedules, star players now flew to matches with their national teams.

After winning the 1998 World Cup at home, the French had managed to win the 2000 European championship, achieving the rare double of keeping players healthy and contented for a two-year stretch. But four? Watching the familiar French stars recoil as they put one foot after the other made it clear that winning championships is the equivalent of dog years.

After one more season with Juventus, the great Zidane had taken even bigger money to join the aging stars of Real Madrid, known as the Galácticos. By my count, he had played in 169 league matches for his clubs since the 1998 World Cup and at least 27 official international matches for France. That would be a total of 196—nearly 50 matches a year, nearly one a week, at the highest level.

Thirty-eight minutes into the friendly with South Korea, Zidane hobbled toward the sideline, touching his left thigh. He sat the rest of the match, with ice packs on his thigh, as France managed to hold off the Reds, 3–2. However, the South Koreans always take their toll, with their energy and the odd elbow or heel where it hurt the most. And they were playing at home. The French were a long way from home.

This was apparent on May 31 in World Cup Stadium. The schedule maker, with a sense of whimsy, had arranged for the defending champions to play their opening match of the tournament against Senegal, a former French colony that supplied footballers to many European clubs. In Senegal's first World Cup match ever, a large twenty-year-old midfielder, Papa Bouba Diop, born in Dakar and a professional in Switzerland, scored the only goal, in the thirtieth minute. France then looked lethargic in a scoreless match with Uruguay and, with Zidane finally back on the field, was hammered out of the World Cup, 2–0, by Denmark.

Watching the French trudge off the field at breezy Incheon, I thought of the best ice hockey team I had ever covered, the New York Islanders, who won four straight Stanley Cup championships from 1980 through 1983. By 1984, all those play-off games had caught up with the Islanders, who seemed to be skating in Slurpees. The French seemed to be running in crème brûlée.

The quick demise of the French opened up the tournament for fresh faces—Turkey, South Korea, and Senegal, plus the sleeping giant from North America.

The 2002 U.S. team can now be seen as a collection of epic characters in a special time. Did Americans really appreciate them?

Straight from its disgrace in France in 1998, the United States entered the final phase of qualifying with a new generation and a new attitude personified by Bruce Arena, the new coach, a former lacrosse goalie and soccer keeper at Cornell University and a highly successful coach at the University of Virginia and DC United. Arena knew his team had to earn its points at home.

The golden age of American soccer began against Mexico in the cold of Columbus, Ohio, on February 28, 2001. The U.S. federation, recalling past embarrassments, tried to place home qualifying matches in modest stadiums in heartland cities, where it could possibly keep down the number of fans from other nations in the Americas.

The first game of the final round, known as the Hexagonal because it included six teams, was held in twenty-nine-degree weather in central Ohio. Despite the best efforts of the U.S. federation, hundreds of Mexicans showed up in the parking lot, wearing warm clothing including serapes and sombreros, the trademarks of these loyal fans. Some had even managed to buy tickets. The American team came out for warmups in shorts. The Mexican team did not come out until game time.

Welcome to the Hex. In the fifteenth minute, Rafael Márquez, the Mexican headhunter, whacked Brian McBride in the eye, forcing him to be replaced by Josh Wolff. Then Claudio Reyna was hurt and had to be replaced by Clint Mathis.

Was this the long-awaited new breed, the product of the youth leagues and the college feeder system? Mathis and Wolff had known each other since they were nine years old, in the youth leagues of Georgia, and both had gone to the University of South Carolina.

Soon after coming on, Mathis spotted his Georgia buddy making a break and unleashed a lead pass that Wolff converted to put the Yanks ahead. Later, Wolff set up Earnie Stewart for a 2–0 victory. Three points taken from Mexico in the frigid air of Ohio. That game is still remembered by Mexican fans as La Guerra Fría—the Cold War.

The Yanks rolled up thirteen points in their first five matches before the trip to Azteca, two days ahead of the return match. Arena did not want to be there long enough for his players to adjust to the rarefied air. In and out.

They would receive considerable police protection on the bus ride from hotel to stadium, but sometimes there was an odd touch:

The man was drunk, he was dirty, he was maybe three feet tall, and he was rolling on a glorified skateboard near the American team bus, shouting things most of us could not understand, which was probably a good thing. The police did not chase him away. Perhaps he was some sort of unofficial greeter to Azteca, the fabled stadium that had already held two World Cup finals.

"What a great place!" one young reporter raved as he walked onto the field for the workout, impressed by the sweep of ninety-five thousand empty seats.

"Try playing here tomorrow," said Jeff Agoos, who was back for a third try at playing in the World Cup. Agoos had his own memories of Azteca: four years earlier, in this same qualifying format, he had received a red card for swinging his arm near a Mexican player. The United States had somehow held on for a 0–0 draw, which was the all-time highlight of seventeen qualifiers in Mexico City—sixteen losses, one draw.

"Altitude, heat, smog, and, on top of all that, you've got the Mexican team, so there are a number of factors why it is difficult," Agoos said. "I think it's also sort of a mind-set. You can make it more difficult than it has to be. If you come in with the idea that you're going to come out on the wrong end of it, then you're going to have a long day. Your mind-set has to be right going into Azteca."

The word *revancha*—revenge—was reproduced all over the city. Revenge for what? Never quite clear in the Hex but most likely revenge for General Winfield Scott and the siege of Veracruz and the loss of 525,000 square miles, much of the modern southwest United States. Stuff like that.

Displaying normal gamesmanship, the groundskeepers kept the tarp on the field when the Yanks reported for their workout. Rainy season, the groundskeepers insisted. Arena claimed his rights by demanding that the tarp be taken off the entire field; then he did not use one end of it. Keep the groundskeepers in shape. Healthy for them. That's the way it works in the Hex.

The next day the place was jumping with ninety-five thousand fans in place, with a vehemence I had never felt in this stadium during the 1986 World Cup. *Revancha.*

In the sixteenth minute, Alberto Garcia Aspe, a longtime regular, just recalled for this match, lofted a floater into the box, where Jared Borgetti, the striker, essentially unmarked, headed the ball into the upper right corner.

"Foolish goal," Arena said. "Poor decision." The goal stood up and Mexico won, 1–0. As the American buses left Azteca, the tiny greeter was still there on his skateboard, still shouting imprecations.

The tactics of the Hex continued on September 1 in Washington against Honduras. To make some money, the United States had put the match in RFK Stadium, a noble soccer venue within driving range of millions of Spanish-speaking fans. To counter that, the federation tried to limit the sale of tickets to Americans only, which annoyed Honduran fans, including the country's ambassador, who raised the possibility of suing for the right to buy tickets in the land of the free and the home of the brave.

"I pay my taxes, but when I call to get a ticket they tell me they are sold out," said Rafael Garcia of Ridgewood, Queens, a fan who had driven down the interstate, blue-and-white banner flapping, horn honking.

Eventually, tickets were made available for some Honduran fans in one distant corner of the upper deck, the loudest and happiest section in the joint, as it turned out.

The Honduran players did not need a ticket controversy to be prodded into an attitude. Every time they came to the States, they screwed up their faces and marched as if on a mission: "Thank you to the Dole Fruit Company for many kindnesses in the past."

This chippy posture helped the Honduran players and fans eat the Americans' lunch in a 3–2 whipping. "I guess there are a lot of Hondurans in Washington," said Landon Donovan, a nineteen-year-old prospect with a temporary gold dye job, who was making his first World Cup qualifier start.

On September 5, the Americans lost in Costa Rica, 2–0. Shortly after that they—and the country—had more important things to think about, with the 9/11 terrorist attacks.

The next qualifier took place on October 7 in Foxborough, Massachusetts, against Jamaica. On a cool autumn day, the mood was subdued

after Arena told the players that the United States was invading Afghan-
istan to seek the people who had planned the attack on 9/11.

Claudio Reyna had witnessed an ugly gesture as he played for
Rangers in Glasgow a few days before this qualifier. As he prepared to
make a throw-in, Reyna saw one Celtic fan moving his hands like an
airplane crashing into a building. The fan was banned from further
matches, and Reyna was shaking his head when asked about it. (John
Terry, the sordid Chelsea captain, had shown his lack of character a day
after 9/11, getting drunk and mocking stranded Americans in an airport bar.)

Reyna wore the captain's band as the United States beat Jamaica, 2–0,
on two goals by Joe-Max Moore, a gritty midfielder from that well-
known soccer bastion of Tulsa, Oklahoma. ("I cannot imagine a better
name for him than Joe-Max," said Eric Wynalda, as Moore was inducted
into the National Soccer Hall of Fame in 2013. "That's what he gave you—
maximum.") The double by Joe-Max gave the Americans the victory that
qualified them for the 2002 World Cup. The long hard road of the Hex
had toughened the Americans for the year ahead.

Bruce Arena had a sarcastic way of employing his Noo Yawk accent. I
had no problem deciphering him because I remembered him as a high
school athlete from my younger reporting days on Long Island.

He usually began his answers to reporters' questions with the word
"Obviously." He also had an eye for talent and speed and change, and he
was fearless and did not act as if soccer was overly complicated.

For example, FIFA had commissioned a new ball, not for improved
aerodynamics or durability but for marketing: the official World Cup
ball would sell around the globe, after consumers saw it on television.
The players, being players, were convinced that the new ball veered like
a space capsule with a buzz on. Keepers hated it. This is a given: every
four years, keepers hate the new ball.

Asked to discuss the new spheroid endorsed by FIFA, Arena refused
to take the issue seriously.

"It's a BAWL," he enunciated.

When Arena said that, I burst out laughing. Everything he said made perfect sense to me. Yuh know what I mean?

During the long march to the World Cup, Arena had upgraded his squad with new players like John O'Brien and Tony Sanneh, most of them with overseas experience.

The new age was personified by Landon Donovan, who turned twenty just before the World Cup. Fleet and opportunistic, Donovan had a decided tropism for his home in Southern California rather than some sleety soccer enclave in Germany, even if it cost him income and growth as a player. Donovan had a mind of his own, but when he broke into stride on an open field he was a thing of beauty.

Another new face was DaMarcus Beasley, out of Fort Wayne, Indiana, who had resisted teasing back home that black American men do not play this sport. Only five feet, eight inches tall, Beasley could dunk a basketball; on the huge grass field, he would track down stray balls deep in defensive corners and come back and lead the fast break, tossing his rubbery body into the mix.

Arena, who had played one game as keeper for the national team, chose three terrific athletes with strong personalities to play his old position, including Brad Friedel of the Blackburn Rovers. Tall and physical, Friedel had helped win a national title at UCLA and had once been invited to be a walk-on member of the basketball team. The man could leap. Kasey Keller, who was now playing for Tottenham Hotspur, felt he had a shot at the first-string job until it dawned on him that Arena was going with Friedel. Arena asked Tony Meola to come back as the third keeper, and Meola responded by practicing hard and teaching younger players what he had learned in 1990 and 1994.

One of my favorite players on that 2002 team was Clint Mathis, out of Conyers, Georgia, who liked the nickname Cletus because of its unabashed pine-woods aura. He had a southern charm and a mind of his own.

Cletus showed up in Seoul sporting a Mohawk haircut, courtesy of his roommate Pablo Mastroeni. This gained him considerable attention from the Korean media and fans. Mathis was a throwback, an athlete who loved attention. The other players would vanish to their families or the private game rooms, but Cletus hung out in the lobby along with his proud mom, Pat. He did not mind when young ladies asked if they could pose for a photo with the southerner with the Mohawk. Sometimes they even had a camera.

His attitude carried onto the field. Cletus was of the firm opinion that a player like himself should not waste too much time digging for the ball in a distant corner when he could be shooting it. American youth leagues do not encourage gunners who fire away, the way kids in real soccer countries learn to do in impromptu sandlot games.

Cletus was one year past a serious knee operation, and Arena questioned whether he was pushing himself hard enough. "I think he's got a real good future if he can just develop some better habits as a professional, and that will happen," Arena said. "That's part of being in an environment where that is required of a player."

Sports Illustrated thought enough of Cletus to put him on the cover of its pre–World Cup issue, making him the first male soccer player on the cover in eight years. He seemed destined to be a star—James Dean in a jersey.

By sheer luck, I saw a lot of the American team. A friend had tipped me off that the United States was staying at the Marriott, with a great pool and located directly above a major arcade and subway station, and I made reservations for myself and my colleague Jeré Longman before the Marriott system began to block reporters.

Staying in the same hotel did not gain us any special access—not with the genial and armed team security agent perched near the elevator bank. However, whenever the team was available, I could pop downstairs without having to commute from another hotel.

One day, I interviewed players about the custom of exchanging jerseys with opponents after a match. Some players told me how they would immediately wear the jersey somebody else had just worn for ninety sweaty minutes, which sounded kind of creepy. Another time, I got permission to visit the recreation room the federation had reserved for the wives and children of the players.

I also chatted with a few survivors of the 1998 château, who appreciated Arena's putting them up in the Marriott.

"We're all adults and we like to have time to ourselves," Keller said. "We were all lolling around trying to keep from going nuts." Then he added, "Here you can walk into a mall and get a Starbucks."

Team officials organized an outing to the DMZ, the demilitarized zone where South Korean and American troops have been on guard against North Korea since the end of the Korean War in 1953. It was not far, maybe an hour on modern roads, in and around mountains and inlets, to go from a modern city with Starbucks to an armed standoff—"the most dangerous place on earth," as President Clinton once called it.

The American federation thoughtfully provided a separate bus and issued guidelines for reporters—no shorts, no logos, no waving at the North Korean side because observers would be taking video, and any expression of friendship would be portrayed as a weakening of resolve. We did not understand until we saw armed soldiers of one side glaring at armed soldiers from the other side, identical faces, only a few yards apart. We were told about the sneak attack years earlier when North Koreans had suddenly mauled South Koreans with hatchets, in a dispute over a few trees. The hatred in the eyes of the soldiers was tangible.

The buses made a detour to a barracks a few yards from the border, where hundreds of fit first-line American and Korean soldiers were resting, waiting. DaMarcus Beasley shook his head. He had no idea it was this tense.

Young South Korean journalists seemed as touched as the Americans. They had been raised with hopes of peace, by parents with long memories they did not necessarily share. Why burden the next generation with fears of war? The young South Koreans shook their heads, as innocent as the Americans.

The Americans stored away their images of the DMZ. They had three matches coming up against Portugal, South Korea, and Poland.

A great source of talent, Portugal had played in the World Cup only twice, finishing third with Eusebio in 1966 and winning one of three matches in 1986. Eleven of the team's twenty-three players earned their living elsewhere in Europe, and twelve played in the very respectable Portuguese league. The star was Luís Figo, who had won the Ballon d'Or as the best player in Europe in 2000 and was now one of the Galácticos of Real Madrid.

There is a theory that it is helpful to play the best team first, before the all-stars learn to play together. According to the FIFA computer, Portugal was the Americans' toughest opponent, ranked fifth in the world while the United States was ranked thirteenth, South Korea thirty-second, and Poland thirty-eighth. What did these rankings prove? The French team that trudged off the team bus was ranked first in the world.

For the match with Portugal in Suwon, near Seoul, Reyna was injured, and Arena held out Mathis because of lack of conditioning. Instead, he sprung Donovan, which may have been the plan all along.

The match began better than anybody could have imagined. Four minutes in, John O'Brien scored after the Portuguese keeper collided with a teammate in the goalmouth.

At twenty-nine minutes, with Donovan putting pressure on the keeper, a Portuguese defender deflected the ball into his own goal—shades of poor Escobar of Colombia in 1994.

At thirty-six minutes, McBride converted a chance, giving the United States a 3–0 lead, but the United States let Portugal back in by surrendering a goal in the thirty-ninth minute. In the second half, at the seventy-first minute, Jeff Agoos—finally playing a World Cup match after his past frustrations—allowed an own goal. The United States held on for a 3–2 victory, which was perceived as one of the great upsets the United States had ever perpetrated, right behind the 1950 victory over England.

The United States now had three quick points against the fifth-ranked team, but next it had to play the host team in Daegu. The entire nation had come to idolize Guus Hiddink, the Dutch coach of the South Korean national team, and just about everybody was wearing a red T-shirt that said "Be the Reds!"

"No host nation has not gotten into the second round, right?" asked Eddie Pope, the American defender. He was right.

Mathis, back in the lineup, scored in the twenty-fourth minute, and

Friedel gave the Americans a huge lift when he saved a penalty kick in the fortieth minute. The United States was still ahead in the eighty-second minute when Ahn Jung-Hwan, a dynamic second-half substitute, rose above Agoos and Friedel, the leaper who could have played basketball for UCLA, and tied the match. Given the energy flowing between the host team and its fans, the U.S. players said they had done well to draw. Privately, they knew that Ahn's goal had rendered them vulnerable.

On June 14, the United States played Poland in Daejon, while a simultaneous match was held in Incheon between Portugal and South Korea. Poland, whose players made a living all over Europe, had not advanced to the tournament since 1986. For some reason, the United States often seemed to play better against more artistic southern European squads—Spain, Italy, Portugal—than against more physical northern and eastern European teams (Czechoslovakia and Austria in 1990, Romania in 1994, Germany in 1998).

This was the case again in 2002. Poland scored in the third, fifth, and sixty-sixth minutes for a 3–0 lead that put the Americans in deep trouble. Under the rules put in after the disgraceful waltz in 1982, the scores of the simultaneous match were not displayed in the stadium, but in the age of the cell phone and the laptop, the Americans were well aware that Portugal and South Korea were playing a scoreless draw that would eliminate the Yanks.

However, in distant Incheon, the referee had tossed out two Portuguese players by the sixty-sixth minute, so there was hope. Four minutes later, Park Ji-Sung scored to put South Korea ahead. Back in Daejon, Donovan scored in the eighty-third minute, essentially a meaningless goal, as the United States lost, 3–1. The team waited out South Korea's 1–0 victory that put the mighty Reds and the wobbly Yanks through to the second round.

"This is a very good day for U.S. soccer," Friedel said, after giving up three goals. "This was also a very lucky day for U.S. soccer," he added.

Three days later, the Americans would play their regional pals from Mexico, not in thundering Azteca or some sleety pitch in the American heartland but down the road in Chonju, a neutral site.

. . .

One upgrade was noticeable about American soccer in 2002—the traveling supporters known as Sam's Army. Mark Spacone and John Wright of Buffalo, New York, had had such a good time at the World Cup in America in 1994 that they went to France in 1998 to cheer on the U.S. team, as wretched as it was. Although Sam's Army welcomed dues-paying members, anybody wearing red was welcome to flock around them at games, with drums and flags and chants.

Red was not such a good choice of color in 2002, since every single person in South Korea was wearing a Reds shirt, so part of Sam's Army switched to blue. Even fans have road uniforms.

For the Portugal match, Bill Starling from Tyler, Texas, and his son, Jeff, from Dallas, had been in the stands in Suwon, wearing blue. Jeff Delp of Atlanta, and his brother, Shawn, from Los Angeles, were there, both in red, with Jeff wearing a floppy red hat straight out of Dr. Seuss.

"I didn't think we'd have that many fans," said DaMarcus Beasley, the most observant of the players. "It's great to hear them."

In decibels, the individual American fan probably measured about one-third of other national fans, but they were trying. They also had idealistic rules of the road, much like Deadheads following the Grateful Dead—do not take a seat away from somebody who has paid for it; let little children stand up front; don't behave destructively.

Sam's Army—and World Cup crowds in general—were a different animal from club supporters, the Ultras and skinheads of Europe. Because the World Cup is a universal event, relatively affluent fans from all over the world attend, bringing the joy and scruples of tourists and pilgrims. Sam's Army tried to yell like the Dutch or bounce around like Koreans or just look good, like the Brazilians. But like its team, Sam's Army was a work in progress.

Heading into the knockout round, the fans could take heart from the reality that the United States was drawing close to its longtime tormentor. Mexico still ruled in Azteca and had an all-time record of twenty-eight victories, nine losses, and nine draws against the United States, but the Americans had won four straight matches on American soil.

The Mexican team still played with intimidation for all past insults and incursions. Also, Mexico does not lack for well-off fans who can afford to travel for a World Cup match, but Sam's Army had passports and dollars and outfits and banners, not to mention lung power.

Arena had to revise his lineup because of injuries and a yellow-card suspension to Frankie Hejduk, the muscular and fiery back known as Frankie Yellow Card. "We won't have any trouble finding two guys who want to play," Arena said of his back line. He dusted off Gregg Berhalter, who had played for Energie Cottbus in the former East Germany, and sent out five midfielders, deputizing Reyna to play on the right side, to cut off the Mexico passes and to counterattack down the right side.

The captain responded with the game of his life. Reyna was a conservative midfielder, at his best distributing the ball and closing down the center, but against Mexico, his team needed more from him. In the eighth minute, Reyna took off down the right side and crossed the ball to Wolff, who diverted the ball to McBride, who scored from twelve yards with virtually no coverage.

The Mexican players lost their edge immediately. They had never seen the United States play like this. The experiences in the Hexagonal had toughened the Americans and many of them had learned to be more aggressive while playing overseas. One example was Tony Sanneh, the right back, whose father had come from Gambia to the United States. Sanneh said he learned in the Bundesliga to take what the opponent gave you, much like Paul Caligiuri, the hero of Trinidad in 1989.

Years later, Sanneh told me that as he ran down the right sideline against Mexico that day, he heard a teammate shout, "Tony! Stay back!"— the traditional by-the-numbers approach that holds back American players. Sanneh claimed he shouted "F—— you!" over his shoulder, as he attacked. He was not a big name in the United States, but fans back home suddenly learned his name from his big-time romps down the right side.

The Mexicans were so flustered by the new American aggressiveness that they made a substitution in the twenty-eighth minute, apparently to raise the intensity. The United States got lucky early in the second half when John O'Brien touched a Mexican corner kick with his right hand, and Mexico screamed for a penalty kick, but the referee did not call it.

Later, O'Brien did not deny he had touched the ball but said his arm was pushed by a Mexican player.

In the sixty-fifth minute, O'Brien played a ball on the left side to Eddie Lewis, who centered it high to Donovan, who scored on a header for a 2–0 lead.

The Mexicans, so accustomed to dominating the Americans, particularly in Azteca, were a long way from home. They collectively lost their minds, and the game turned nasty, with the referee issuing five yellow cards against the United States and five against Mexico. In the eighty-eighth minute, Rafa Márquez head-butted Cobi Jones in the jaw, a cheap shot not worthy of a captain. Márquez was tossed with a red card, and Mexico spent the final minutes shorthanded, chasing the ball. The Mexicans had been publicly depantsed, in perhaps the most satisfying victory the United States had ever achieved against them.

"The rest of the world used to call us a sleeping giant," said Robert Contiguglia, the nephrologist who was president of the U.S. federation. "I think the sleeping giant has woken up."

Now the Americans would play Germany. The Americans had great respect for the Bundesliga and the country's soccer culture; many of the Germans spoke English and vacationed in the United States. This would be a World Cup quarterfinal, not a regional grudge match.

The U.S. writers had a charter bus to take us to the match in Ulsan, down the east coast. For a while we bantered: Filip Bondy of the *New York Daily News* waved a yellow card when Michelle Kaufman of the *Miami Herald* was tardy. After nearly two hundred miles, we approached the stadium, and you could feel the energy kick in; writers get up for the big game, too.

As the German team came out on the field—Oliver Kahn with his fright mask of a face; Michael Ballack, large and sleek; Miroslav Klose, deceptively bland-looking—they seemed purposeful. This is not some leftover wartime stereotype, I hasten to add, but a respectful judgment earned from one World Cup to another. Those guys would run over their opponent; those guys would never quit.

The Americans held them off for thirty-nine minutes but then Germany gained a free kick, and Ballack headed the ball into the net.

Germany was still ahead in the fiftieth minute when the United States suffered a piece of terrible luck. Reyna put a corner kick near the goal, and then Sanneh headed it at the keeper. Gregg Berhalter stuck out his left foot for the rebound and volleyed it back at Kahn, who managed to deflect the ball as he dove to his right. Torsten Frings, a German midfielder, was guarding the left post, his left arm extended, and he deflected the ball, and Kahn dived on it, protecting it from the frantic kicks by the Americans.

After Kahn cleared it, Berhalter and his teammates pointed at Hugh Dallas, the Scottish referee, and shouted for a handball. The replay on our screens did not indicate that Frings had blatantly stuck out his arm, but his arm was clearly out there, at an angle that worked to Germany's extreme advantage. It was the kind of non-call that affects a match and changes history. There was still no provision for instant replay, as there was in American football. Play on, the ref said.

Arena threw in all his firepower—Mathis in the fifty-eighth minute, Jones in the sixty-fifth, Stewart in the eightieth, but they could not penetrate. Raging at the non-call, the Americans left the field, and the tournament, with a 1–0 loss.

"It should have been a penalty," Berhalter said afterward. He comes from a soccer family, is an establishment guy. "I don't know what view the referee had," he added. "Don't blame it on him."

Somebody reminded Berhalter about O'Brien's obvious handball against Mexico.

"I'm not complaining," Berhalter said. "You win some, you lose some."

The players had lived out their destiny for this World Cup, and now they were headed back to Seoul. Then something happened in the media room that still gives me a chill. A small group of German reporters packed up their laptops and prepared to move on, but first they stopped by our desks to commiserate. Roland Zorn, a German columnist who used to be based in New York and speaks colloquial English, told us that the Americans had outplayed the Germans and deserved to win. His buddies nodded their assent.

"The score was 1–0," I said. "Your guys won."

In the ballet-critic world of soccer writing, there is a concept of the just result, which team deserved to win, based on effort and artistry. In Zorn's considered opinion, the just result would have been an American victory. It is that kind of big-picture bond that unites professionals from different countries. I told Roland I would see him at the semifinals.

The American writers piled into our bus for the long haul back to Seoul. I remember darkness, cars speeding past in the night, our bus pulling into a rest stop so grim and oily that it could have been the New Jersey Turnpike. At dawn, we arrived at the Marriott, where my wife had juice and pastry waiting.

A few hours later, Bruce Arena held the last press conference in Seoul before everybody grabbed a flight to vacations, to Major League Soccer, to the rest of their lives. As deadpan as ever, the coach praised his players, saying they got a tough call, saying it was a good World Cup. He also reminded us that this nice run in no way meant that the United States had reached the top level of world soccer.

The wires were carrying stories that the German legends Franz Beckenbauer and Jürgen Klinsmann, with their ties to the United States, were saying that a handball should have been called on Frings.

"Whatever," Arena said. "It wasn't called. That's life."

Somebody noted that a few German players had stopped Arena after the match and told him the Americans had outplayed them.

"That's nice to hear," Arena said with a tinge of Noo Yawk sarcasm.

In other words: It's a BAWL.

And on that note, the brief Golden Age of American soccer was over.

This was South Korea's time. I had fallen in love with the country in 1988 during the Olympics in Seoul, catching the last vestiges of the old generation that had survived the wars, the elders with their bright gowns and bizarre stovepipe hats, strolling the ancient lanes of the city. I loved the passions of the Korean people, who sometimes traded punches in the national legislature, and I loved the mountains and the urban hikers and the bittersweet unofficial national anthem, "Arirang."

Susan Chira, the regional correspondent for the *Times* in 1988, and her writer-husband, Michael Shapiro, had taught me to love Korea. Michael once said that Koreans reminded him of relatives back in New York. They got up close to you, they argued, they laughed, they cried. That's why Koreans make great New Yorkers.

Fourteen years later, Seoul was still a hoot, a great city with three stadiums on the subway line. On June 4, while the Reds were holding off Poland in the southern port city of Busan, hundreds of young fans jammed into a subterranean plaza, screaming in front of a large television. When the match ended, the young people disposed of every scrap of paper, every soda can, and went their way.

The city was expanding everywhere, with young people chattering on cell phones in the subway, getting reception through the deep rock substrata under the Han.

People were friendly and tried out their English on us. In one museum, Marianne met a young woman named Juin who adopted her as an auntie; the two of them ran around town for the next few weeks.

Early in our stay, Marianne looked out the hotel window and spotted a humble restaurant next door, patronized by Koreans, sitting cross-legged at low tables, eating, waiting for buses back to the countryside. We walked past and saw them eating the same dish—roast duck, out of clay pots, with purple rice and various nuts and fruits, including plums, one of the great ethnic dishes we have ever tasted. We have never encountered the specialty in New York; if you know where to find it, please let me know.

One sweet day, we went to the arts center nestled in the hills, away from the bad air of central Seoul, and attended a *pansori* concert, men telling tall tales as energetic women pound on drums. Korean rap, I called it. Very cool.

This was my sixth World Cup, and I had never seen so much pride and hope from the host nation. The psychic core of a people was on display.

Seoul was connected to the rest of South Korea by a fine rail system, with special trains back from night games. One of my trips was to the first World Cup match ever for China, coached by everybody's good friend

Bora Milutinović, now on his fifth different World Cup squad. Bora's team had been training on Cheju Island, the traditional Korean site for newlyweds, but China's venture would have a very short honeymoon.

Exactly thirteen years after the demonstrations in Tiananmen Square, I took the train to Kwangju, itself the site of a dreadful massacre of protestors in 1980. I sat on the train next to a young stockbroker from Shanghai, who pointed out his fellow yuppies, a fashion writer, a doctor, a banker, all with electronic gadgets and stylish clothes, making me look even more shabby and outmoded than usual.

Unfortunately, China was not very advanced in men's soccer, hanging with Costa Rica for a half and then surrendering two goals. China would finish with no goals and nine goals allowed and has not been back to the World Cup since.

That night I learned something that would serve me well for the rest of the tournament—don't touch the wretched faux-Western food at the stadium. There was a better alternative at every train station, no matter how late: a couple of older women would be selling noodle soup for the long ride back to Big Town. These *ajummas*—grannies, babushkas—were more outgoing than other Asian women, with ruddy cheeks, frizzy hair, big smiles, dropping lines on me that were undoubtedly funny, maybe even bawdy, while plopping shrimp into my container. I still wonder what they were saying.

Meantime, a whole other tournament was going on in Japan. From what I heard, the Japanese were diligent hosts but did not seem to have as much invested psychically in the dual enterprise as the Koreans did. A few young Japanese friends of ours, who had lived near us in New York and now worked for international corporations in Tokyo, said their bosses demanded they be at their desks. But the young people insisted on watching at least the Japanese matches, and their bosses relented.

My first contact with the Japanese end of the tournament came on June 7, when I flew from Incheon to Osaka to Sapporo for the match between Argentina and England, a reprise of the quarterfinal in 1998 when David Beckham earned a red card by kicking at Diego Simeone. Beckham had played his way back into the hearts of the English fans and was on the team.

In Sapporo, one of the few cities in Japan with a grid layout, police were guarding against any outbreak of Falklands-Malvinas hostilities, but the fans were polite in this neutral place. This dream first-round pairing was held in the Sapporo Dome, the first indoor World Cup match since Michigan in 1994, and FIFA sent in a superstar to ride herd on the other stars. Pierluigi Collina of Italy, a referee noticeable for the absence of hair due to a rare disease, alopecia, had his own Web site, his own fan club, and his own watch commercial.

Life does not always provide opportunities to redress mistakes, but, indoors, on the other side of the world from Saint-Étienne, Beckham had his chance. In the forty-fourth minute, Michael Owen reprised his jitterbug runs of 1998, breaking inside the Argentine defenses, hurtling himself toward the goal, and causing contact with an Argentine defender (not Simeone). The great Collina blew his whistle and sent England to the penalty-kick disk. Owen and Beckham conferred briefly, but Beckham was the best free-kick specialist in this sport and had been lusting for redemption for four years. Of course he would take the kick. Simeone, ever the antagonist, tried to shake Beckham's hand, to mess with his mind, but Beckham ignored the antics. He let the keeper make his move, then plunked the ball straight down Sapporo High Street for what would be the only goal of the evening. After the match, Beckham celebrated. Four years was a long time.

Both Japan and South Korea had advanced into the knockout round, a matter of pride for both countries. Japan went out quickly, 1–0, to Turkey, one of the many outsiders in this tournament.

The other host team played Italy in the main stadium in Seoul, a night that would test FIFA's campaign against the grand spectacle of diving.

To its credit, FIFA had been raising the professionalism and fitness of officials, calling them in for periodic training sessions, lowering the retirement age into the forties, and preparing them with seminars and training

films. Just before the tournament, reporters were invited to the end of a
three-day training session in Seoul, where I got to interview Brian Hall
from Gilroy, California, who had been assigned to officiate the Italy-
Ecuador match and would be the fourth official for Argentina-England,
a high level of trust.

"This is a brotherhood," Hall told us, praising Collina.

The refs had been told to crack down on the diving—*simulazione* in
Italian. In recent years, bad acting had reached epidemic stage.

"My intent is to protect the good players," Hall said, adding, "You
judge the location of the field and the score at the time. If a team is losing late in the game, they try to use gamesmanship. If you watch the
video, you can see a player realize he has lost control of the ball, and
then he drags his toe or his heel and does a flop. Then they look up to see
if you are watching."

Hall, who worked in the credit card and computer fields, came to his
strange sideline the way most officials do, by accident. As a thirteen-
year-old keeper in California, he was asked to fill in when one of the refs
did not show up. He declined, until the other ref reminded him that he
would earn a seven-dollar fee. Hall had worked his way past the stereotype that the United States was not soccer territory, and now he and his
colleagues had their orders: cut down on the acting.

Byron Moreno of Ecuador was the referee for Italy–South Korea.
Christian Vieri scored in the eighteenth minute, and Italy seemed to be
tightening its traditional defense. But the Reds, inspired by crowds chanting *"Tae-han Min-guk"*—Republic of Korea—chased the ball until they
scored in the eighty-eighth minute.

Given its own ghastly record in three straight World Cup shoot-outs,
Italy was not counting on that mode for salvation. Italy began firing the
ball toward the goal and pulling out all the tricks, the operatic death
scenes that work for the top teams in the chummy world of Serie A.

Thirteen minutes into extra time, Francesco Totti of AS Roma went
into spasms on the ground, his arms and legs shaking violently, as if he
were being riddled by machine-gun bullets. The referee, warned about
histrionics, observed Totti's death rattle. Moreno had flashed the yellow

card at Totti in the twenty-second minute for another infraction; now he waved it again, meaning Totti was automatically expelled.

The Italians screamed but had to play one man down, which caught up with them at the twenty-seventh minute of added time, when Ahn Jung-Hwan scored the winning goal. The Italians went off the field raging at Moreno.

Italian fans had no idea the referees had been told to cut down on faking; the cynical *tifosi* who saw strange calls in their home league suspected favoritism in the yellow card brandished at an Italian player in Seoul. This is the way the world works, *vero*?

Since FIFA had ordered the refs to clamp down on diving, it seemed logical that a leader would back up his people the next day. Instead, Sepp Blatter undercut his referee.

"Totti's sending off against Korea was neither a penalty nor a dive," Blatter told *La Gazzetta dello Sport*. He added, "A referee with a feeling would not have shown him the card, bearing in mind the same player had already been booked."

In a sense, Blatter was right. Refs generally hand out yellow cards early in a match to calm the lads down and then use discretion late in the match. On the other hand, a player with a yellow card in his dossier ought to be smart enough to shut down some of the gratuitous violence or yapping, but sometimes they forget—like Boniek of Poland in 1982 or Harkes in 1994.

Now Blatter was publicly telling the world that his ref should have observed a double standard. The refs came to Moreno's defense. The highly rated Anders Frisk of Sweden praised his colleague for making the right call and could not help noting that both Totti and Vieri missed easy shots late in the match.

Many Italians insisted that Moreno must have been paid off to allow the Reds to advance. Blatter said that this was ridiculous but since he had already said the referee made the wrong call, Blatter and his staff made sure Moreno did not ref any more World Cup matches.

In the months to come, Moreno was exposed as a shady character. Back home in Ecuador, he allowed nine minutes of injury time when a highly favored team was behind. After he gave up refereeing, Moreno was caught with $700,000 worth of heroin on a flight from Ecuador to New York in 2010 and served twenty-six months in prison. But nobody could have predicted his downfall on that furious evening in Seoul, when Totti flopped.

That night I wrote that Totti had been guilty of bad acting. Then I began receiving e-mails.

"*Devei morire*," one of them began. You must die. Terrific. It gave me a chance to use my rudimentary Italian to write back to my new pen pals.

The quarterfinals included three regulars (Brazil, England, and Germany), one perennial disappointment (Spain), and four outsiders (South Korea, the United States, Turkey, and Senegal). Never had four nations from so far outside the power structure reached the quarterfinals. Why did this happen?

- Opening up the competition to thirty-two teams gave outsiders the chance to upset somebody.
- The increase of sponsor and television money in the best leagues in Europe and the Bosman court decision, allowing players to move to clubs in other countries, gave players experience and confidence when they played for their national teams.
- Contemporary technology and electronics allowed nations to be more effective in training and teaching their players.
- National teams recruited coaches from established nations like Brazil and the Netherlands. South Korea, once known as the Hermit Kingdom for its resistance to outside influences, had been unable to improve in soccer until it hired Guus Hiddink, the Dutchman who had coached at Fenerbahçe in Turkey and Real Madrid, as well as the 1998 Dutch team that went to the World Cup semifinals.

When the Reds began to get results, Hiddink was hailed as a genius—a Western genius, at that, whose management style included spreading responsibilities to assistants and conferring with his players, a radical change for the Koreans.

Bruce Arena said being the home team in the World Cup was worth two goals—one to get you out of trouble in the first round; another to beat a team you might not have beaten otherwise. South Korea had a lot going for it.

On June 22, Hiddink went from genius to downright immortal as the Reds held off Spain for 120 minutes and then won in penalty kicks, 5–3, another World Cup failure for Spain. Going to the semifinals was a great moment for South Korea because it surpassed the stunning romp to the quarterfinals by North Korea in 1966.

Another outsider was guaranteed a place in the semifinals, as Turkey was meeting Senegal in Osaka. Senegal was coached by a foreigner, Bruno Metsu, a Frenchman who had played in France and Belgium and later coached in France, Africa, and the Middle East. Twenty of the twenty-three Senegalese players worked in the French league.

Turkey was also having its best World Cup. The domestic league had intense competition among three teams based in Istanbul, but the national team had been marginal until coached by Şenol Güneş, a former national team keeper from the Trabzonspor team. Eight of the twenty-three Turkish members played in Germany, while its best striker, Hakan Şükür, had played for Torino, Inter Milan, and Parma but mostly for Galatasaray.

In the quarterfinal of outsiders, Turkey outlasted Senegal, 1–0, on a goal in the fourth minute of added time. The world was still waiting for a semifinalist from Africa.

I opted for the Brazil end of the semifinals, and by evening, we were ensconced in Ginza, which was glowing, as usual. It was great to see Japan. I had decided that holding the European championships in adjacent countries may be fine, but the sea between South Korea and Japan was too great a barrier for a World Cup.

Brazil appeared to be gathering steam under Luiz Felipe Scolari, known as Big Phil. Managing Brazil is always tricky because *jogo bonito* is a national patrimony. Every time Brazil looks vulnerable on defense, the public calls for hunkering down, but when a nation produces a left back like Roberto Carlos, it's hard not to deploy one of the most murderous left-footed shots in history.

Brazil was powered by tall sturdy Rivaldo and a brash newcomer with glistening curls named Ronaldinho, along with the resurrected superstar Ronaldo, who had survived his apparent trance in the 1998 final to become the great striker of his time, a lethal mix of six-foot power and balletic grace.

Like most artists, Ronaldo had his flaws, including his taste for roaming, which would eventually produce at least four children by various companions and wives. His other flaw was his knees. Injuries and operations had held him to only sixteen matches in 2001–2, but in a way that meant he was fresh for the World Cup. He had scored in four straight matches before missing against England. He had an injured thigh, but was expected to play in the semifinal against Turkey—a rare rematch in the World Cup format.

The two teams had met in their group, producing charges of world-level faking. When Luizao went sprawling in the eighty-seventh minute, he convinced the Korean ref to give a penalty kick, which Rivaldo converted for a 2–1 victory. In the closing minutes, a Turkish player directed a ball into Rivaldo's shins, and Rivaldo clutched his face with great elaboration, shades of Croatia's Slava Bilić in 1998. The ref went for Rivaldo's agony, flashing a red card, which ruled the Turkish player out for the next match.

"Oriental Hospitality," proclaimed the headline in a Rio paper, referring to the regional proclivity for generous gift giving. Needless to say, the Turkish players and fans remembered Luizao's dive and Rivaldo's mortal injury.

The two teams were training in new stadium in Saitama, at the edge of the Tokyo sprawl, where the Japanese had built a subway line, exactly the kind of excesses the World Cup and Olympics foist upon host nations. For a few yen, I traveled from glittering Ginza to the end of the line in Saitama, in actual farmland. In the dusk, I walked along a quiet sidewalk, hearing the breeze whistle through the crops, birds singing vespers, a farmer finishing up for the evening, with the glow of the new stadium up ahead.

Brazil was working out in the mostly empty stadium on this sweet, eerie evening, with the major noise coming from Brazilian radio reporters, who swarmed and chattered, keeping track of Ronaldo's thigh, Ronaldinho's banishment because of a dangerous tackle against England, and a collision between the regular keeper and a reserve during training. (The keeper would recover.)

After the workout, I walked back through the farmland and took the subway back to Ginza, where the lights put me on sensory overload. I caught up with the televised semifinal in Seoul, between Germany and the Reds.

In the seventy-first minute of a scoreless draw, Captain Ballack sacrificed himself when he took down a Korean player on a fast break, a tactical foul, worth a yellow card. He had accumulated a yellow card in the team's earlier match when a Paraguayan player initiated contact, so Ballack would be out for the final, if Germany made it that far. Four minutes later, he made sure his team would reach the final, putting in a rebound. In South Korea, an estimated seven million people watched—and groaned—in public plazas.

The next evening, some Turkish fans living all over the world splurged for last-minute air tickets to Tokyo and then splurged for outrageous scalper tickets, just to be in the corn and soy fields of Saitama for Turkey's first World Cup semifinal.

Ronaldo, ailing thigh and all, spun two defenders in the fourth minute of the second half and placed a shot into the corner for the only goal. Then he celebrated with a raised index finger and his gap-toothed grin, described by my colleague Howard French as resembling Alfred E. Neuman, the *Mad Magazine* icon.

Big Phil replaced Ronaldo for a fresh defender in the sixty-eighth minute, and Brazil held on for the 1–0 victory. The honorary Brazilians in the stands, from Japan, South Korea, China, everywhere in the world, celebrated in their blue-and-yellow kits, the colors standing for grace, music, enthusiasm. Brazil was back in the finals.

. . .

Normally, I am not interested in the third-place match, but the Reds and Turkey had provided fresh energy and new faces. From Tokyo, I watched them play in far-off Daegu, as Şükür, the Bull of the Bosporus, scored the fastest goal ever in the World Cup, 10.8 seconds into the match.

After Turkey held on for a 3–2 victory, its players summoned the South Koreans to take the victory lap with them. The players put their arms around one another, saluted the fans, absorbing the lusty cheers from the stands. Bravo to the Turks for acknowledging the last thrilling month.

The championship match was in Yokohama, the ancient port for Westerners, with its foreigners' cemetery. Marianne and I met our Japanese friends in Yokohama's Chinatown before I headed for the stadium.

After all the new faces, the final belonged to Germany and Brazil, with seven championships and five runner-up finishes between them. Ronaldinho was back from his suspension, but Ballack was serving his, an ominous imbalance.

The great Collina was assigned to work the final, since he would reach the retirement limit of forty-five before the next World Cup. He took control of the match right away, wielding a yellow card to Roque Junior in the sixth minute and to Miroslav Klose in the ninth. The boys got Collina's point and did not test him after that.

Germany took the play to Brazil for more than a half, counterattacking, conceding nothing, but without Ballack, it could not score. Big Phil's tactics—the defense, and, who knows, maybe even the celibacy—had focused the Brazilians, with their offense coming from Big Ronnie, Little Ronnie, and Rivaldo, from everywhere.

In the sixty-seventh minute, Germany made its first blunder. Rivaldo fired a left-footed shot that skipped off the soggy turf to Kahn, who normally would have gathered the ball. Instead, he deflected it to Ronaldo, who flicked it into the empty corner. (Later, there were suggestions Kahn had been playing with an injured ring finger on his right hand, but, tough guy that he was, he would not say.)

In the seventy-ninth minute, *jogo bonito* emerged. José Kléberson centered a cross toward Rivaldo, who feinted as if to shoot, but he dummied the ball, letting it roll through his long legs, leaving the German defense leaning. The ball went to Ronaldo, who tapped in his second goal. Big Phil took him out in the ninetieth minute, as all Brazilians, honorary and real, applauded his comeback from the horror of 1998.

"We missed this joy," Ronaldo said after being awarded the Golden Boot trophy as the tournament's outstanding player. "We said to ourselves, 'We cannot miss it.' Not only our joy is in first place but the joy of the Brazilian people."

The journalists waited in the mixed zone for words of wisdom from the Brazilian players. Eventually, they paraded through the corridor in a wiggly line, dancing the samba, blowing on horns, singing, but they never stopped to talk, and that was fine. At the end of a World Cup of outsiders, Brazil was making music and dancing again.

14

THE HOME I WAS
ALWAYS SEEKING

NEW YORK, 1997–2008

For one magic decade, I was taken inside a society with all the finer things in life—soccer, the Italian language, and Sicilian orange-flavored rice balls.

In the fall of 1997, my friend Massimo Lopes Pegna, the American correspondent for *La Gazzetta dello Sport*, told me about the café that was a truce zone for fans of all Italian squads. In their usual state of *ansia*, the Azzurri still needed at least a draw against Russia in the final match of 1997 to avoid the disgrace of not qualifying for 1998.

On a cold Saturday in November, this match was a godsend to Pino DiBartolo, the proprietor of L'Angolo café—the Italian word for "corner"—in Greenwich Village. Pino was legally not allowed to charge admission for watching the match on the modest television set propped high above the bar. However, Pino could charge a reasonable amount for a sandwich and a drink. The place was packed when I arrived, with mostly Italian spoken, but some English and Russian, too. Pino reserved a seat at the bar alongside some journalist friends who made things easier for me by speaking English, even to one another. The seat nearest the television was reserved for a fervent fan named Maurizio, who contorted himself into corkscrew positions whenever the ball took an ominous turn.

Fear and anguish filled the air. Even the Americans had already qualified, six days earlier, by beating Canada, 3–0. If the United States had been eliminated, most sports editors would have delightedly printed the score with the knowledge that they would not have to think about soccer for another four years. For Italy, the honor of the nation was at stake.

We peered up at the tiny set, noting that coach Cesare Maldini had started a willowy assortment of defensive-minded players. For more than a half, the two teams jostled each other without scoring, disaster only one mistake away. Then Italy counterattacked, and Demetrio Albertini caught up with the ball in full stride and blasted a left-footed shot past the keeper—shades of Paul Caligiuri in Trinidad.

In L'Angolo, most of the fans celebrated. In far-off Naples, the Italian defenders went into some version of *catenaccio*, and at 4:36 p.m. New York time, Italy clinched a 1–0 victory to ensure the berth in France. The television revealed a banner in Italian reading, Another Caesar Is Going to France.

As the patrons vanished into the bleak November afternoon, I remained to file my column via laptop. I loved L'Angolo even more now that it was mostly empty, revealing faded cushions on ancient wicker chairs, scuffed tables, blinds askew over dusty windows, with Pino bringing another strong espresso.

I had never been a regular at any bar or café since college. As a young reporter, I had been jealous of my pals in Manhattan who hung out in the Lion's Head in Greenwich Village (a young actress named Jessica Lange waited tables there in 1973), but I always felt I was on a one-night pass.

The Village had been a beacon since one snowy night in college, when I wandered into a bookstore to check out the Cavalier poets, the incense, the girls working in the shop. A few years later, my wife and I would drive to the Village, and our firstborn would gurgle and smile as we drank coffee at midnight. She was six months old and knew it was cool.

The Village. Bobby Zimmerman from Minnesota had found it. Now I was rediscovering it, via L'Angolo. I quickly got to know Riccardo Romani, a freelance writer, and Sandro Simone, who worked for an

Italian television channel, both of whom had played soccer in Italy as teenagers. And always there was Pino, a small and bespectacled native of Castellammare, Sicily, plying me with succulent *arancini*, the orange-flavored rice balls he claimed had been flown directly from Palermo, but even if they were made in Bensonhurst, they were delicious.

Epic days in L'Angolo: the 1999 Champions League final, when the Bayern Munich coach subbed out Lothar Matthäus to preserve a lead as the German fans groaned. *Never take out your best player.* Sure enough, Manchester United scored twice late, and Massimo and I had to go on suicide patrol, convincing the Bayern fans not to throw themselves under the crosstown bus.

L'Angolo was great for meeting writer pals and soccer mates, great for interviewing or being interviewed. Home. People said Steve Nash, the great point guard, who had a flat downtown, would slip into L'Angolo to watch a match, but I never saw him because I was always at the World Cup.

And if there hadn't been *arancini* and soccer, I still would have gone there to chat with Paola, the waitress, who was tall and beautiful and smart (and quite a team handball player, it turned out).

I imagined bringing my grandchildren, introducing them to Pino, making them speak a few words of Italian and learn to love rice balls. I could grow old there, like the wicker chairs.

There were warning signs. The city passed rules against smoking in public places, a blessing to our health but a disaster to Pino. *People come in, they have one beer and go outside to smoke, and maybe they find something else to do.* Landlords raised the rent on corner properties in the Village. You can never have enough Starbucks. Or nail shops.

Con Edison, with its ancient slogan of Dig We Must for a Better New York, began an excavation directly in front of L'Angolo. Jackhammers drowned out the games. The big dig lasted so long we assumed archaeologists were seeking Xi'an terra-cotta warriors from the other side.

Paola got a job running a restaurant, uptown. Riccardo got on his motorcycle and drove to Rome. Massimo got married.

One day L'Angolo was closed.

Pino moved to Florida for a while and then went home to Castellammare, where he runs the Soho Lounge. Nowadays, I hang around Foley's at Herald Square, on Irish pub dedicated to baseball, if you can imagine such a thing. It's a lovely place, but it doesn't serve Sicilian rice balls.

15

SCANDAL AND
HEAD-BUTT

GERMANY, 2006

This was close to a perfect World Cup—except for the bizarre way Germany became host and the ugly way the final ended.

Germany was chosen after FIFA expanded the tournament to thirty-two teams and encouraged emerging soccer nations to bid for future World Cups. Sepp Blatter went on record that if he were needed to cast a tie-breaking vote for 2006 he would choose South Africa. He was bucking for a Nobel Peace Prize, and this could be his ticket.

It never came to that. In 2000, Charles Dempsey from New Zealand, one of the twenty-four voting members of the FIFA executive committee, was instructed by his Oceania region to pick South Africa. However, the night before the vote, Dempsey vanished from Zurich. There being no provision for a proxy vote, Germany prevailed by a 12–11 margin.

This meant Blatter did not have to pick sides, which was highly convenient for him. Accusations of financial irregularities within FIFA were surfacing in Europe, where a few journalists were beginning to cover soccer politics seriously, as big business with a dark side. With Germany and England competing to be the host for the World Cup in 2006, Blatter's promised tiebreaker for South Africa would have made the European bloc quite unhappy. Since he was up for reelection in 2002, Blatter wanted his home continent to be happy with him.

When Dempsey resurfaced in New Zealand, he claimed he had been under terrible pressure and had opted not to be remembered as the delegate who caved to one side or the other. Was he threatened with harm? Was he overwhelmed by conflicting offers? We do not know. What we do know is that the vanishing delegate worked out for Sepp Blatter.

Two years later, Dempsey was given a lifetime status with FIFA, which included lucrative travel privileges and expenses. A nice bonanza for a member who had disgraced the organization.

However it happened, Germany proved to be a worthy host. Its Bundesliga was among the top leagues in the world, with modern, elegant stadiums, a railroad system that allowed fans to flit from match to match, and central cities with affordable hotels that somehow escaped the normal gouge by "official" FIFA hotels.

My wife and I sampled the new Germany in 2005 when we flew in for the draw ceremony in Leipzig, in the former Deutsche Demokratische Republik, East Germany, which had disintegrated in 1990. As soon as our train slid into the former East Berlin, everything looked half a century behind the times—weary land, faded buildings. When we arrived in Leipzig, with the St. Thomas church, where Bach worked, and the outdoor Christmas market with mulled wine, we were transported back in time.

The made-for-TV ceremony was held in a looming convention hall, with Heidi Klum flashing her cheekbones and Franz Beckenbauer booting souvenir balls into the stands. Once again, the United States was drawn into its own personal Group of Misery, if not outright death.

Since the United States had humiliated Mexico in the 2002 round of 16 and had given fits to Germany in the quarterfinals, there was reason to think that the FIFA seeding committee would consider those results. Being seeded in the top eight was a huge advantage because it meant facing potentially inferior opponents, but there was a snag: the host team was always placed in the first tier. Germany, rebuilding under its new coach, the retired striker Jürgen Klinsmann, was ranked sixteenth, but had to be placed in the top bracket. When Bruce Arena, back for a second World Cup, realized that Mexico had been seeded in the top tier, he knew his squad was headed for the lower depths.

"That means we play one seeded team, one European team, and one team from the other pot," Arena said in classic New York I've-been-around fatalistic tones.

Amid the flashing lights and thudding sound system of the ceremony, Arena learned his fate: the U.S. team was drawn into a group with the second-ranked Czech Republic, fourteenth-ranked Italy, and fiftieth-ranked Ghana.

The American journalists crowded around Arena, hoping he would pop off.

"We're pleased," Arena said.

Why in the world was he pleased?

"We know our opponents," he said with his normal smirk. "Now we can prepare."

When asked about his own Italian roots, Arena allowed himself thirty seconds of sentimentality, recalling being six years old in the Brooklyn grocery of his maternal grandfather, Salvatore Schembre, who kept a poster of the Azzurri on the wall. Now Arena was a national coach, and he thought of his second opponent as a powerful three-time champion, not as his ancestral homeland.

Early in 2006, Arena began to choose his squad.

Clint Mathis was gone. His aggressive goals in 2002 had earned him a look in the Bundesliga, until his inner Cletus emerged. Sent into a match late, he produced a game-tying goal, but he could not resist racing past his own coach and tapping an imaginary wristwatch, as if to say, "Why don't you cut it a little closer next time?" That pretty much finished Mathis in Germany, and Arena did not choose him for 2006.

The mainstays were back—Reyna, Donovan, McBride, Beasley, Pope. Keller was back in goal. There was one intriguing new face—Clint Dempsey, a hard-edged kid who played with appealing desperation from growing up with mostly Mexican immigrants in East Texas. Steve Cherundolo, small and unobtrusive, had quietly made himself into a very decent right back at Hannover. One of the new faces was Oguchi Onyewu, known as Gooch, an introverted Clemson University player with Nigerian roots, who was the biggest defender the United States had—six foot four and 210 pounds.

As he had done in Seoul in 2002, Arena treated his players like adults, housing them in the bustling heart of a great city, Hamburg, the northern port where they could go shopping, check out the parks and water views, maybe even visit the Reeperbahn district, where the Beatles had emerged four decades earlier.

Their first match was in Gelsenkirchen, an industrial city, against the second-ranked team in the world. The Czechs, with four players from major western European leagues, did not take long to exploit the Yanks.

Pavel Nedvěd came out flying, bringing the game to Gooch, who had the unfortunate effect of making people bounce off him. Nedvěd, who refined his tumbling repertoire with Juventus, hit the deck, bestowing a yellow card to Gooch in the fifth minute.

Within the same sixty ticks of the clock, Jan Koller, four inches taller than Gooch, lumbered into scoring position near Onyewu, who looked hesitant to get ejected so early in the match. Koller, whose large bald head earned him the nickname of Dino (as in dinosaur), stuck out that cranial appendage and hammered home a header. Petr Čech shut out the Yanks, 3–0, but Koller tore up his thigh and was done for the tournament.

"We lost to the second-rated team in the world," Keller said afterward, trying to find the bright side.

In the emerging world of social media, something amazing was happening back home. People were ticked off at Our Lads. Just as English fans hated their Swedish coach, and German fans were not sure how they felt about the Americanized Klinsmann, so American fans were turning mutinous over Bruce Arena.

This was a stunning development. Soccer was catching on with younger Americans, who had played a tame version of the sport in their suburban youth leagues and now possibly played in adult leagues but certainly had some discretional cash to sit in pubs and form opinions.

Back in the United States, electronic mobs were roaming the virtual countryside, flicking cranky messages with their thumbs rather than brandishing wooden pitchforks. The new breed wanted Bruce Arena gone, wanted to know why he had not used Eddie Johnson and John O'Brien until the United States was down a couple of goals. Where the heck was Freddy Adu? Why had Nike invested in the great savior of American soccer if he was not on the playing field in Gelsenkirchen? Get us Bruce Arena's head! Yesterday!

After the drubbing from the Czechs, the Americans prepared to play Italy in Kaiserslautern, not far from the U.S. Air Force base at Ramstein. I visited the base and met Allison Hardwick, who piloted C-130 transport planes on their tight and perilous descent into Baghdad. A defender in the intramural league on the base, Hardwick said she was planning to attend the Italy match—"a dream of mine."

With American servicepeople in the stands, waving flags and chanting "U-S-A," the Americans played a nasty and ultimately brave match. Italy scored first, in the twenty-second minute, and then surrendered an own goal in the twenty-seventh minute. One minute later, Daniele De Rossi flung an elbow at Brian McBride's head while they were up in the air, and McBride went down, bleeding. The referee, Jorge Larrionda of Uruguay, wisely asked for input from one of the sideline assistants, who had seen the elbow flying, and Larrionda tossed De Rossi with a red card.

A world power would know how to exploit that extra player, but the Yanks squandered it—and worse. Just before halftime, Pablo Mastroeni took out Andrea Pirlo with a lumbering cleats-up tackle and was handed a red card, so the United States and Italy went into the locker room at the half even in score and ejections. Two minutes into the second half, Eddie Pope, one of the steadiest defenders ever to play for the United States, committed a two-footed tackle, worthy of a yellow card. Already playing with a yellow from earlier in the game, Pope was sent off, to his horror.

Down a player, the Americans took the play to the Italians, with Keller punching or swatting or catching everything that flew near him, securing a 1–1 draw that earned the respect of everybody in the stadium, including the Italian fans.

Within an hour, in this new electronic world, I received e-mails from a friend in Greece and another in Italy, saying the Americans deserved better than a draw.

After two matches, the United States needed a victory over Ghana in Nuremberg to have any chance to advance. In the twenty-second minute, Captain Claudio Reyna twisted his knee near midfield, and Ghana scooped up the ball and scored. Reyna tried to continue but had to come out in the fortieth minute.

Dempsey scored in the forty-third minute, and it seemed the Yanks might overcome the bad start. But, two minutes into injury time in the first half, the Curse of Gooch struck again. As Onyewu headed the ball out of the box, he made minor contact with Razak Pimpong, nine full inches shorter than him. The German ref, Markus Merk, saw Pimpong bouncing away and called for a penalty kick, which Stephen Appiah converted. The 2–1 score stood up, and the loss sent the Yanks home.

We reporters had been around these players for weeks in Germany, and for years before that. It was not fun to stand in a mixed zone and ask Keller, Donovan, and McBride to explain things, but they were cooperative; we all had jobs to do.

Arena had become more sarcastic, more withdrawn, as the tournament went on, and he bristled when asked why he had moved Eddie Lewis and DaMarcus Beasley from their comfort range on the left side.

The new president of the U.S. federation, Sunil Gulati, was uncharacteristically terse near the mixed zone. Gulati was a soccer lifer, born in India, childhood in Connecticut, amateur player and referee, official and fan. I used to see him in the bleachers at Columbia University on Saturday mornings, bickering and bantering with Paul Gardner. Gulati was also an economist and college professor, with ties to the Kraft family of football and soccer. I knew him well enough to sense he was not pleased with three-and-out.

Arena had warned us in 2002, after that quarterfinal loss to Germany, not to assume the United States had arrived as a power. Arena was right; he often was. There is some question whether coaches should serve a second term with the national team because the players grow tired of the same lectures, the same tactics, the same inflections. ("It's a BAWL.")

Many coaches choose to make their tenure a one-time-only deal and move on to their next club gig. Arena had chosen to come back; he and Gulati would part ways a few weeks later.

There were many new and appealing teams in this World Cup, including Angola, Togo, Ivory Coast, and Ghana, plus three European squads competing for the first time since being spun off from their former amalgamations—the Czech Republic, Ukraine, and the short-lived Serbia and Montenegro. For me, the most enjoyable new team was Trinidad and Tobago.

After witnessing Paul Caligiuri's booming goal in 1989 in Port of Spain, I had never stopped hoping that T&T would get to the World Cup. In the fall of 2005, T&T was once again close, meeting Bahrain in a special play-off, with the winner going to Germany.

A friend knew some Trinidadians who would be watching in an apartment in Brooklyn, and we wangled an invitation. A few days ahead, I called Caligiuri, now coaching at Cal Poly Pomona, and asked if he would say hello to some fans in Brooklyn. Caligiuri said he, too, had been rooting for T&T ever since that sunny afternoon in 1989.

"Every place I go, there's somebody from Trinidad," Caligiuri told me. "They look at me and say, 'I am Trinidadian.' I just want them to win so I can get off parole."

On the day of the match, I sat in Derek Marshall's apartment in Flatbush and handed my cell phone to him and said, "Hey, it's Paul Caligiuri." The men in the apartment delightedly passed the phone around, and Caligiuri wished them luck, and the match began.

Early in the second half, Dwight Yorke, who once ran down David Beckham's crosses for Manchester United, took a high, curving corner kick that connected with the head of Dennis Lawrence, who towered at six feet, seven inches tall, and the ball glanced past the Bahrain keeper. This time, T&T won the deciding match. In Derek Marshall's apartment, I joined the cheer "Ger-ma-ny! Ger-ma-ny!"

Germany felt the same way about T&T. That most international city of Hamburg was the base for the Soca Warriors, who scheduled a friendly with St. Pauli, the counterculture lower-division team. On a sweet late spring afternoon, I squeezed into the St. Pauli stadium along with a lot of Germans and Trinidadian ex-pats. It was the kind of moment before a World Cup when spontaneous love for the sport is in the air, like an old Beatles love song from a few blocks over.

The good vibes did not last once the World Cup matches got under way. After T&T shocked Sweden in a 0–0 opening draw, several players claimed they heard Jack Warner—the very same Jack Warner who had printed more than ten thousand extra tickets in 1989—promise to issue bonuses. When T&T lost to England and Paraguay, the money did not materialize. The curse of Caligiuri was exorcised, but the curse of Warner was still in effect.

My wife and I loved strolling around Hamburg and walking down to the mighty Elbe, where so many Europeans had left for the New World. But this was not one of those World Cups where I could hunker down in one place. It was time to move on to Essen, the city of the Krupps, a short ride to Gelsenkirchen, the site of the first U.S. match.

I had an ulterior motive in choosing Essen.

As a child, I had never taken much interest in family roots—children rarely do—but now that my mother was gone, I regretted not knowing more about her Belgian Irish cousins, Florence and Leopold Duchene, whom she had known as a child. I knew the family had been caught harboring Scottish soldiers in Brussels during World War II, in their home on Rue Sans Souci, French for "Street Without Care."

While investigating on the Internet, I had discovered photos of my aunt Florrie and learned that her name is chiseled on a monument to Belgian resisters in Ixelles, just outside Brussels. Gert de Prins, a historian with the Belgian Department of War Victims, wrote to me that my aunt had been sent with twenty other Belgian and Polish women to Ravensbrück and then to Mauthausen and on to Bergen-Belsen, where she died in April 1945, just short of her thirty-ninth birthday.

I also learned that Florrie's trial had lasted from June 8 through June 11, 1943, in Essen. The aunt I had never met had once been in this city.

On the sixty-third anniversary of the start of her trial, we checked into a nice hotel across from the Essen railroad station and walked a few blocks to the Old Synagogue, now a Holocaust information center run by the government. The lobby contained photographs of the last worshippers in this building—youthful faces from the early 1930s who looked exactly like my classmates in Queens in the early 1950s. As I thought of our innocent flirtations, weekend subway outings to museums, bar mitzvahs, and ball games, tears began flowing.

I knew it was possible that I had Jewish ancestry through my father and his mysterious adoption. This World Cup was giving me a chance to visit a great contemporary nation that reminded me, perhaps more than any other country, of my own. A helpful government worker who spoke good English looked through a few ledgers and said that while the trial was held in Essen, my aunt technically was considered a prisoner of war, not a victim of the Holocaust, and therefore the trial records were stored in Düsseldorf. I knew I could not get there, not with the World Cup starting, so I paid homage to my aunt and all those children of the synagogue the only way I knew, with a highly personal column that expressed how I never could have been as brave as my mother's family.

The real star of the German World Cup was the Deutsche Bahn. Coming from a nation that regards railroads as a socialist plot, I loved being able to scoot around a more compact country, using my rail pass and media credential to see a match almost every day; fans were scuttling around Germany the same way.

Check out this itinerary. (For every train ride, factor in one large juicy, spicy wurst on a roll with mustard and colorful, noisy crowds surging through the stations.)

Starting in Essen on June 10, I commuted down the line to Frankfurt to watch England beat Paraguay. The old hooligans were losing their steam. Only eighteen of them were arrested, mostly for drunkenness.

On June 12, I took the train north to Gelsenkirchen to witness the United States get waxed by the Czechs.

On June 14, I commuted to Dortmund for the Germany-Poland match.

The Germans were not expected to be a factor, even as hosts, but the 4–2 opening victory over Costa Rica in Munich had touched off national sporting pride, chants, and flag waving that had felt psychologically verboten for six decades. Jürgen Klinsmann, the German coach, was often criticized for spending much of his time in that famous old German soccer hub, California am Pazifik, where his American wife and children lived. He had gone native, stunning his German players by actually talking to them. *Was ist los*?

At the Dortmund station, the driver of the media bus made a German joke. His vehicle was packed, no room for anybody else, but the schedule said departure time was still five minutes away. In English, the driver said: "I do something very un-German. We leave now." To the sound of applause, this anarchist eased out of the space, sensibly delivering his full load to the stadium. *Was ist los*?

There had been rumors of Polish skinheads crossing the border to do battle with German skinheads in a forest; apparently, this is what skinheads do. The modern skills of law enforcement made sure nothing happened; Polish and German fans wore their respective jerseys in the old streets of Dortmund, and nobody fought. *Was ist los*?

One minute into extra time, David Odonkor lofted a perfect pass to a sliding Oliver Neuville, who nudged the ball into the net to defeat shorthanded Poland. Odonkor was the son of a German mother and Ghanaian father. *Was ist los*?

No skinheads materialized in Dortmund. No hooligans. No German-Polish truculence in sight. On the jammed train back to Essen, a father was standing with his weary son of five or six, both wearing the red of Poland. A young German fan stood up and offered his seat to the Polish father. People nodded in approval. *Was ist los*?

The railway journey continued as my wife and I moved down the line to Frankfurt, from where I made two day trips to Ramstein and Kaiserslautern for the U.S.-Italy match.

On June 20, we took the train to Cologne and visited the beautiful cathedral where a midday peace Mass was being held. Then I covered the Sweden-England match, a 2–2 draw with both teams already through to the second round.

On June 21, we took the train down to Nuremberg, where my wife scouted out a nice hotel alongside a park.

On June 22, the Americans played Ghana in Nuremberg, alongside Hitler's old rally grounds, one of the rare times on this trip that I got the creeps from the past.

When the Americans were eliminated, I took the day train to Munich, where Germany eliminated Sweden, 2–0.

The next day, I was back in Nuremberg for a real stinker: Portugal 1, Netherlands 0, the ref losing control of two nasty squads, doling out sixteen yellow cards and a record four red cards; it was straight out of the Red Queen in *Alice in Wonderland*: off with their heads!

On June 27, I was back in Dortmund. The Ghanaian players had looked forward to meeting their role models from across the ocean. Final score: Brazil 3, Ghana 0.

Teams disappeared like a blip on the radar, before I could ever see them. Also on June 27, Spain did what it often did—scored the first goal against France and then lost, 3–1. With all that talent, Spain still lacked the discipline, the belief in its own skill. Zidane had announced his retirement after the World Cup; now he seemed energized, a throwback to the lithe twenty-six-year-old dancer of the 1998 final.

On June 28, Marianne and I took the train from Nuremberg to Berlin, to a hotel in the Charlottenburg section. The hotel had a cigar club off the lobby, and the fumes seeped into our room, but rooms were hard to find, so we stayed. We loved the energy and youthfulness of emerging Berlin, but just to remind us of the recent past, a movie theater across the way had a huge advertisement for the current film, *Das Leben der Anderen* (*The Lives of Others*), a gloomy memory of the eavesdropper state of East Germany.

Scandal hung over the World Cup. Gianluca Pessotto, the former Italian national player now serving as general manager of Juventus, had jumped out of a second-story window at team headquarters in Turin and survived. Pessotto's despair was linked to an ongoing investigation of Italian soccer, with four teams, including Juventus, accused of influencing matches.

Luciano Moggi, the general manager of Juve, who had been so helpful during my Maradona mission when he was running Napoli in 1990, had been taped bargaining with league officials for friendly referees to work Juve matches; he once locked a referee in the changing room after a match because he was unhappy with the man's work. Moggi's five-year prison sentence was eventually reduced, and he did not have to serve time.

Thirteen of the twenty-two Italian players at the World Cup played for the four squads involved in the scandal—Juventus, AC Milan, Fiorentina, and Lazio.

Two of the key Juventus players—Gianluigi Buffon, the expressive keeper, and Fabio Cannavaro, the stocky defender—had been interviewed by authorities. Buffon admitted he had gambled on matches outside Italy until 2005 but insisted he had stopped betting when the Italian federation banned all gambling by players. Buffon was a great player and charismatic competitor, but let's put it this way: the position any gambler would most like to influence is keeper.

Also, Massimo De Santis, who was supposed to have officiated in Germany, had his credential rescinded after his name came up as one of the friendly refs Juve chose for its matches. (Referees cannot work their own nation's games in the World Cup.)

None of these charges shocked me after some of the strange calls I had seen in Serie A, such as the ref racing to the disk to let a Juve player take a penalty kick in the closing minutes.

Italian players seemed to thrive on turmoil. I had seen this in 1982, the year of Rossi's comeback from suspension; and 1990, the year of Totò Schillaci; and 1994, the year of Baggio's rescues. Never count out Italy in a World Cup.

On June 30, I took a fast train from Berlin to Hamburg, inhaled the heady air of the Elbe, and watched Italy annihilate Ukraine, 3–0.

Meanwhile, back in Berlin, Argentina took an early lead on Germany, but its coach, José Pékerman, took out his stylish playmaker Juan Riquelme, yet another example of coaches who do not value offensive players who can control the ball. Nine minutes later, Miroslav Klose scored on a header, and Germany won a shoot-out to reach the semifinals, as flags fluttered around this suddenly patriotic nation.

On July 1, I took the train down to Gelsenkirchen for the quarterfinal between underperformers—Portugal vs. England. Portugal had been a semifinalist only once, in 1966, the same year England won its only World Cup.

This was the match of the drama kings—Cristiano Ronaldo and Wayne Rooney, teammates at Manchester United for two seasons, one known for his flops, the other for his rages.

With his tinted tufts and supercilious smirk, Cristiano Ronaldo is the most annoying great player in captivity, but he is also a wonderful talent—big and mobile and selfish, the way an offensive star should be. He materializes out of nowhere to blast a header from high in the air, like Michael Jordan or LeBron James making a dunk. (He reminds me of Alex Rodriguez of the Yankees, a combination of ability and narcissism. In fact, has anybody ever seen Ronaldo and A-Rod together?)

The referee, Horacio Elizondo of Argentina, met the assorted dives and laments with a stern glare and upraised palm, or he just plain ignored the quivering bodies. When Ronaldo realized he could not sway Elizondo, he and his teammates worked at getting into the knotty head of Rooney. With the ref monitoring him at close range, Rooney gave Ronaldo a shove, and the poor lad hit the ground in apparent mortal pain. The ref brandished a red card at Rooney.

Rooney's shove was a throwback to the petulant kick by Beckham in 1998 against Argentina and predated the cheap-shot knee in the back wielded by Chelsea's captain, John Terry, in the 2012 Champions League semifinal. What makes English stars lose their cool?

After playing sixty-one scoreless minutes down a man, England predictably lost the shoot-out, which sent hundreds of English fans raging into the narrow lanes of the old coal and steel town. I slipped through the melee, found my nightly wurst in the station, and avoided the louts waiting for the overnight train to Berlin.

On July 2 at dawn, the train arrived at the modern glass terminal in Berlin. Sunday morning. Summer in the city. Cyclists were already hoisting their bikes onto the S-Bahn for a ride in the greenbelt. After a shower and a nap and some coffee, Marianne and I wandered around Berlin, checking out the architecture and the markers for the vanished Wall.

Some strollers were wearing German jerseys. (How much did it cost for the fourteen letters of Schweinsteiger?)

My colleague Jeré Longman was covering Germany-Italy on Tuesday night in Dortmund, so I watched in my hotel room. For an American, it was like watching the future because everybody knew that one day Klinsmann would be working from his adopted home in California. Germans tended to believe that Klinsmann's tactics were supplied by his assistant, Joachim Löw, known as Jogi. But Klinsi—his nickname made him sound like a wood sprite in a Grimm fairy tale—was more than a cheerleader. From his long career, he understood that strikers do not score on their own. He believed in the system. He was not exactly a new age hippie.

As the scoreless draw went on, Marcello Lippi clearly was not settling for another tiebreaker, not after Italy lost shoot-outs in three previous World Cups. He sent in three players with ball skills, including, in the 104th minute, Alessandro Del Piero, nicknamed Il Pinturicchio after the Renaissance painter. Lippi was going with artists. Bravo, maestro.

Italy cut it close. In the 119th minute, Pirlo gathered up a weak German clear and directed it sideways for Fabio Grosso, who curled a left-footed shot around Jens Lehmann's dive. Lippi's two other subs paid off during injury time, as Alberto Gilardino found Del Piero, who chipped in the second goal. Italy had responded to the gathering scandal by knocking off the host team.

Late at night in Berlin, I needed to write a column. I wandered out of the hotel and waited outside the Quasimodo Café on Kantstrasse—isn't that wonderful, a street named for a philosopher?—until six people wearing Deutschland T-shirts emerged.

"The Italians played well," one man told me, in English.

"Even though we lose, it's a win," another man said.

I asked how they were going to face this hour of loss.

"A curry!" they said, in unison, as they headed for the all-night stand near the Zoologischer Garten train station.

Their team had taken them a long way; the fans had not lost their appetite. There was no sense of that national devastation that I had felt in Spain, Mexico, Italy, and South Korea in past World Cups, when the home team was eliminated.

. . .

I had to sleep fast because on July 5 I caught a fast train from Berlin to Munich for the other semifinal, France against Portugal, the latter team making its first appearance in the semifinals.

This match turned on a fancy piece of footwork by Thierry Henry in the thirty-third minute. Henry was dribbling through traffic, and Ricardo Carvalho, the Portuguese defender and no angel, tried to poke it away, his left foot extended, easily within a kilometer or two of Henry's ankle. Carvalho could see the injustice coming: as he fell backward, he waved his index finger at the referee, the classic European gesture that means *No freaking way; don't even think of it.*

Too late. Henry artfully let himself get entangled with Carvalho's outstretched leg and sold his dive to the referee, Jorge Larrionda of Uruguay.

Zidane took the penalty kick, impassively, going for the low left corner, evading the fingers of the Portuguese keeper, who had guessed correctly. That was all France needed for the 1–0 victory that sent it to the finals.

Zidane was conducting a seminar on how to go out on top. At the age of thirty-four, one championship behind him, he seemed like the coolest man on the planet. His penalty kick was a textbook example of how it should be done: Head down. No visible emotion. No elbows flapping. No knees knocking. Deliberate but not timid-looking. Just whack the ball into a corner.

I had memories of the 1998 final, when Zidane danced gracefully through the Brazilian defense; I could only assume he would go out dancing against Italy.

The World Cup is never separated from its setting. The Mexico World Cup of 1970 was held two years after the massacre of what may have been thousands of protestors at Tlatelolco just before the 1968 Olympics; the Argentina World Cup of 1978 was held as families of hundreds of *desaparecidos* (disappeared ones) staged protests in the plazas of Buenos Aires. The world remembers, bears witness, but, rightly or wrongly, does not stop the games, even after the massacre of the Israelis in Munich during the 1972 Olympics.

The past materialized for the 2006 World Cup final in Berlin, in Olympic Stadium, where Adolf Hitler had presided over the 1936 Summer Olympics and Jesse Owens had won four gold medals.

"The history is there, the totality of the buildings is there," Gunter Gebauer, a sports sociologist, told BBC News in 2004. Gebauer added: "The whole Nazi landscape has not disappeared. There are towers like in a fortress, and people who come will always ask where the Führer sat."

Olympic Stadium is located in a lovely greenbelt just outside downtown. I was pleased to note that a road outside the stadium is named after Owens, who used to claim he waved at Hitler after each gold medal. In fact, Hitler ducked a medal ceremony for two other black Americans, and the International Olympic Committee requested that he not congratulate any winners after that.

I was creeped out by two large statues of athletes outside the stadium— Aryan art from the Nazi era. Then I climbed the inner stairway to the press box, recalling how Hitler bolted down the stairs, fleeing the medal ceremony.

That was where he sat, somebody familiar with the stadium told me. That was where he departed.

What would the Führer have thought of this French team, more than half of them men of color from far-flung French islands or the projects ringing French cities? I recalled how Jean-Marie Le Pen had mused in 1998 that the World Cup champion was a fine football team, although not necessarily French. I bet the Führer and Le Pen would have understood each other.

Now Les Bleus were back in the finals, led by the old master, Zidane, who was about to play his last match, and his new target, Henry, a little-used sub in 1998 but a superb striker now. They would test the defense of Italy—Cannavaro, the muscular defender who was abandoning Juventus as it faced banishment to the lower depths, and Buffon, the emotional keeper who insisted he had stopped his gambling when the authorities asked him and was sticking with Juve.

One thing I had come to feel about any World Cup: by the final, much of the energy and wonder has been expended on outsiders and hot teams and adventures along the road. There is almost never a true surprise team in the finals; the question is how they can possibly produce something beyond the sum of their two parts. I hoped these two squads would play an artistic match but acknowledged the alternate possibility, based on their familiarity with each other, that the final could deteriorate into the dives and fouls that had marred that World Cup.

Almost right away, on a muggy afternoon, the chin of spindly Thierry Henry collided with the shoulder of sturdy Fabio Cannavaro. There is an Italian theory called *dietrologia*, meaning there is usually more beneath the surface. It is safe to say that the Cannavaro-Henry collision was not an accident.

Referee Horacio Elizondo of Argentina presumably wanted no more of that, and three minutes later, he awarded a penalty kick after the hard-edged Italian defender Marco Materazzi bumped a French player from behind.

That set up a classic confrontation—Zizou Zidane against Gigi Buffon. The two knew each other from when Buffon was at Parma and Zidane was at Juventus. Buffon guessed low, and Zidane calmly chipped the shot high, almost too high. It hit the bottom of the crossbar and softly dropped just inside the line to put France ahead, 1–0, as Zidane became only the fourth player to score in two World Cup championship matches.

Both teams showed high energy and creativity for a while. In the nineteenth minute, Andrea Pirlo, the Beckham of Italy, bent a perfect corner kick from the right side, and Materazzi, in a perfect act of atonement for his foul, found a seam in the defense and headed the ball past Fabien Barthez, the bald, twitchy French keeper.

So much for energy and creativity. The long season and the hot July weather and the fear of failure kicked in. With Henry trudging along, Zidane appeared to be the only player on the field capable of raising the level, but he was hounded by the buzz bomb Gennaro Gattuso and growing in frustration. Several times Zidane gestured to the official that he was being manhandled, but the ref waved him off. Zidane's body language was nothing compared to the histrionics of born whiners like Cristiano Ronaldo or Wayne Rooney, but in retrospect his frustration was evident.

The game slogged into extra time. Zidane disentangled himself in the penalty area and jogged upfield, trailed by a blue-shirted shadow, Materazzi, who liked to refer to himself as the Matrix. Materazzi seemed to be tugging at Zidane's shirt, standard stuff; Zidane shrugged and shuffled a few feet away.

Then, in the center of the field, in the center of the universe, with two billion people watching, Zidane performed a crisp little about-face and advanced on Materazzi, tucking his head down slightly. Moving forward, he drove the top of his head into the chest of Materazzi, a blatant assault, designed to injure, nothing subtle about it.

Materazzi, trained by twenty years of Italian soccer to flop to the earth, arms and legs flailing, actually had reason to fall down. No Totti *simulazione* here. The ref flashed a red card at Zidane, who was watching impassively. Zidane did not protest or explain. He walked straight off the field, passing the glittering Jules Rimet Cup, the trophy of the World Cup, only a few inches from his right elbow. If this were professional wrestling, Zidane would have dashed the trophy to the ground, but he just kept walking, his career over.

While the crowd buzzed at this inexplicable act, the teams concluded the final ten minutes and prepared for the shoot-out. Given Italy's three straight failures in 1990, 1994, and 1998, there was no reason for confidence. Then again, just about every soccer power has a complex about shoot-outs—*we never win them*. Yet somebody must.

With no Zidane available, France was shorthanded. David Trezeguet, who had replaced the weary Henry, went second, and pinged his shot off the crossbar. Grosso calmly made the fifth straight, and Italy was the champion for the fourth time. In the soccer way of thinking, the Italians won a "just" victory because, although devious, they did not lose their minds.

Why did Zidane do what he did? The French manager professed not to know but clearly did not appreciate the self-destructive act by that great player. Zidane did not come anywhere near the media to explain himself. And when Materazzi marched through the mixed zone, he was carrying a boom box, with the volume turned up.

Some journalists invited lip-reading experts to analyze the video of the head-butt. A few said Materazzi was speaking Italian, which Zidane spoke, and had dropped a yo-mama comment on Zidane. Maybe also a yo-sister remark.

None of that excused Zidane's meltdown. It was not exactly a military secret that Zidane had lost his cool before—his two-game suspension in the 1998 World Cup for stomping on the head of a Saudi player, a five-game suspension for a similar head-butt in the past.

The French fans cheered him when the team returned to Paris and he appeared in public. Three days after the final, Zidane appeared on the French cable TV network Canal Plus and calmly gave his version: "He grabbed my shirt and I told him to stop," Zidane said in conversational tones. "I told him if he wanted I'd swap it with him at the end of the match."

Zidane continued: "That is when he said some very hard words, which were harder than gestures. He repeated them several times. It all happened very quickly, and he spoke about things which hurt me deep down."

Zidane told the interviewer that he apologized to children and people around the world for his behavior. When asked if that meant he would not do it if he had the chance again, he said politely but adamantly: "I can't regret it because if I do it would be like admitting that he was right to say all that. And above all, it was not right."

This match never had good vibes. Maybe it was the long march to the final; or maybe it was statues, the whiff of the sulfurous past. Either way, 2006 will be remembered not for Italy's play but for Zidane's balding head, a human projectile.

NELSON MANDELA
MEETS FIFA

NEW YORK, 2008

Danny Jordaan, the chief executive of the South African World Cup committee, was flying to New York on November 4, 2008. Jordaan was of mixed race, part Dutch and part Khoikhoi, a pastoral tribe that has been called one of the most oppressed in South Africa.

On the long flight from Johannesburg, Jordaan learned that Barack Obama was leading the U.S. presidential election and was about to become the first black American president.

That reminded Jordaan of another election. "I was forty-six when I cast my first vote in 1994," Jordaan said, after arriving in New York. Then he added the punch line: the first time he was able to vote, "I was elected to Parliament."

Both nations had come a long way. South Africa had been banned from many sporting competitions because of apartheid, but now it was preparing to host the World Cup in 2010, mostly because Nelson Mandela was probably the most respected human being in the world.

Mandela demonstrated grace and wisdom while enduring twenty-seven years in prison. He shared the Nobel Peace Prize and became the first black president of South Africa. He also had to put up with the machinations of FIFA.

In 2004, two and a half months shy of his eighty-sixth birthday, Mandela was pressured to fly across the ocean to serve his country once again. To the people who run FIFA, he was just another public figure who needed to be manipulated before his country could be honored. According to Sepp Blatter, it was time for Africa to stage the World Cup, but South Africa had lost out four years earlier when a FIFA delegate mysteriously left Zurich and Germany won the election, 12–11.

Now it was time to vote for the 2010 host, but first Mandela had to fly to Port of Spain, Trinidad, to pay homage to Jack Warner, the leader of the regional confederation, CONCACAF. Yes, the same Jack Warner who had sold over ten thousand extra tickets to the big match in 1989, putting people in danger in an overcrowded stadium.

The survivor of Robben Island had to visit Trinidad to prove that Jack Warner was a big man, a very big man.

Other soccer officials now wanted to get in on the act. Warner's long-time ally in the confederation, Chuck Blazer, the American who, as general secretary of CONCACAF, handled television contracts and other business, flew in from New York for the festivities. Sepp Blatter rushed in from Zurich to make sure he was in the group pictures.

Mandela—blacks and whites reverently called him Madiba, his tribal name—had survived prison by being able to control circumstances. Toward the end of his captivity, he had been negotiating his release and the future of his country from upgraded living quarters within prison. He walked out not only a free man but a national leader. So, yes, he understood the use of power.

He also understood sports, boxing as a young man and also playing tennis, later admitting his lack of speed and power in both. As a prisoner at Robben Island, he negotiated with the guards to paint tennis lines in the yard and hang a net for regular matches among the prisoners. Later, guards and politicians were eager to play against the famous prisoner.

Mandela never played rugby, which was regarded in South Africa as the white man's sport, but he understood the importance of that game. In 1995, as South Africa prepared to be host of the Rugby

World Cup, the first black president was presented with the green peaked cap of the Springboks and he wore it proudly as the national team improbably won the World Cup in Johannesburg. He was building a nation.

In 2004, Mandela understood the message from FIFA that soccer and Africa needed to grow together. He knew he was being manipulated, but he got on the plane to appease the regional bosses, to give them the photo opportunity their egos needed.

"This is my last trip abroad—I am here to plead," Mandela said upon arriving in Port of Spain on April 29. He posed for pictures, spoke for fifteen minutes, and went to his hotel to rest.

On May 15, Mandela was in Zurich for the vote, along with the country's current president, Thabo Mbeki, and his fellow Nobel Peace Prize winners F. W. de Klerk and Archbishop Desmond Tutu. Mandela said the World Cup would be "the perfect gift to celebrate ten years of democracy in South Africa."

South Africa's chief rival for the bid was Morocco, whose champion was Alan Rothenberg, the previous head of the U.S. federation and, before that, the leader of the 1994 American World Cup. "We all appreciate him and his place in history, but that is it—Mandela is not a man of the future. He is a man of history," Rothenberg said.

The "man of history" was a major reason his homeland won the FIFA vote, an affirmation that FIFA was expanding the club to include Africa. Now South Africa had to prepare for a monthlong party in 2010. It had to perform the ruinous dance of the World Cup and Olympics: grovel first, overspend, throw a great party, and after the final whistle try to figure what to do with all those buildings and all those debts.

The talent, will, and money of South Africa went to work on infrastructure that would help the nation far more than stadiums ever would—roads, buildings, air terminals, rail lines. And the talented younger cadre of the organizing committee began going out into the world to tell the nation's story.

As a young man, Jordaan had gotten an education, advanced in soccer just far enough to be rebuffed by the white establishment of the pre-Mandela time, and became an activist against apartheid. He never went to jail but waited decades to become anything close to a full citizen. Now Jordaan was in charge of the 2010 World Cup. The venerable Nelson Mandela had done his duty with his long trips to Trinidad and Zurich. It is safe to say that FIFA officials were not embarrassed.

SPAIN MAKES A BREAKTHROUGH

SOUTH AFRICA, 2010

I don't usually indulge in predictions, too many things can happen, but just before the 2010 World Cup I wrote, "I'd like to see Spain meet the Netherlands in the final—two pleasing contenders, one new champion—but in the end I see Brazil. I always see Brazil, until proven otherwise."

Fair enough. Spain was the great slacker, always coming into the World Cup with artistic scorers from one of the top leagues in the world, and then getting whacked before the semifinals.

I once read an article by a social scientist or psychologist who theorized that Spain's national players seemed to lack *corazón*, heart, perhaps because Spanish mothers doted too much on their sons, rendering them not tough enough, not resourceful. Okay.

Now, before our eyes, Spain had become something else. All the strengths had finally kicked in—the talent, the passion, the money, the rival cultures of Castile and Catalonia, the artistry of Barça, the influence of the Galácticos of Real Madrid, and the legacy of the Dutch.

Spain openly acknowledged its debt to the Total Football of the Netherlands that had not quite won the World Cup in 1974 and 1978. Rinus Michels and Johan Cruyff had imported the style from Ajax to Barcelona, and now it was embedded in the Spanish national team.

"I am Dutch," Cruyff would tell *El Periódico* of Spain during the World Cup. "But I will always defend the football Spain play."

The Spanish coach was Vicente Del Bosque, an unassuming former Real player and coach, who used a quorum of Barça players with everybody buying into the premise of keeping possession with short, intricate forward passes. The players did not need to make hipper-dipper runs through the defense or dump the ball downfield and try to muscle it away from the other side. Spain believed in possession, enlightened possession. With that talent, it looked simple.

And Spain was coming into this World Cup with credentials as a champion. In 2008, I watched the Euro finals in a Manhattan tapas restaurant with Reggie Williams, a former star linebacker in the NFL, who was in town recuperating from his latest knee surgery. (Reggie stuck his Velcro antibiotic pouch onto the wall of the restaurant to ensure maximum flow. The waiter was not about to ask a man that large to hide his antibiotics pouch; he brought us our tortillas and chorizo and cerveza. The surgery and medication saved Reggie's knee.)

On that warm afternoon in New York, the tapas patrons cheered the blond, ruddy-faced whippet, Fernando Torres, as he infiltrated the German defenses and won the European championship for Spain. Now the Spaniards were trying to take their edge from the Euros to the World Cup. Give them this: the Spaniards were one of seven nations that had qualified for six consecutive World Cup tournaments. Those powerhouses, those dynasties, were Argentina, Brazil, Germany, Italy, South Korea, Spain, and (roll of drums, please) the United States.

Of course, the United States had been helped to some degree by the automatic inclusion as host in 1994, but so had Germany, Italy, and South Korea in the same period. It could be argued that the Yanks were qualifying from a lesser confederation, but try pushing that theory on a nasty afternoon in Central America while dodging missiles and maledictions.

At any rate, the Yanks were back, with a new coach. Bruce Arena had moved on to coach the Red Bulls (and later would win championships with the Galaxy). Sunil Gulati wanted to hire Jürgen Klinsmann, who had stepped down as German coach, but Klinsmann was not ready to deal with all the soccer jurisdictions in this sprawling democracy, or maybe there was a financial gap.

So Gulati hired a homegrown coach, Bob Bradley, from New Jersey and Princeton and MLS, who was smart, experienced, in great shape, and wary. I'm old enough and secure enough to understand public figures who put up a wall. I liked Bradley. When he responded with clichés, I found myself smiling. He was in there, somewhere.

Not that this got Bradley the job, but his son Michael, a midfielder with an attitude, was working his way from MLS to Europe and was clearly going to be a mainstay on the national team for years to come. Michael once filled out a team questionnaire that asked him to name his favorite player, and he answered "Roy Keane," the Irish former captain of Manchester United. The kid wanted to be a hard-ass like Keane-o. That could win a match sometime.

The qualifying began on February 11, 2009, in that winter soccer haven of Columbus, Ohio, with weather right out of *The Wizard of Oz*—evil green clouds, snow, rain, thunder, lightning, wind, warnings to seek shelter, a full crowd, and Mexico as the opponent. Michael Bradley roamed the field, whacking opponents and scoring both goals in a 2–0 victory, and nobody was blown away by the weather.

There was another epic qualifier in El Salvador on March 28. The United States fell behind, 2–0, but Jozy Altidore got one back. Then the United States played a long ball into the box, presumably for Altidore, who is six foot one, but long-haired Frankie Hejduk, all of five foot eight, vaulted on the back of his taller teammate and planted the goal for a draw and a point on the road. In August, the United States lost, 2–1, in Azteca, with Mexican fans reviving their hatred of Landon Donovan, particularly since he had been filmed urinating on the field during a practice in Guadalajara in 2004. By now, many Mexican fans believed Donovan did it during a qualifier in Azteca—all part of the lore, false or accurate, of the Hex. The Americans clinched a spot in the World Cup with a 3–2 victory in Honduras on October 10.

Three players who helped the Americans qualify did not make it to South Africa. Hejduk's aging body wore out; Charlie Davies, a mobile forward who worked so well with Altidore, was injured in an auto accident that killed a young woman in the fall of 2009, and he would never be the same player; and Conor Casey, a husky striker who scored two goals in the clincher in Honduras, did not make the squad for 2010. It is a fact of life of the World Cup: help the team qualify, then watch it on television.

Soccer had grown so much that ESPN staged an extravaganza in May 2010, at the network's campus in Bristol, Connecticut, to introduce Bradley's squad on live television. I was happy to see DaMarcus Beasley, a force on the 2002 and 2006 teams, the guy I look for in the mixed zone. He had wandered from Europe to Mexico and now he survived the final cut. Feeling almost paternal, I told him I was happy for him.

It was important for a reporter to be around the American team through qualifying. After the players saw you at practices or games, they figured maybe you were not a total idiot or a total stranger. I had kept up with the American players over the years, and I had tried to keep up with some of the South African officials. Let us know when you come over, they said.

About six months out, I discovered I was not being assigned to cover the first stage. The editors were sending good people—the *Times* always does—but just not me, not at first. I had been looking forward to getting around South Africa before the games, to write journalistic postcards, giving readers the feel of a place, as I did in my first seven World Cups.

Knowing I needed to keep sharp for when I arrived, I decided to write every day from New York, watching matches with fans in various ethnic settings.

For the opener, I went to the Paley Center for Media in Manhattan, where South Africans cheered a 1–1 draw with Mexico.

On Saturday, I sat in my den and watched the United States gain a 1–1 draw on a gaffe by the English keeper—a point from nowhere.

On Sunday, my teenage grandson George and I played a tripleheader, starting with breakfast in a sports bar on Manhattan's Second Avenue, joining a group of Slovenians for a 1–0 victory over Algeria. Then we drove across the river to a Ghanaian restaurant in the Flatbush section of Brooklyn, where fans danced to celebrate a 1–0 victory over Serbia. Then we drove to an Australian pub in the Park Slope section of Brooklyn to watch Germany romp over Australia, 4–0. George assured a cluster of cool German architects behind us that they would win the whole tournament.

On Monday, I went to the old Italian oasis in Corona, Queens, to Leo's Latticini, known to everyone as Mama's. There I met a favorite son of the neighborhood, Omar Minaya, then the general manager of the New York Mets, who had played baseball in Italy and loves the culture. We watched as the Azzurri bounced back for their usual opening draw.

By midweek, I was thoroughly annoyed with the vuvuzelas, the long plastic trumpets blaring incessantly through the television speakers. The networks were trying to strain out the noise, which sounded like racing cars going round and round in your brain, but there was no banning the horns in the stadiums. South Africans were defending vuvuzelas as an ancient tradition—and indeed they were. Plastic horns, based on an older wooden version, had been on sale in that nation since at least the 1990s. My wife could not stand being in the same room with the whine of the vuvuzelas; she handed me a pair of soft ear plugs, which would cut the noise in half when I reached the open-air press sections of the South African stadiums.

On Friday I watched at home as the United States fell behind, 2–0, to Slovenia but then came back for a 2–2 draw. A third goal in the eighty-fifth minute, on a gorgeous curling kick by Landon Donovan that was converted by Maurice Edu, was waved off by the referee. On television, with its multiple replays, there was no obvious foul or offside. As usual, FIFA did not back up controversial calls with an explanation.

On Sunday, while waiting for my flight to South Africa, I watched New Zealand take an early gift goal from Italy, but then Daniele De Rossi spun to earth after a minor shirt pull, and Italy converted for a 1–1 draw. Two matches. Two points. Italy was cutting it close. *Tutto normale.*

After a long flight, it was late autumn in Johannesburg. A young volunteer drove me to the suburb of Melrose, a glitzy mall with hotel, shops, restaurants, and apartments, behind barricades.

I had thought of renting something for my wife and myself, and a friend in Johannesburg had given me the e-mail address of somebody who might be renting a house in a nice neighborhood. When my e-mail went unanswered, I asked my friend what had happened, and he said, Oh, she was backing out of her driveway and was carjacked and shot dead. Not this World Cup, I told my wife.

Instead, the *Times* booked a room for me in the hotel where the U.S. federation was ensconced. The hotel was in a mall that felt like the Buckhead section of Atlanta or some other cold, nouveau, yuppied-up enclave— economic apartheid, not racial apartheid. I called it the Walled-Off Astoria.

Because the United States needed a victory to get through to the second round, the paper asked me to write from the Algeria match. Two days after arriving, I took the media bus to the old rugby stadium in nearby Pretoria and, fighting off jet lag, I tried to keep an eye on the ball.

As the scoreless match raced into injury time, Tim Howard made his save and clearing pass. Then came Donovan's run and pass, Altidore's cut and kick, Dempsey's cannonball roll through the goal area, and Donovan's arrival to push the ball into the goal.

The Americans killed off the last three minutes, and the Algerian players trudged off the field without accomplishing their purpose, a lethal draw.

In the mixed zone under the stands, we could hear shouting from the adjacent locker room, where former president Bill Clinton was congratulating the U.S. team. Ultimately Donovan came out, seemingly embarrassed to be the center of attention. He had come through a rough year, separating from his wife, Bianca Kajlich, an actress, and often referring to their ongoing closeness, his private and public lives overlapping. "Those experiences can harden you and can help you grow if you learn from them," Donovan said. "I spent a lot of time and work to get something out of those experiences. I think it all kind of came together tonight."

By the time we got back to the Walled-Off Astoria, we learned that in the knockout round the Yanks would be playing Ghana, the same team that had beaten them in 2006.

The next day, the U.S. reporters were invited to meet President Clinton behind high walls and barbed wire at a safe home in the posh suburb of Sandton. Clinton told us he was doing a favor for his good friend later that day, giving a talk at the Nelson Mandela Centre of Memory. The former president was even more hoarse than usual, sipping tea and honey after cheering the day before. He told us how he had been sitting with Sepp Blatter and Issa Hayatou of Cameroon, the top-ranking African member of FIFA, and he knew that dignitaries from Algeria and the Middle East were nearby. They all understood the code.

"I was very diplomatic," Clinton said. "Till they scored."

As the honorary chairman of the U.S. bid committee for the 2018 or 2022 World Cup, Clinton, ever the politician, pushed the bid by stressing the varied backgrounds of the U.S. players and the diversity of the country. "We got you a home team," he said with his let's-make-a-deal fervor, referring to fans from around the world. "We'll suit you up."

Asked if he was a big fan, Clinton gave us a short history of the sport, saying he had been reading Franklin Foer's fine book, *How Soccer Explains the World*. He hung around to schmooze after breakfast, and, in a casual conversation, I found myself calling him "Man." When we took a group photo, my female colleagues clustered near him. I thought it must be nice to be Bill Clinton.

Three days later the writers joined a charter bus caravan out to Rustenberg, with its casinos and golf, the Las Vegas of South Africa. When we arrived at the stadium, I noticed Ghanaians, some now living in the United States or Europe, waving their own flag or specially made banners blending the Ghanaian and American flags. Upscale World Cup crowds are not the brawling mobs traditionally seen in Europe and elsewhere. Americans chanted the ubiquitous "U-S-A" while Ghanaians smiled and applauded, on an adventure together, just about the nicest crowd I have ever seen at the World Cup.

The United States was in trouble almost immediately—in fact, before the match. I voiced disapproval when Bob Bradley's lineup was distributed, showing Ricardo Clark, shaky in previous outings, starting at midfield. In the fifth minute, the ball got loose near Clark in the American end, and Kevin-Prince Boateng swooped in and shot past Howard. The United States often fell behind—even more lethal in the knockout round.

Clark was so jittery that he picked up a yellow card, and Bradley had to replace him with Edu in the thirty-first minute.

The United States steadied itself, Donovan converted a penalty kick in the sixty-second minute, and the game veered into the double fifteen-minute overtimes. Three minutes in, Asamoah Gyan scored on Howard. Now the United States had to score or go home.

Desperation had worked three days earlier against Algeria. Howard, the dunker, moved forward to try to put his high-flying forehead on the ball. In a scene that seemed borrowed from pro basketball, Howard and Richard Kingson, in their gaudy keepers' kits, flew into the air, but the United States could not put the ball past Kingson, and Ghana held on for the victory. The players embraced, and the Ghanaian and American fans trooped out together. Good luck was over.

After a long haul in heavy traffic back to its camp in Johannesburg, the U.S. team was up early the next morning. Before everybody went home, Bob Bradley calmly explained that he thought Clark was the best man for that midfield spot. Parent to parent, I told Bradley, in private, that his son had been one of the very best players on the team. I think he knew it but would never say it. He let his pride show, for a few seconds.

Sunil Gulati, the federation president, gave a group interview a day later. Without throwing tantrums or making provocative comments, Gulati let us know he was not happy. "It was all in front of us," he said, adding that after Donovan converted the penalty, "I was sure we would win," mostly because of fitness, but the anticipated finishing kick did not materialize. Gulati did not say anything about the status of his coach, but it was clear he was going to look around.

Where was the United States going in this sport? Between World Cups, it had some success in qualifying and the Confederations Cup, even beating a weary Spain in 2009 in South Africa. The Yanks had been ranked seventh in the fall of 2005, but by September 2010, they would be ranked eighteenth—and that was charitable.

Forty-four years since the debatable Geoff Hurst goal, FIFA still did not have an adequate way to monitor the goal line. On the afternoon after the American loss, I was with a group of reporters in the hotel media room, watching Germany take a 2–0 lead over England. Then Matthew Upson scored for England in the thirty-seventh minute and two minutes later, Frank Lampard banged a shot off the bottom of the crossbar, with the ball obviously landing a full foot inside the line and ricocheting back to the German keeper. The only person who could not see it was a goal was Jorge Larrionda of Uruguay, who, unfortunately, was refereeing the match.

The closest assistant official kept his flag down, enraging the England players. Was this some cosmic payback for the Hurst goal in the 1966 final? More likely, it was a case of human error, with the television camera documenting what the officials' eyes could not process. Ultimately, Germany went on to win, 4–1, but who knows what would have happened if Lampard's shot had brought England even at halftime? (Most English fans, long conditioned to be grimly realistic, concluded that their lads would have lost anyway.)

Afterward, Sepp Blatter said he was sorry for that wretched call. He was also sorry for a missed offside that helped Argentina beat Mexico, 3–1. Blatter was often sorry. Perhaps he was even sorry for the unexplained call that had nullified a winning American goal against Slovenia.

A few days later, Blatter had morphed into Sepp the Damage Controller, saying he would consider technology for goal-line calls in the next World Cup.

The old order—emphasis on the "old"—slinked out early. France, one finalist from 2006, was disgraced by bickering among its players and lost to South Africa; it blessedly went out after the first round. The overconfident defending champs from Italy were eliminated by Slovakia. And now England was gone after the round of 16.

Argentina was still around, once again a sideshow because of its endless fascination with Maradona. The aging star was the reincarnation of the fabled Russian monk Rasputin, who in 1916 was poisoned with cyanide, shot three or four times, beaten and perhaps stabbed, then tied up and tossed into the icy Neva River. When his body was recovered, it was determined that Rasputin had drowned trying to claw his way to the surface through the ice. A tough man to put away.

So was Diego Armando, who had worn out his welcome at several clubs, survived several suspensions for performance-enhancing drugs, gone through repeated rehabilitation for so-called recreational drugs, been treated for heart trouble in Cuba, become a folk hero for the most blatant handball goal in history, gone through domestic crises, including at least one illegitimate son. Plus, the Italian government accused him of owing $53 million in back taxes. (He disputed the charges, blaming the Italian system.)

Now he was the coach of the Argentina team. Seriously. On the advice of his daughters, he stopped wearing a clunky track suit on the sideline in favor of a business suit, but somehow he still looked as if he was wearing a track suit.

In good form, upon arriving in South Africa, Maradona revived a feud with the South Korean coach, accusing him of employing taekwondo tactics on him in 1986; he warned the refs to protect his stars, Carlos Tévez and Lionel Messi; he advised Pelé to "go back to a museum"; and he juggled his lineup with the same quirky independence he had shown finding open space. "They said I had no idea and suddenly I'm winning four matches and people see me as someone else," Maradona said. "I'm still the same person."

With all that talent, Argentina won four straight matches by a 10–2 combined margin. Then Argentina lost to Germany, 4–0, and Maradona was sacked by the same federation that had been enabling his behavior for more than three decades. As he left, he said he had been betrayed.

Because of my late start, I was way behind in getting a feel for South Africa, but I was trying. One free morning, a few of us went to the Apartheid Museum, where the admission line is arbitrarily divided in two, to give visitors the feel of the bad old days. Our young college-educated driver, white, watched films of police and horses rampaging through downtown Pretoria, raining blows on protestors, black. The young man shuddered, suggesting to me that the new generation barely knows how bad things were, back then.

Going into the stadium in Pretoria, Grahame Jones of the *Los Angeles Times*—on his eighth straight World Cup, just like me—heard a female security officer talking in very brusque tones to black employees who were inspecting bags. Grahame, who was born in England but spent his childhood in Cape Town, quietly told the officer, "I don't like the way you are speaking to those people." In Afrikaans. She seemed quite shocked to have an American chastise her in her language.

Jeffrey Marcus, who writes for the *New York Times* Web site, and I watched the Iberian derby between Spain and Portugal at a *braai*, a sausage restaurant. We consumed copious amounts of sausage—soft, spicy, sweet, chewy, thin, thick, with Castle Lager to wash it down—and the waitresses were pretty and solicitous; a couple of German guys at the next table thought it amusing that two Yanks knew a bit about their sport. Spain, which usually fell apart about this time, broke through for a 1–0 victory.

To atone for not bringing my wife to South Africa, I promised Marianne I would not have any fun. I violated my solemn vow on a rest day between rounds. Three young writers and I took a day trip with Witek, a Polish-born guide, to the preserve in Pilanesburg, a couple of hours out in the countryside. Witek parked alongside the elephant walkway as a dignified and watchful family tramped slowly past us, keeping their right eyes directed at us, their trunks swinging. Witek also found a water hole, with the rib bones of an elephant that had just been picked clean; the lions were probably in that clump of bushes on the other side of the water hole, but we did not get any closer to investigate.

On July 2, I watched the tube as the Netherlands eliminated Brazil in a quarterfinal match. Then I covered the Uruguay-Ghana match, when Luis Suárez of Uruguay blatantly swatted away a goal during extra time. As punishment for the handball, Suárez would have to miss the next match, but that seemed like a fair exchange after Asamoah Gyan, who had scored the winning goal against the United States, banged the penalty kick off the crossbar. Uruguay won in penalty kicks, and the Ghana players cried as they left the field.

My first live glimpse of Spain came on July 3, in that grand old rugby palace of Ellis Park, the scene of South Africa's rugby championship in

1995. (I had prepared for South Africa by seeing the Clint Eastwood movie *Invictus*, in which Morgan Freeman plays Mandela, building a nation by openly following the white man's sport.) Once Spain was the bull; now it was the matador, wearing down Paraguay, its players trusting one another to be there for the next short, lovely pass.

My new favorite player—Baggio and Zidane were gone—was Andrés Iniesta, from Barcelona, of course. At first, I was not impressed with Iniesta, baldish and moonfaced, unexceptional in physique or demeanor, but eventually I realized how purposeful he was, always in the right place.

I quietly started counting consecutive touches by Spain—one, two, three, all the way to nineteen, opening up the field, making Paraguay work. It took a while, and a lucky bounce or two, but ultimately Spain controlled the ball for 60 percent of the match. David Villa scored after a deflection in the eighty-third minute, and the Spanish keeper Iker Casillas made a superb kick save for the 1–0 victory that put Spain into the semifinals, at last. They looked even better in person, as they used the whole field, and you did not have to depend on what the television director let you see. There goes Sergio Ramos down the right side. Xavi puts the ball on his instep.

In my first seven World Cups, relative outsiders had often reached the semifinals, including Portugal in 2006, Turkey and South Korea in 2002, Croatia in 1998, Bulgaria and Sweden in 1994, Belgium in 1986, and Poland in 1982. But never the nation of Real Madrid, the land of Barça. The only time Spain had finished in the top four was 1950, when it qualified for a four-team round robin—and finished last.

After the Paraguay match, Pepe Reina, the backup goalkeeper, who played for Liverpool and spoke decent English, graciously served up quotes to the teeming Anglophone horde of reporters. "We are proud to be here," Reina said. "And we are still hungry. Now we play Germany, the best team in the tournament."

He talked as if the European tournament had been a tiny dish of tapas. Players often become old or sated or unlucky in the two years between the Euros and the World Cup, but Spain had done the opposite. It was maturing, improving, before our eyes.

. . .

One of the saddest parts of my short stay was having to choose between two cities, two semifinals. Friends of mine from Cape Town, who live in New York, let me know that I was insane to miss their beautiful city, and I probably was, but I knew I had to see Spain face Germany, and so I chose to go to Durban.

This trip involved a door-to-door car ride, with Jeffrey Marcus driving. I admit, I thought about Chris Clarey's running into a dead horse on the highway. True story. The only way Clarey had been able to get from one match to another was via an overnight drive from Port Elizabeth to Durban. Seeing warnings of a slowdown ahead, Chris remembered being told never to stop at night. So at fifty miles per hour, he plowed straight into a dead horse in the road and lived to tell the tale in the *International Herald Tribune*. Made it to the next match, too.

On July 4, I was once again on the road on my birthday, not mentioning it to anybody. Marcus drove the toll road, with two lanes in each direction and often nothing but a yellow line separating us from the oncoming traffic, at a closing speed of 150 miles per hour. Jeffrey is a good driver, and I relaxed as we sped through the dry wintry highlands. As it grew dark, we started to descend, passing the wreckage of four or five cars, and then I opened the car window and could smell the sea.

At our hotel, on the so-called Golden Mile, two pert clerks greeted us with smiles and chatter. Omigosh, I thought, I was in India. I knew Mahatma Gandhi had made his activist start in Durban, with its large Indian population. My wife has been to India thirteen times as a child-care volunteer; we have an adopted Indian granddaughter; and I have learned to love the chatter as well as the curry. I was home.

The next morning I looked out and saw the Indian Ocean—Mumbai 4,275 miles across the water, wide sidewalks and piers and the beach, a sign showing the midday temperature at seventy-eight degrees. Somebody told me the Golden Mile had another nickname—Mugger's Mile—but it had been cleaned up for the World Cup. I put on my shorts and T-shirt and sneakers and my headset and went to the beach, choosing

Brian Wilson's quirky comeback album, *That Lucky Old Sun*, sounds of Southern California, different ocean.

I saw elaborate sand sculptures made—a lion gnawing on a stag, a snakelike beast devouring the upper torso of a woman in a thong, a little weird. One sculptor posted a sign, Support the Arts, so I did, with 10 rand (about $1.29). I saw dozens of surfers, most white, some black, in the roiling waves. African women along the boardwalk tried to sell me stuff. Two Spanish fans in matador costumes attracted gawkers along the boardwalk. At lunch, Wayne, the gregarious hotel manager, was wearing a Manchester United jersey, talking about changes in South Africa, mostly for the good of people of color, he said.

The next day, we watched the semifinal in Cape Town on TV, as the Netherlands outlasted Uruguay, 3–2, displaying a much chippier game than the old Orange version of Total Football. And on Wednesday, I covered the semifinal in Durban between emerging Spain and perpetual Germany, managed by Joachim Löw, with his Beatle mop haircut and his reputation as Klinsmann's strategist in 2006. Löw had the right idea—go out and get the ball, which cut Spain's possession rate from 60 percent against Paraguay to 52 percent. But Spain was patient, too.

Arriba, Puyol! Right behind the open media section, a Spanish fan kept exhorting the powerful defender with his ringlets flapping. Carles Puyol was a product of the Barcelona youth program, relatively short, like Franco Baresi, only five feet ten inches tall, but able to stay with the German mastiffs up front. Total Football lived in Puyol's stout Catalan heart. In the seventy-third minute, he moved forward after a nice run by Iniesta, his teammate from Barça, to set up a corner kick by Xavi, another Barça stalwart.

Arriba, Puyol! He elevated himself above Germans many inches taller than him and, with his curls flying, headed home the only goal of the match.

Afterward, gracious as ever, Löw put things in perspective: "The past two, three years, Spain has been the most skilled team of all, and they showed it tonight. They circulated the ball quickly, and we weren't able to get back to our plan. We had our inhibitions. I think Spain deserved to win this match, absolutely."

Löw's demeanor showed why Germany was the solid gold standard of these World Cups. They were almost always there; they were almost always classy.

I hated to leave Durban, particularly upon checking out with the same chatty Indian clerks who had greeted us three nights before.

"I'm going to miss you," I said.

"Well, why don't you take us with you?" one of the clerks said.

I love the saucy Indian sense of humor.

"If only we could . . . ," I said.

Jeffrey drove back from pungent salt air to the wintry chill of Johannesburg. My travel agent had let me down. In the entire fortress of Johannesburg and Sandton not a hotel room was to be found, so she put me up in a suburban bed-and-breakfast, run by a pleasant young couple. My quarters were private, spacious, modern, with great breakfasts, but behind barbed wire atop thick walls in a pretty neighborhood that was also a fortress. I immediately developed a massive case of claustrophobia.

The next day I did venture out for a walk to a shopping street with restaurants, where I noticed a few black women and white women having lunch together in the emerging South Africa, the gift of Mandela, something far more precious than a tournament.

On Sunday, I took the media bus out to Soccer City, a stadium in Soweto Townships, rebuilt and expanded for this event.

Before the match, Nelson Mandela, about to turn ninety-two, was given a victory lap to celebrate the World Cup—and the nation he had helped create. After the tribute, it was time for the kickoff between two grand soccer nations that had never won a World Cup, the two nations I had mentioned before the tournament, the two nations linked by style and history.

"I think Spain is the country playing the best football in the past few years," Netherlands coach Bert van Marwijk had said Saturday. "I've been the coach of the national squad for two years now, and during that time, it has crossed my mind that I would love to play Spain, and now it is happening."

While praising Spain, Van Marwijk apparently made the calculation that his team could not possibly match Spain in artistry so it would have to overwhelm it with crudity.

The spirit of Johan Cruyff, Marco van Basten, and Ruud Gullit howled in the cold township night as the Dutch kicked and shoved and elbowed the Spanish. The tactic held down the offense, with Spain accumulating five yellow cards against eight for the Netherlands, and both teams were scoreless after regulation time, the horror of any final.

In the 109th minute, the bill came due for the Dutch. John Heitinga picked up his second yellow card and was ejected, leaving way too much open space to the spiritual grandchildren of Cruyff. Seven minutes later, Cesc Fàbregas, a late sub, pushed the ball ahead to the very smooth Iniesta, who got to the right of the decimated Dutch back line and crossed a shot inside the post. The Spaniards held on for a 1–0 victory, not only shedding their reputation for folding but in a way punishing the Netherlands for violating its own heritage of positive, offensive soccer. With short passes and trust and optimism, Spain had expanded the sport, taken us to a new age.

As I packed to leave South Africa, I thought about the farewell press conference on Saturday, when Danny Jordaan, the head of the organizing committee, assured us that everything had been safe and positive. I could not argue with that. People who run World Cups don't like to talk about the bills that arrive after everybody leaves town.

But there was something else. Jordaan, with his mixed Khoi and Dutch ancestry, had been classified as "coloured" well into middle age. Now he had helped his homeland become the first African nation to stage the World Cup.

Jordaan often used an African word, *ubuntu*, which means "we are all interconnected." On Saturday he had quoted John Donne's "Meditation XVII," which includes the words "No man is an island." I took Jordaan's voice and Donne's words as my lasting memory from this first African World Cup, in the homeland of Mandela.

BLATTER SCORES AN
OWN GOAL

NEW YORK, 2013

For a highly political survivor, Sepp Blatter made a stunningly stupid move in 2010: he mandated a double vote for the sites of two future World Cups—a European host for 2018 and a host for 2022 from what could be called the third world of soccer.

As a consequence, the delegates chose Russia to host the 2018 World Cup and Qatar to host the 2022 World Cup; the latter choice soon came to be seen as impractical, perhaps also tainted. After half a dozen top officials, close associates of Blatter's, left soccer in financial scandals, every action by FIFA was suspect.

Theoretically, skipping the old bastions of Latin America and Europe and opening up the World Cup to other regions had been an idealistic move, much as FIFA had done in choosing South Africa as the host in 2010. However, anybody who had studied political science in junior high school could have told Blatter that the linked votes inevitably encouraged deal making. European candidates were sure to seek support from outside their region for 2018 in return for European support for 2022.

The United States was a bit player in world soccer, partially because of its lack of success on the field and also because its sunshine laws and moderately open business customs frightened FIFA. Considered part of the outer circle, the United States submitted a bid for the 2022 World Cup that followed its successful blueprint for 1994, featuring stadiums, hotels, and electronics already in place, plus American corporations eager to sponsor and a world full of tourists eager to visit America. This time, the United States also had a growing domestic league in place.

Qatar has neither a significant national soccer league nor a significant national team nor a supply of soccer stadiums. What Qatar does have is oil and money. It based its bid on building stadiums in the desert, for matches to be played in the heat of summer (average high 105 degrees Fahrenheit, but daytime highs of 130 in the desert). Why not? Qatar certainly had the oil to run the proposed air-conditioning systems. Qatar promised to dismantle the stadiums at the end of the World Cup and give them to poor nations.

After the last decade, there was considerable reason to be suspicious of anything FIFA did, what with the mysterious disappearance in 2000 of the New Zealand delegate that gave the 2006 World Cup to Germany and the blatant forcing of Nelson Mandela to visit the big man Jack Warner in Trinidad in 2004 to lobby for the 2010 bid.

Also, Blatter's public squashing of his own secretary general, Michael Zen-Ruffinen, and his refusal to listen to critical delegates during the FIFA meeting in Seoul in 2002 had exposed Blatter's autocratic style. Now, with this double vote for 2018 and 2022, nations and delegates and power brokers were openly lobbying with one another.

In order to become the host in 2022, the U.S. Soccer Federation needed votes from its regional federation, CONCACAF, which was run by the odd couple—Jack Warner, the president, from Port of Spain, and Chuck Blazer, the general secretary, a New Yorker who handled much of CONCACAF's financial and television dealings, usually without benefit of legal or accounting oversight.

"For two decades, Blazer and Warner had been close allies," wrote the *New York Times*. "They had grown Concacaf from a nearly insolvent regional governing body to one with a yearly income averaging $40 million and headquarters in Trump Tower in New York." Blazer also lived in that expensive Trump building and had an apartment in Miami's

South Beach and at a gambling resort in the Bahamas, all subsidized by CONCACAF.

As the 2010 vote approached, two of the twenty-four voting FIFA members were barred after the *Times* of London caught them offering to sell their votes. The BBC ran information from Andrew Jennings, a persistent reporter from England, who claimed that three executive members—Ricardo Teixeira of Brazil, Issa Hayatou of Cameroon, and Nicolás Leoz of Paraguay, the longtime leader of the South American federation—had taken payoffs in the past from FIFA's defunct marketing agency, International Sports and Leisure (ISL). They denied the charges.

The United States was courting the support of Michel Platini, once an elegant star for France and Juventus, now the highly ambitious president of the European federation, UEFA. But French president Nicolas Sarkozy was strongly in favor of Qatar.

"Sport does not belong to a few countries," Sarkozy said weeks before the vote. "It belongs to the world. . . . I don't understand those who say that events should always be held in the same countries and the same continents."

It was subsequently learned that on November 23, 2010, Sarkozy held a luncheon at the Élysée Palace with guests including the crown prince of Qatar, along with Platini, and, according to French journals, a representative of the investment fund that owned the prominent club Paris Saint-Germain.

On December 2, 2010, in Zurich, Russia was chosen as host for 2018, and Qatar won the vote for 2022. Sunil Gulati, the president of the U.S. federation, an economist with a world view, politely praised FIFA for moving the World Cup to a new region. What else could he say?

This vote seemed to catch Blatter by surprise. The International Olympic Committee, in choosing its host cities, presents voluminous analysis of all the bids, even if the eventual voting is secret. FIFA's standards were far more opaque.

After the vote, reporters and gay-rights activists around the world pointed out that Qatar had strong laws against homosexuality. Asked whether gay fans should attend the tournament in Qatar, Blatter blurted out, "I would say they should refrain from any sexual activities." He quickly apologized, but his latest verbal blunder seemed to move him even further from the Nobel Peace Prize, for which he had been lobbying for years.

Qatar was suddenly a player in world soccer. Six weeks after the vote, Qatar purchased the Paris Saint-Germain club, and in 2012, the Al Jazeera television network, owned by Qatar, introduced a French sports channel, beIN Sport, with the rights to televise French soccer until 2016.

FIFA was now in the spotlight as never before.

In 2011, the *New York Times* described FIFA this way: "Since its founding in 1904 in Paris, FIFA has grown into an extremely rich organization, with reserves of almost $1.3 billion and revenues last year of $1.2 billion from the sales of television and marketing rights all over the world. It has also benefited from a tax exemption for Swiss sports organizations, a bountiful perk that is beginning to raise political heat in the local cantons in light of the various corruption scandals."

When pressed for details about FIFA, including his salary, Blatter often cited the legal codes of Europe, which give far more privacy to companies and tax-exempt nonprofits than the United States did.

FIFA generally had not been pursued by investigative journalism, but in recent years, Blatter had a bit of bad luck when the British reporter Andrew Jennings turned his attention from the International Olympic Committee to FIFA. Blatter tried to ban Jennings from press meetings and generally discredit him, but Jennings began to discover gems like this:

In 1996, before a crucial vote of FIFA, the Haitian delegate, Jean-Marie Kyss, could not travel from Haiti to Zurich. Knowing that, Horace Burrell, the president of Jamaica's federation, arranged for his girlfriend, Vincy Jalal, who was neither Haitian nor male, to use Kyss's credential. The next time a vote was needed, Burrell used a male voter. Kyss apparently found out much later that others had voted in his place. There was no indication Blatter knew of this chicanery, but it was the way FIFA was run in the age of Blatter. Most people cut their own deals.

Jennings also began to ask questions about International Sports and Leisure, the marketing partner of FIFA, which collapsed in 2001 with the disappearance of many millions of dollars, sometimes estimated at

$300 million. There was no suggestion that Blatter had profited, but FIFA and ISL were close partners, and millions of dollars had vanished somewhere.

Shortly after Qatar was chosen in 2010, powerful soccer figures began to vanish as well. The leader of its World Cup bid, Mohamed bin Hammam, announced he would run against Blatter for president of FIFA. Soon after that, bin Hammam was banned for life for bribing delegates in that presidential election although he and FIFA both denied that Qatar had bribed voters in choosing the host for 2022.

In 2011, João Havelange, the imperious Charles de Gaulle lookalike who had served as the president of FIFA before Blatter, and his former son-in-law, Ricardo Teixeira, both came under investigation in their homeland of Brazil and also in Switzerland, the home of FIFA. Andrew Jennings testified in Brazil, claiming that Havelange had taken upward of $50 million in bribes or commissions through a front company called Sicuretta. Days before an ethics committee of the International Olympic Committee was to convene, Havelange resigned as a member.

Teixeira resigned from FIFA in March 2012 and was said to be living in Miami. He and Havelange repaid some money to FIFA but because commercial bribery had not been a crime in Switzerland in the mid-1990s, they were not prosecuted.

Havelange's disgrace was particularly inconvenient for Brazil, inasmuch as the country would be hosting the 2014 World Cup and the main Olympic Stadium for Rio de Janeiro in 2016 had been named for him.

Jack Warner's star began to dwindle when he supported bin Hammam's audacious run for president against Blatter, who ultimately was reelected without opposition. In the words of Machiavelli, "Never do an enemy a small injury."

In 2011, a British parliamentary committee reported allegations of corruption, adding, "FIFA has given every impression of wishing to sweep all allegations of misconduct under the carpet." Prominent European soccer officials began to connect Blatter with the laissez-faire climate in the organization he had led since 1998. "Mr. Blatter always knew that Warner was an embarrassment, but he had thirty-five votes," said John MacBeth, a former president of the Scottish soccer federation.

On April 19, 2013, CONCACAF's special Integrity Committee issued a report on the financial activities of the longtime allies Warner and Blazer. "I have recounted a sad and sorry tale in the life of CONCACAF, a tale of abuse of position and power, by persons who assisted in bringing the organisation to profitability but who enriched themselves at the expense of their very own organizations," said Sir David Anthony Cathcart Simmons, the former chief justice of Barbados, who was the chairman of the Integrity Committee.

Warner had taken money from Havelange and erected the Dr. João Havelange Centre of Excellence in Trinidad, ostensibly to foster soccer among the poor people in the region. But Warner had never registered the complex as property of FIFA. In fact, it was built on land belonging to the Warner family. "Approximately $26 million of CONCACAF funds went into Center of Excellence and that is no longer an asset of CONCACAF," the Integrity Committee reported.

The Integrity Committee also concluded that Blazer "misappropriated at least $15 million in compensation payments" from CONCACAF. Some of this money went to support his various apartments. According to the Integrity Committee, Blazer also mixed his personal and business accounts on his American Express card so he could gain all the membership points—worth $29 million at last count.

The two former allies faced possible legal action as well as FBI and Internal Revenue Service investigations. Blazer resigned his position with FIFA, and Warner said he was now gone from soccer and could not locate any records pertinent to his work for CONCACAF.

Another powerful FIFA official, Nicolás Leoz, age eighty-four, the longtime head of the South American confederation known as CONMEBOL, was said to have offered his vote for England as 2018 host if the legendary British club championship, the FA Cup, was named for him. As a Paraguayan, Leoz had no history whatsoever with the FA Cup. The former chairman of the British Football Association, Lord Triesman, claimed Leoz had asked for a knighthood in exchange for his vote for

England in 2018. In 2013, Leoz resigned from FIFA, citing health problems.

With so many powerful figures departing from FIFA, Damian Collins, a member of the British parliament who had been investigating FIFA corruption, told the *New York Times,* "This shows that FIFA can't be trusted to run their own investigation." He added, "This demonstrates that they have totally failed. This means we will never know the truth about what happened."

In July 2012, FIFA hired a new lawyer to conduct an internal investigation: Michael J. Garcia, a partner with Kirkland & Ellis of New York and Washington, who from 2005 to 2008 had been the United States attorney for the Southern District of New York. FIFA also hired Hans-Joachim Eckert, a highly regarded judge from Munich, to handle any information Garcia might develop.

Early in 2013, Garcia turned in a four-thousand–page report to Eckert, who soon issued a scathing judgment of Havelange, Teixeira, and Leoz. Eckert wrote: "There are . . . no indications whatsoever that President Blatter was responsible for a cash flow to Havelange, Teixeira or Leoz, or that he himself received any payments from the ISL Group, even in the form of hidden kick back payments." But he continued: "It must be questioned, however, whether President Blatter knew or should have known over the years before the bankruptcy of ISL that ISL had made payments (bribes) to other FIFA officials."

The most striking link between Blatter and the money flow was noted in Eckert's report: a payment of 1.5 million Swiss francs ($1.6 million) which was sent to FIFA's offices in Zurich in 1997 and earmarked for Havelange. When the payment was brought to Blatter's attention, he ordered it returned to ISL. This connection of Blatter's awareness of money intended for his predecessor had been developed by Andrew Jennings. Blatter told the investigator he did not suspect the money was a payoff or bribe.

Eckert concluded, "President Blatter's conduct could not be classified in any way as misconduct with regard to any ethics rules. . . . The conduct of President Blatter may have been clumsy because there could be an internal need for clarification, but this does not lead to any criminal or ethical misconduct."

In April 2013, Havelange resigned as honorary president of FIFA for "health and personal reasons."

Blatter put out a release saying he had been exonerated, but the word "clumsy" has been attached to him ever since. His stewardship includes game rigging and gambling scandals around the world that surfaced in recent years, including in Italy, where Juventus was forced to play in Serie B for one season after indications of favoritism in the choice of referees. In 2012, news broke of a gambling ring, presumably based in Singapore but extending into eastern Europe and Italy and run by Tan Seet Eng. More than 100 matches from 2008 to 2011 in Italy's three top leagues were suspect, as part of 680 matches under investigation by law enforcement. Again, there was no suggestion that Blatter was directly involved or knew anything about these gambling rings, but his supervision of FIFA, including game influencing, would seem to deserve Judge Eckert's well-chosen legal word "clumsy."

With his longtime comrades going down all around him, Blatter began shooting off an unprecedented number of press releases—FIFA was in favor of education, FIFA was in favor of women playing soccer, FIFA was in favor of friendship between Israel and Palestine, FIFA was in favor of building stadiums in impoverished lands, and most of all, FIFA was against the racist chants heard in many stadiums across the globe.

Blatter also took his head out of the sand regarding technology. The World Cup had a heritage of questionable goal-line calls—the highly debatable goal by England's Geoff Hurst in the 1966 final and the shot by England's Frank Lampard that clearly crossed the line in 2010. Yet Blatter remained stuck to his position of 2002 about goal-line technology: "I will make sure that no technical help will be introduced in refereeing, because we shall rely on persons and human beings."

There was another terrible call during the 2012 European tournament, when a shot by Marko Dević of Ukraine clearly crossed the goal line but was not allowed by the officials. England received the inadvertent gift, and Ukraine, one of the cohosts, was eliminated. With tennis, American football, and baseball increasingly using technological aids, in 2013 Blatter announced that FIFA would use modern goal-line technology in the 2014 World Cup. He was trying to morph into Sepp the

Techie. At the same time, he had to cope with FIFA's choice of Qatar for the World Cup of 2022.

Showing the same fluid moves that had made him such a great player, Michel Platini was now claiming that his vote in 2010 for Qatar had been conditional. This was *très drôle*, since Platini had given head fakes that he might favor the American bid but had clearly gone along with the French tilt to Qatar. By March 2013, Platini was suggesting it might not be wise to put a World Cup in the desert in the summer. Instead, Platini suggested, Qatar should move the event to January, when the weather would be better. "Also, the neighboring emirates must be included so that the World Cup is staged throughout the entire region," Platini added.

In early September 2013, Blatter conceded it "may well be that we made a mistake" in awarding the 2022 World Cup to Qatar, and he began to talk about moving the tournament to cooler months. He had to know this move would disrupt the September-to-May club schedule, the backbone of the sport in Europe and also the economic support for players from all over the world who work in Europe.

It was hard to know when Blatter was serious. He was famous for asinine statements, like urging female players to wear tighter uniforms to appeal to male fans and proposing to hold a World Cup every two years. When FIFA belatedly opened its executive board to three female officials, Blatter said, "We now have three ladies on the board. Say something, ladies! You are always speaking at home. Say something now!"

Now he began to address the Qatar issue. Sepp the Burgher from Zurich was morphing into Sepp the Revolutionary, a regular Che Guevara. "If we maintain, rigidly, the status quo, then a FIFA World Cup can never be played in countries that are south of the equator or indeed near the equator," Blatter said. "We automatically discriminate against countries that have different seasons than we do in Europe. I think it is high time that Europe starts to understand that we do not rule the world any more, and that some former European imperial powers can no longer impress their will on to others in far away places."

It was highly unlikely that FIFA would come up with direct evidence about payoffs or trade-offs for the 2022 World Cup back in 2010. For obvious geopolitical reasons, FIFA did not want to displace Qatar, not in a world already inflamed by regional and religious tensions.

Now that Blatter had identified a problem, he was in a rush to move Qatar to a late autumn date in 2022. He wanted to make the decision at a board meeting in October 2013 but ran into criticism from an unusual source—the United States.

Sunil Gulati, the unpaid president of the U.S. federation, was elected a member of FIFA's twenty-five-person executive committee in 2013, replacing Chuck Blazer, who had left in disgrace. Born in 1959, Gulati had relative youth and international credentials that could make him a positive force within FIFA. He had expressed disillusionment at the revelations about Blazer, his longtime ally and fellow New Yorker, and spoke in favor of openness, including financial details. Now he went further, questioning the need to move quickly on moving the dates of the 2022 World Cup.

"I don't see at this stage, frankly, how I or any member of FIFA's executive committee could make a sensible decision," Gulati told the *New York Times*. "We don't have enough information, and there are too many questions. I don't see how anybody in a position of responsibility can take a position without some answers." Gulati was well aware that American-based television networks and sponsors had based their bid for the 2022 World Cup on a summer date, not during the American football season. "If the position I'm taking—which is that we need a lot more information—is rocking the boat," Gulati said, "then I'm going to be rocking the boat." He continued to rock the boat by saying that FIFA needed to clarify the bidding process and rely on technical evaluation of national bids. "Otherwise, it's an unnecessary expenditure of funds and time," he said.

This was the strongest public stand the U.S. federation had ever taken within FIFA. And when FIFA's committee met in Zurich in October, it faced the greatest scrutiny in its history, with papers like the *Guardian* and the *New York Times* writing about FIFA as if it were a rogue parliament or congress that bore considerable watching. Qatar was under siege after reports that many foreign laborers had already died, and more could be injured, by building stadiums in the desert heat. Qatari officials insisted that they could construct modern cooled stadiums for a summer

World Cup without endangering migrant labor. FIFA, faced with complaints from European leagues and major television networks, seemed hesitant to disrupt the traditional schedule, although Blatter remained firm that the 2022 World Cup would take place in Qatar. After the public reservations from Gulati and others, Blatter postponed a decision until after the 2014 World Cup in Brazil.

At no point did the United States call for the 2022 World Cup to be moved, taking the high road like nations that have lost elections they thought they should have won—Greece for the 1996 Olympics, South Africa for the 2006 World Cup. The reward for tact and patience could turn out to be a North American World Cup in 2026, with host cities ranging from Toronto to Mexico City, assuming that nations still believe hosting a World Cup is worth the trouble.

The biggest crowds in Brazil are usually for celebrations, moving to the samba beat. Carnival every year. Winning the World Cup five times.

In 2013, Brazilians were protesting as far as the television cameras could go, in dozens of cities. It started with a mundane incident; unrest often does. The despair of a fruit vendor in Tunisia. Anger in Egypt and Libya and Syria. Plans to remodel a park in Istanbul. The raising of bus fares in Brazil.

As millions of people took to the streets in Brazil in 2013, they made a leap in logic that had never quite been made before. The demonstrators linked the corruption in their daily lives to their patrimony, their sport, *jogo bonito*, the beautiful game, the World Cup, the biggest sports event on the planet.

Suddenly, with the zeal of *citoyens* in France in the time of the revolution, crowds were asking if they really needed to turn their country into a giant television studio and resort so billions of people could watch a soccer tournament, with the bills arriving later. The crowds focused their anger on Sepp Blatter as the epitome of Brazil's colonization.

"I can understand that people are unhappy," Blatter said in a speech in Rio de Janeiro. "But football is here to unite people. Football is here to build bridges, to generate excitement, to bring hope."

The crowd booed Blatter; Brazilians also criticized Pelé, the greatest symbol of talent and joy the sport has ever produced, for urging people to "forget the protests." Soccer had been very, very good to Pelé. Now he was seen as a shill for the power brokers who run the sport.

Could the inequities of the world be approached without taking a look at the world's biggest sports event? In 2013, people were asking this question as perhaps never before.

Blatter, who had long said he would retire after his fourth term ended in 2015, was now talking of running for a fifth term. In January 2014, Jérôme Champagne of France, a former official of FIFA, said he planned to run against Blatter, and Pelé immediately endorsed Champagne. The impracticality of Qatar was hanging over FIFA. The organization had reached to New York for a lawyer and to Munich for a judge to assess the scandals. One key word in Judge Eckert's findings seemed likely to stick with Sepp Blatter for a long time: clumsy.

THE AGE OF KLINSMANN

CONCACAF REGION, 2013

In 2003, a fleet blond striker registered for a fast Southern California league under the name Jay Göppingen. The man had moves—and a German accent—and scored five goals in eight games for Orange County Blue Star.

Pretty soon everybody figured out he was really Jürgen Klinsmann, the retired German star (born in Göppingen, Germany), who lived with his family in the area. Nobody seemed to mind the assumed name— that was charming—but Jay Göppingen could not make all the matches because he was often away on business trips, coaching the German national team, ultimately to third place in the 2006 World Cup.

When would the United States produce its own Klinsmann? For that matter, was the experience of Klinsmann transferrable to American players? Sunil Gulati, the president of the national federation, believed it was time to do something different. He courted Klinsmann after the 2006 World Cup but could not convince him to sign on, so the job went to Bob Bradley, who deserved it, and did fine. But was it enough for the United States to be among the seven nations to have qualified for all six World Cups starting in 1990? The sour look on Gulati's face in Johannesburg seemed to speak for ambitious American fans: they wanted the Yanks to do better in Brazil in 2014.

After a few mediocre matches following the 2010 World Cup, Gulati went back after Klinsmann, offering him a base pay of $2.5 million per year through 2014, as opposed to the base salary of $515,647 received by Bradley in 2010. (Bradley did make another $345,000 for reaching the Confederations Cup in 2009 and the World Cup in 2010, along with other bonuses and compensations.)

Gulati was no naïf. He knew that German fans believed Klinsmann had depended heavily on Joachim Löw for strategy during the lovely run in 2006. One of the more secure people in coaching, Klinsmann was often the first to credit his friend. But he had also been fired by Bayern Munich during his first season, after poor results and criticism from the front office that he spent too much money and attention on American-style PowerPoint technology and nutrition and training programs for individual players.

Klinsmann spoke many languages. When he played for Monaco early in his career, he took a French language course; he studied computers. He was one of the better ex-players to coach a national team, and American players would respect his star status.

Some fans in the States were convinced that a big-time coach from overseas could impart the magic chord, the secret of life that would suddenly elevate the lads to world level. Could Klinsmann transfer the spring in his legs, the experience in his active head, to the American players?

From watching Arena and Bradley, hardly touchy-feely types, I believed the United States needed a coach attuned to the American mentality. Most European coaches have come along in autocratic systems and would be put off by the American question, "Why?" I could not see Alex Ferguson, chomping gum as if he were grinding the egos of his hirelings, speaking the psychological language of Americans. But the theory was that Klinsmann, whose children were growing up in California, might work out in this culture.

. . .

The United States Soccer Federation was no longer the small-scale operation it once had been, with a few employees in a hole-in-the-wall office in the Empire State Building. It had moved to Colorado Springs for a time and then in 1991 to two mansions in the historic millionaire enclave of Prairie Avenue on the South Side of Chicago. Its net assets were estimated at $57 million in 2012, and it employed more than one hundred people. The federation made considerable expenditures on refereeing clinics and programs for millions of youths and had produced the championship women's teams and in 2013 a promising under-twenty team coached by Tab Ramos.

But how was the U.S. federation to be judged? In some ways, it was gaining in power and prestige with Gulati on the executive committee, but in the pragmatic world of soccer, the United States would mostly be judged by the results of the men's team. After all the projects and academies, after the grand run in 2002, the United States had continued to produce admirable players who had learned the sport without much of an informal sandlot base where they could grapple and struggle and improvise, making moves on their own without Coach screaming in one ear and helicopter parents screaming in the other.

Motivated, well-trained, intelligent players were proving themselves overseas, but the McBrides and Reynas had retired, and the United States was still waiting for an even higher level. One indicator of success used by the federation is the number of national players close to Champions League level, playing for the top four clubs in the top four best national leagues in Europe—Italy, England, Spain, and Germany. By the end of the 2012–13 season, both Spain and Germany had nearly seventy stay-at-home stars on their top four squads, but the United States had just four players in top clubs, none of whom quite fit the definition: German-born Jermaine Jones with fourth-place FC Schalke 04; Brad Friedel, now the second-stringer at Tottenham and no longer playing for the national team; Michael Bradley, who was highly respected by fans of AS Roma, which finished sixth in Serie A; and Clint Dempsey, an occasional starter with fifth-place Tottenham.

One category that the United States has exported is superior keepers: Kasey Keller, Brad Friedel, Tim Howard, and Brad Guzan have all gone to the Premiership, partially because athletes with size and reach can be taught to play keeper. Talent is much more difficult to develop at the ten other positions.

Probably the best American field player of the twenty-first century has been Landon Donovan, who had a productive spurt on winter loan to Everton but remained a homebody in California. In 2012–13, Donovan took a walkabout from the national team and the Los Angeles Galaxy, saying he needed to reconnect with his family as part of his growth as an adult. While the United States was preparing for the Hex, Donovan took a trip to Cambodia.

Donovan's sabbatical seemed like a classical American need-to-find-myself journey—"On the Road," or "The Midfielder in the Rye." Bruce Arena, the coach of the Galaxy, was characteristically sarcastic about Donovan's "bad plan."

Establishing himself as the American coach, Klinsmann, while living in Southern California himself, came off as a demanding Bundesliga coach, the stern German papa. In an interview with Matthew Futterman of the *Wall Street Journal*, Klinsmann spoke of the need for higher competition within Major League Soccer.

"We would say it would be great if our eighteen- or nineteen- or twenty-year-olds would have an environment where they get pushed every day, where they are accountable every day, where they understand what it means to be a pro, where they have eleven months of training, games, training games, where they have a chance to build their stamina to build their systems so you can really take in the game as a leading component, not just seven or eight months and then I go on vacation," Klinsmann said.

Major League Soccer was doing fine, producing players like Omar Gonzalez, Matt Besler, and Graham Zusi, who jumped to the national team in 2013 without taking the advanced course in Europe. Ultimately, these players might follow the money trail to Europe, but that is part of the process anticipated by MLS since the first season of 1996.

The level of play had improved incrementally in MLS, going into the 2013 season, its eighteenth, one longer than the North American Soccer League survived. MLS now had fourteen soccer-specific stadiums, with another expected in San Jose. The seventeenth season was the best ever, with an average attendance of 18,807, the seventh-highest league average in the world.

Commissioner Don Garber has talked of wanting a rivalry in the New York area, and in 2013 the league committed to a twentieth team as a rival for the Red Bulls, who were based just across the Hudson in New Jersey. The new club would be owned by the New York Yankees of baseball and Manchester City of the Premier League, which is itself owned by the ruling family of Abu Dhabi. The new owners were planning another soccer-specific stadium, perhaps in Queens, with its ethnic enclaves, but more likely near Yankee Stadium in the Bronx. However, urban priorities and a new mayor would determine if even more land was to be turned over to a private business like soccer.

Meanwhile, investors owning the legendary Cosmos brand seemed to have missed the chance to get into the league, casting their fate with a secondary league. Ultimately, Cosmos is only a name. Pelé and Beckenbauer and Chinaglia are not coming back.

Klinsmann did not insist that Americans leave for European clubs while still in their late teens, saying, "I was not ready to go abroad until I was twenty-four," but he also noted that Michael Bradley had been ready to grow in Europe at nineteen. Klinsmann also said that Major League Soccer could not provide the twenty-four-hour indoctrination to soccer that the European system does: "This is the problem we have because we are not socially so connected so deeply to soccer in the daily life. They think, you get a tryout in Europe with West Ham, this is huge, you made it. No, you haven't even made it if you have the contract with West Ham. And even if you play there and if you become a starter, which would make us happy, that still doesn't mean that you made it."

Klinsmann began his tenure by recruiting in the territory he knew best—German players with an American parent who had never played with the German national team and were therefore eligible for the U.S. squad. The best of them was Jermaine Jones, a swaggering, broad-shouldered version of Rafa Márquez of Mexico and Claudio Gentile of Italy—every squad needs a hard man—but Klinsi's Germans came off as Hessians, hired hands, who did not necessarily display commitment when they jetted in for a match.

When the United States advanced to the Hexagonal in 2013, Klinsmann began to put his signature on the team by benching the popular captain, Carlos Bocanegra, before a dreadful 2–1 opening loss in Honduras and then not calling Bocanegra for subsequent matches. Klinsmann made an innovative move in calling up DaMarcus Beasley, a veteran of three World Cups, from his club in Puebla, Mexico, and moving him from wing to left back. Beasley was sometimes overmatched on defense, but he played the entire field, darting into open space, a true footballer. Klinsmann revived the national career of Eddie Johnson, who had moved to the Seattle Sounders in MLS.

The coach seemed to have critics, including within the American locker room. A story broke in the *Sporting News* claiming that some anonymous American players were finding Klinsmann erratic, not clear in his expectations. The coach was remarkably sanguine about the criticism, dismissing it as normal. Public criticism of Klinsmann's fluctuating lineup was a sign that some American fans were still not familiar with the normal World Cup cycle. The fans wanted to see a set lineup of familiar faces, but the reality is that the path to every World Cup involves constant revision. Some players are just not available because of club schedules, injuries, slumps, coaching experiments, or personal and family priorities. Or the coach wants to take a look at somebody else.

The long march of the Hexagonal moved from a sloppy loss in Honduras to a match with Costa Rica in a developing snowstorm in Colorado. FIFA officials probably should have called the match beforehand, but given the tight schedules of the assembled players, there was huge pressure to get the match done. With snow covering the field, Clint Dempsey scored a goal, and the United States held on for a victory. Costa Rica protested holding the match in the snow, but the complaint was denied by CONCACAF officials, and the United States had three points at home.

Four nights later, still at altitude in Azteca, Major League Soccer paid off marvelously, with two home-based defenders, Gonzalez and Besler, negating the inefficient Mexican strikers, and Brad Guzan of Aston Villa filling in for the injured Tim Howard, making saves near the end of a 0–0 draw.

With the team earning a point in that hard place, criticism of Klinsmann abated. He named the taciturn Clint Dempsey captain, suggesting that it was time for Dempsey to step up his leadership and
acknowledging that Tim Howard and Michael Bradley were going to be
leaders anyway.

Klinsmann also let it be known that he was losing patience with Jozy
Altidore, the big striker who had finally found a home with AZ Alkmaar
and was the top scorer in the Netherlands with thirty-one goals in all
competition but had not scored for the United States on Klinsmann's
watch. The criticism may have motivated Altidore: after a stinker of a
friendly against Belgium, he scored in five straight matches, including vital Hex victories, one a 2–0 victory over Panama in Seattle in
mid-June—a breakthrough of sorts for American soccer. The Sounders—
a grand old Seattle soccer name—have been producing huge and boisterous crowds for their Pacific derbies against Portland and Vancouver.
The national federation had tried to duck most big cities and stadiums,
fearing that Latin American fans might show up, but the Hex qualifier
in Seattle drew 40,847 fans, most wearing red and chanting and standing the entire night.

The television cameras in Seattle showed Panamanian fans proudly
displaying their flags and jerseys in the stands, unmolested. The mood
was positive, like the U.S.-Ghana match in South Africa in 2010, when
fans mingled and some even displayed both flags. By contrast, on the
same night as the Panama match in Seattle, frustrated Mexican fans were
heaving missiles out of the stands in Azteca to protest another wretched
showing by the home team.

With the United States in great position, thirteen points in six matches,
Klinsmann had a major project over the summer of 2013—evaluating
Landon Donovan, who had rejoined the Galaxy in the spring. Klinsmann
echoed Arena, saying Donovan needed to prove he could still play in MLS
before even thinking of rejoining the national team. Sir Alex Ferguson or
Fabio Capello or José Mourinho could not have been more blunt. Then
Klinsmann added Donovan to a B-list roster for the Gold Cup tourna-
ment, the odd-year summer competition in the CONCACAF region.

My guess was that many of the American players who had been on the field when Donovan made some of his greatest runs, including against Algeria in 2010, were more pragmatic than their coach. They had experienced the way Donovan could transform a match. Now Klinsmann was getting empirical evidence that Donovan had not lost his speed and pace and touch, as he scored five goals and made seven assists in the American sweep through the Gold Cup. Later, Klinsmann said, "He earned every compliment he got in this tournament." When asked about Donovan's chances of playing in the four remaining World Cup qualifiers, Klinsmann said, "There is a high probability he joins us."

The Gold Cup tournament provided a new insight into the coaching ability of Jürgen Klinsmann. The great striker demanded that his second-tier players move the ball forward, expecting teammates to materialize in open space, and they began to show confidence and aggression rarely seen on American squads.

"Collectively, they're a very good team," said Agustín Castillo, a Peruvian coaching the Salvador national team, after a 5–1 loss in the Gold Cup semifinal. Castillo added, "They almost play by memory. They can find the spaces. It almost seems like every time they pass the ball into a space it's going to nobody, then somebody appears and actually meets the ball. Good work, good movement. They're the best team I've seen in this tournament. They are a candidate to win it all."

It almost sounded as if Castillo was talking about Spain, the way its players trusted one another to keep advancing.

The stern face of Klinsi returned in late August when Clint Dempsey left the Premier League, accepting a contract for $5,038,567 for each of the next four years with the Seattle Sounders of MLS. This salary would have been unimaginable in the socialist single-owner entity of MLS of seventeen years earlier, but the league was now paying to retain its homegrown stars.

Klinsmann was not enthusiastic about Dempsey's return. "There is always another level," the coach had said, earlier in 2013, speaking about Dempsey. "If you one day reach the highest level, then you've got to confirm it, every year. Xavi, Iniesta, Messi. Confirm it to me. Show me that every year you deserve to play for Real Madrid, for Bayern Munich, for Manchester United. Show it to me."

Dempsey declined to apologize for taking the high salary and the chance to raise his children in the United States. Klinsmann had to know from observing the cranky screwface Dempsey displayed in public that this was no moonbeam of a player. Dempsey played with a poor boy's drive, having grown up in East Texas, playing against older Latinos in highly physical and nasty matches. Still, Klinsmann reserved the right to goad the man he had named captain. This was the Bundesliga way.

The qualifying round resumed in early September, with the United States losing, 3–1, in Costa Rica, where fans and players seethed with resentment over the snow game in Colorado earlier in the year. Michael Bradley rolled his ankle taking a kick in warmups and would miss four weeks. Altidore, now playing for Sunderland in the Premier League, reverted to immaturity by taking a needless yellow card in extra time, which meant he was out for the Mexico game four days later in Columbus, Ohio.

After winning the 2012 gold medal at the Olympics in London, Mexico was a stunning disappointment in 2013. Hours after his team coughed up two counterattack goals to Honduras in a rainy Azteca, coach José Manuel de la Torre was fired.

Short on leadership, maybe also short on talent, Mexico seemed to have never recovered from being humiliated by the Yanks, 2–0, in the knockout round of the 2002 World Cup in South Korea. Some loyal Mexican fans brought their sombreros and their aspirations and managed to buy tickets for the qualifier in Columbus, the scene of three previous qualifier defeats, all by scores of 2–0—the same score as the World Cup loss. Hence a new American chant for their neighbors from the south: "*Dos a cero.*"

The impact of Jay Göppingen, the former striker for the Orange County Blue Star, was evident against Mexico. In the absence of the injured Michael Bradley, players were expected to take control of their positions, move the ball forward, make something happen, and the constantly rebuilt defensive line rebuffed Mexico's unimaginative long balls.

In the forty-ninth minute, the resurgent Eddie Johnson met an outswinger corner kick from Donovan and blasted home a header, after the keeper had strayed in pursuit of the ball. Later, when Johnson felt woozy after a collision, he was replaced by Mix Diskerud, a Norwegian whose mother was from Arizona, which made him eligible to play for the United States. Two minutes after coming into the match, Diskerud showed the empowerment from his coach by turning the corner from the right side and releasing a perfect low pass in front of the goal, where Donovan converted it. The fans chanted "*Dos a cero,*" and later in the evening, after the two other qualifiers were finished, the United States celebrated qualifying for its seventh consecutive World Cup.

With the stadium in Columbus shimmering with red-clad fans, I remembered that dismal loss to Costa Rica back in 1985, when Gregg Thompson asked his coach when the United States would ever feel like the home team, and poor Alkis Panagoulias could only respond, "Never." Now it was happening. The United States had developed fans worthy of its players and vice versa.

"The biggest change in American soccer in the last ten years has been the fans," said Hank Steinbrecher, the American federation executive who had blistered a television official for ignoring the American women at the 1996 Olympics. Steinbrecher was talking not only about the numbers but also the way fans now chanted and bounced up and down for a full ninety minutes, passionate but generally sportsmanlike.

Klinsmann had raised the expectations—testing Donovan, prodding Dempsey, dropping Bocanegra, all the self-aware actions of a man who has played and coached at the highest level. Maybe the question for American soccer was not merely how to recruit better athletes away from basketball, football, and baseball. In the time of Klinsmann, the issue seemed to be how to demand more from players already succeeding in their life's work.

The United States had not produced a Maradona, swirling through the English defense in 1986, or a Zidane of the dancing feet, levitating for headers in 1998, the feral genius who wants control of the ball. In musical terms, American women had already evolved into talented divas, our Barbra, our Aretha, our Loretta, but where was our Chuck Berry, our Johnny Cash, our Frank Sinatra, doing things his way?

Still, America was accumulating its own highlight film of epic moments—Joe Gaetjens's flicked goal against England in 1950, Paul

Caligiuri's boomer at Port of Spain in 1989, the desperate full-field rally against Algeria in 2010.

That latest *dos a cero* victory over Mexico demonstrated that American fans were becoming conditioned to the reliable run, the dependable stop. Genius might have to wait.

On October 11, 2013, the Americans clinched first place in the Hex with a 2–0 victory over Jamaica in the new high-tech soccer stadium in Kansas City. The United States now lobbied for better seeding in 2014.

However, the rules of the draw once again worked against the United States. Placed in the same pool as the generally weaker Asian and CONCACAF teams, the Americans wound up with a killer draw of Ghana, Portugal, and Germany. Yes, the same Ghana that had eliminated the Yanks in the past two World Cups.

Group of Death? This one was pretty lethal. It did not make Americans feel better that Mexico, which barely slipped into the last spot in the World Cup, emerged with a much softer schedule in its group.

"We hit the worst of the worst," Klinsmann said. "It's one of the most difficult groups in the whole draw." The competitor in him emerged, and he added that this is the reality of the World Cup and he hoped to surprise people. However, progress from the first round seemed very difficult.

"If we're not playing in the round of 16 in 2014, we're not doing well," Sunil Gulati had said early in 2013. But after the crushing draw at the end of the year, Gulati proactively extended Klinsmann's contract through 2018 and added the role of technical director for U.S. soccer, which meant Klinsmann would have major input into the supply chain. This extension and new title were a sure sign to players and fans alike that Klinsmann had already made his impact on the national team and would be around no matter what happened in Brazil. When Michael Bradley returned to Major League Soccer in January 2014, for a stunning $36 million for six years, he made sure to explain the move to Klinsmann before it went public. The standard for 2014 was surely miles higher than it had been in 1990, after Caligiuri's goal took the Americans to their first World Cup in forty years.

Bit by bit, the United States was raising its presence in the biggest sports event on the globe. The century was still young.

EPILOGUE:
BACK TO THE ROOTS

QUEENS, NEW YORK, 2013

Jamaica High School has been phased out by the New York City Department of Education, in all its wisdom; four smaller schools now nest in the grand old building. But for varsity sports, the schools still come together as one team. The combined Jamaica team had a game one afternoon in the fall of 2013.

I called the captain.

"Aw, I can't make it," Bob Seel said in the high-pitched voice that used to scream instructions at me. "One of my grandkids has a game. You should see them. They're better than I was."

Nobody is better than Bob Seel, I thought. Better he should watch his grandkids. I would go alone.

Jamaica was playing Queens High School of Teaching, located adjacent to a municipal farm. A pungent odor of vegetables and animals wafted across the soccer field, which had almost no grass, no white lines. If the ball went wide or long, one of the players had to search for it in the brush.

The Jamaica road uniform was a very dark blue. I missed the ratty red long-sleeved jerseys of my time, and thought of our school song, to the tune of "Aura Lee" (also "Love Me Tender"): "Red and blue / Red and blue / School of red and blue . . ."

Before the game, two female coaches gave instructions to their teams. I thought of our little old coach, Mr. Harrington, opening up the ball bag and sending us out to play. Jamaica's coach was Dana Silverstein, twenty-five years old, trim and energetic, a former player for the University of Rhode Island. "It's like I have twenty kids of my own," she had told me in a phone conversation. I said it was cool to see two women coaching boys, and Silverstein replied, "I'm sure they had never had a woman coach in their life. They tell me now, 'We thought it was a joke.'" She added, "The respect level is high."

Jamaica took control from the opening whistle. Down at the other end, the Jamaica keeper shouted "*otro lado*" (other side) and "*corre, corre*" (run, run). He got bored and squatted on his haunches. I thought: don't do that, son.

Suddenly, a Queens defender thumped a long clearing shot that bounded downfield. The old terror came back—the autumn haze, the chill when the sun went behind a cloud, how safe the field seemed from my defender position, until hordes of Grover Cleveland attackers came marauding.

I have been watching World Cup games from the press tribune, as Sócrates and Baggio and Donovan moved forward like Pac-Men on electronic rampage, but down here on terra firma it happened fast.

A fleet Queens halfback gathered the long ball at full speed, got a step on the Jamaica defender and let fly—a few inches wide of the goal, rocketing into the underbrush.

Soon, Jamaica reasserted itself in shifting powerful triangles, with deft short passes, bing-bing-bing, advancing on the far goal. After decades of watching all those games, I could recognize the familiar clues, the potential of a goal. Jamaica took a 2–0 lead by halftime.

In the second half, the teams changed ends. Jamaica players swooped in to take corner kicks, a few feet from where I was standing, out of bounds. I still whack a ball around with a grandchild now and then, proud I can use either foot. I had the illusion of being in the game, felt my competitive side turn on.

The ball skittered across the dirt boundary, toward me. I saw a Jamaica player hustle over, eager to maintain pressure. I extended my right instep and tapped the ball to him. He scooped it up, planted his feet, and made a quick throw-in.

For a rare time at a Jamaica soccer match, I did not screw up.

The touch of ball on instep made me think: I love this game.

The whistle sounded on a 4–2 Jamaica victory, and the teams went through the handshake line. Afterward, Silverstein summoned the players for her critique. Then she introduced me as a former player.

"I was terrible," I told them. "Now I'm writing a book about soccer."

They crowded around, happy to have won a game to stay in contention. They reassured me that even with four smaller schools inhabiting the same building there is a sense of unity.

I remembered the polyglot Jamaica team of my years. Silverstein had told me she heard at least thirteen different languages in the building and said sometimes one player would translate for a teammate. I asked the young men to name their favorite squads, and they shouted "Barcelona," "Arsenal," "Chelsea," "Juventus"—the powerhouse teams they see on television these days.

The players packed up and headed toward the city buses that would take them to all corners of Queens. I remembered our long treks back from the Metropolitan Oval and Brooklyn.

That night, I downloaded a few photos I had taken and transmitted them to five or six teammates I could locate.

"These guys are good," I told them. "We won."

APPENDIX:
EIGHT WORLD CUPS

1982 • SPAIN

    SEMIFINALS: Italy 2, Poland 0

                West Germany 3, France 3
                (West Germany wins on penalty kicks, 5–4)

    FINALS: Italy 3, West Germany 1

1986 • MEXICO

    SEMIFINALS: Argentina 2, Belgium 0

                West Germany 2, France 0

    FINALS: Argentina 3, West Germany 2

1990 • ITALY

    SEMIFINALS: Argentina 1, Italy 1
                (Argentina wins on penalty kicks, 4–3)

                West Germany 1, England 1
                (West Germany wins on penalty kicks, 4–3)

    FINALS: West Germany 1, Argentina 0

1994 • UNITED STATES

SEMIFINALS: Italy 2, Bulgaria 1

Brazil 1, Sweden 0

FINALS: Brazil 0, Italy 0
(Brazil wins on penalty kicks, 3–2)

1998 • FRANCE

SEMIFINALS: Brazil 1, Netherlands 1
(Brazil wins on penalty kicks, 4–2)

France 2, Croatia 1

FINALS: France 3, Brazil 0

2002 • SOUTH KOREA/JAPAN

SEMIFINALS: Germany 1, South Korea 0

Brazil 1, Turkey 0

FINALS: Brazil 2, Germany 0

2006 • GERMANY

SEMIFINALS: Italy 2, Germany 0

France 1, Portugal 0

FINALS: Italy 1, France 1
(Italy wins on penalty kicks, 5–3)

2010 • SOUTH AFRICA

SEMIFINALS: Netherlands 3, Uruguay 2

Spain 1, Germany 0

FINALS: Spain 1, Netherlands 0

*Details of all World Cups can be found at http://www.fifa.com/worldcup/archive/index
.html and http://www.fifa.com/womensworldcup/index.html.*

*The matches of the 2014 World Cup can be found at http://www.fifa.com/worldcup/
matches/index.html.*

BIBLIOGRAPHY

The chief source of this book is my own memory, backed up by the files of the *New York Times*. In many other cases, I called or e-mailed colleagues, whom I mention in context or in the acknowledgments.

In this wonderful new world of technology, when I want to re-create my impression of Zidane's dancing feet in the 1998 final or the American goal that beat Algeria in 2010, there are amazing videos out there on the Web, at YouTube and elsewhere. I often marvel at working in an age where I can see plays that happened years ago.

BOOKS

Anderson, Chris, and David Sally. *The Numbers Game: Why Everything You Know About Soccer Is Wrong.* New York: Penguin, 2013.

Biss, Levon (photographer). *One Love: Soccer for Life.* Foreword by Steve Rushin. Tielt, Belgium: Lannoo Publishers, 2006.

Bondy, Filip. *Chasing the Game: America and the Quest for the World Cup.* Cambridge, Mass.: Da Capo Press, 2010.

Buford, Bill. *Among the Thugs: The Experience, and the Seduction, of Crowd Violence.* London: W. W. Norton, 1990.

Burns, Jimmy. *Hand of God: The Life of Diego Maradona, Soccer's Fallen Star.* New York: Lyons & Burford, 1996.

Foer, Franklin. *How Soccer Explains the World: An Unlikely Theory of Global-ization.* New York: HarperCollins, 2004.

Galeano, Eduardo. *Soccer in Sun and Shadow.* London and New York: Verso, 1998.

Gardner, Paul. *The Simplest Game: The Intelligent Fan's Guide to the World of Soccer.* New York: Macmillan, 1996.

Glanville, Brian. *The Story of the World Cup.* London: Faber and Faber, 1993.

Harkes, John, with Denise Kiernan. *Captain for Life: And Other Temporary Assignments.* Chelsea, Mich.: Sleeping Bear Press, 1999.

Hirshey, David, and Roger Bennett. *The ESPN World Cup Companion: Every-thing You Need to Know About the Planet's Biggest Sports Event.* New York: Ballantine/ESPN Books, 2010.

Hornby, Nick. *Fever Pitch.* London: Penguin Books, 1992.

Jennings, Andrew. *Foul! The Secret World of FIFA: Bribes, Vote Rigging and Ticket Scandals.* London: HarperSport, 2006.

Kuper, Simon. *Football Against the Enemy.* London: Orion House, 2004.

Lange, Dave. *Soccer Made in St. Louis: A History of the Game in America's First Soccer Capital.* St. Louis: Reedy Press, 2011.

Longman, Jeré. *The Girls of Summer: The U.S. Women's Soccer Team and How It Changed the World.* New York: HarperCollins, 2000.

Mandela, Nelson. *Long Walk to Freedom: The Autobiography of Nelson Man-dela.* Boston: Little, Brown, 1994.

Markovits, Andrei S., and Steven L. Hellerman. *Offside: Soccer and American Exceptionalism.* Princeton, N.J.: Princeton University Press, 2001.

McGinniss, Joe. *The Miracle of Castel Di Sangro.* Boston: Little, Brown, 1999.

Oxenham, Gwendolyn. *Finding the Game: Three Years, Twenty-five Countries and the Search for Pickup Soccer.* New York: St. Martin's Press, 2012.

Schaap, Jeremy. *Triumph: The Untold Story of Jesse Owens and Hitler's Olym-pics.* Boston: Houghton Mifflin Harcourt, 2007.

Vecsey, George. *A Year in the Sun: The Games, the Players, the Pleasure of Sports.* New York: Times Books, 1989.

Weiland, Matt, and Sean Wilsey. *The Thinking Fan's Guide to the World Cup.* New York: HarperCollins, 2006.

1. THE GOAL THAT CHANGES EVERYTHING

Longman, Jeré. "Desperate Hope, Dramatic Ending." *New York Times.* June 24, 2010.

Vecsey, George. "A Foreign Game Looks Very American." *New York Times.* June 24, 2010.

2. THE MAKING OF A FAN

Goal! The World Cup. Film documentary. Directed by Ross Devenish and Abidin Dino. Written by Brian Glanville. 1967.

Decker, Duane. "Off His Rocker About Soccer." *Sports Illustrated.* January 10, 1955.

Vecsey, George. "Backtalk; A Soccer Shrine Is Captive to a Mushrooming Tax Bill." *New York Times.* October 17, 1999.

Suarez, Ray, moderator. "America's Interest in Soccer Perks This Year After the World Cup." *News Hour.* Pbs.org. July 10, 2006.

Vecsey, George. "Soccer Is Welcome at Home of Sox." *New York Times.* July 25, 2012.

3. THE BEST GROUP EVER

Gardner, Paul. *The Simplest Game: The Intelligent Fan's Guide to the World of Soccer.* New York: Simon & Schuster Macmillan, 1976.

Vecsey, George. "Boniek Is the Whole Show for Poland." *New York Times.* June 29, 1982.

———. "Equal/Opposite." whatahowler.tumblr.com/post/24698119812/vecsey -equalandopposite. 2012.

Sampson, Paul. "82: The original and harshest Group of Death." fourfourtwo .com/blogs/worldcupwonderland. May 13, 2010.

Vecsey, George. "Endless Dancing in the Streets." *New York Times.* July 4, 1982.

———. "Kissinger's New Mission: Bring World Cup to the U.S. by 2022." *New York Times.* March 30, 2009.

"Cualquier Tiempo Pasado . . . Año 1982." jesusmesloquehay.blogspot.com. October 17, 2012.

Nash, Nathaniel. "Edgy Outpost: Life in the Falklands; Unease Tempers Prosperity in Falklands' Postwar Years." *New York Times.* June 15, 1991.

http://www.i-azzurri.com/specials/articles/item/249-best-of-italy-germany -matches-in-history.

4. NOT READY FOR PRIME TIME

New York Times. "Team America Is Taking Shape." February 23, 1983.

Vecsey, George. "Dodge City Time in Soccer." *New York Times*. May 15, 1983.

———. "Strangers at Home." *New York Times*. June 2, 1985.

Bell, Jack. "The Long, Hard Struggle to Mold an American Team." *New York Times*. September 27, 2006.

———. "Team America." *Howler Magazine*. Summer 2012.

5. THE KID COMES BACK

Burns, Jimmy. *Hand of God: The Life of Diego Maradona, Soccer's Fallen Star.* New York: Lyons & Burford, 1996.

Hero: The Official Film of the 1986 World Cup. A Drummond Challis/Tony Maylam Film. 1987.

Chaudhary, Vivek. "Who's the Fat Bloke in the Number Eight Shirt?" *Guardian*. February 17, 2004.

Raggio, Nora. "Pre-Columbian Sacrifices." Sjsu.edu. San Jose State University. 2000.

Vecsey, George. "The Old and the New." *New York Times*. May 30, 1986.

———. "Mexico Was Only a Winner." *New York Times*. June 1, 1986.

———. "Iran: On the Road Again." *New York Times*. June 3, 1986.

———. "It's Happening in Monterrey." *New York Times*. June 5, 1986.

———. "Italy and Argentina Play to a 1–1 Tie." *New York Times*. June 6, 1986.

———. "Speaking for a Nation." *New York Times*. June 30, 1986.

"Messi Is the Most Expensive Athlete in History." Tierraunica.com. 2005.

"Maradona—Goal of the Century." Wander-Argentina.com. 2013.

Vecsey, George. "It's About the Air." *New York Times*. June 8, 1986.

———. "Only Yank in the World." *New York Times*. June 10, 1986.

———. "Denmark Beats W. Germany." *New York Times*. June 14, 1986.

———. "World Cup; France Easily Dethrones Italy." *New York Times*. June 18, 1986.

———. "The Real Number One." *New York Times*. June 29, 1986.

Crooks, Eleanor. "Goal-Line Technology to Be Sanctioned: The Famous Goals That Never Were from Geoff Hurst to Frank Lampard." Telegraph.co.uk. July 5, 2012.

Crouse, Lindsay. "Who Made That? Cleats." *New York Times Magazine*. June 7, 2013.

6. THE SWEETEST FANS

Vecsey, George. "Where U.S. Pride Rests on One Game." *New York Times.* November 19, 1989.

———. "U.S. Advances to World Cup." *New York Times.* November 20, 1989.

Jennings, Andrew. *Foul! The Secret World of FIFA: Bribes, Vote Rigging and Ticket Scandals.* London: HarperSport, 2006.

Longman, Jeré, and Doreen Carvajal. "Power Broker Steps Down After Years of Whispers." *New York Times.* June 21, 2011.

Lewis, Michael. "Forty-Year-Old Virgin." *Howler Magazine.* Summer 2013.

7. MARKING MARADONA

Janofsky, Michael. "Tiny Village Welcomes U.S." *New York Times.* May 27, 1990.

———. "For U.S. Coach, Budapest Hits Close to Home." *New York Times.* March 19, 1990.

Vecsey, George. "Soccer's Little Big Man." *New York Times.* May 27, 1990.

———. "Reality Cannot Kill the Soccer 'Passion.'" *New York Times.* June 11, 1990.

———. "The Meolas Come Home with a Son." *New York Times.* June 14, 1990.

———. "A Defeat Revives a Dream." *New York Times.* June 15, 1990.

Mellinger, Sam. "Soccer Always Special to Sporting KC's Vermes." *Kansas City Star.* November 3, 2012.

Covitz, Randy. "Stirring Day for Vermes." *Kansas City Star.* October 12, 2013.

Vecsey, George. "Maradona Has Arm (Maybe) in Victory." *New York Times.* June 14, 1990.

———. "The Old Man Waited for the Shadows." *New York Times.* June 24, 1990.

———. "Last Look at Italy's World Cup." *New York Times.* July 8, 1990.

Janofsky, Michael. "Lion-Hearted Cup Team Gives Hope to Cameroon." *New York Times.* June 18, 1990.

Vecsey, George. "And Maradona Was Waiting." *New York Times.* June 25, 1990.

Lawton, James. "The Father of 'Total Football' Who Let His Players Run Free." *The Independent.* March 4, 2005.

8. MR. BLATTER COMES TO AMERICA

Vecsey, George. "Friendly Suggestion from the Home Office." *New York Times.* August 19, 1990.

Dwyre, Bill. "Analysis: Forget World Cup: This Was 'Circus of the Soccer Stars.'" *Los Angeles Times.* December 20, 1993.

Lewis, Michael. "The 1994 Bid: How the U.S. Got the World Cup—Part 1." *World Cup Soccer,* 1994.

"U.S. Soccer Mourns Loss of Werner Fricker (1936–2001)." Ussoccer.com. June 1, 2001.

9. THE BIG EVENT

Cart, Julie. "Germany Wins, 2–1, in Tropical Silverdome." *Los Angeles Times.* June 20, 1993.

Yannis, Alex. "There's Something for (Almost) Everybody at World Cup." *New York Times.* November 21, 1993.

Vecsey, George. "Soccer Junkie Files His World Cup Flight Plan." *New York Times.* December 20, 1993.

Raver, Ann. "Grass Struggles Back (Thanks to Soccer)." *New York Times.* June 5, 1994.

Longman, Jeré. "U.S. Ties for First Cup Point Since 1950." *New York Times.* June 19, 1994.

Rhoden, William C. "Simpson's Sad Drama a Puzzle." *New York Times.* June 18, 1994.

Vecsey, George. "Yank Recalls Old Victory over Brazil." *New York Times.* July 4, 1994.

Hughes, Rob. "Crime and Punishment: FIFA Edits the Book." *New York Times.* July 8, 1994.

Vecsey, George. "From Deep in His Serbian Heart." *New York Times.* April 18, 1999.

———. "John Harkes Knows the Feeling of Having to Sit Out an Important Match." *New York Times.* July 5, 2010.

Moran, Malcolm. "Baggio Brings a Last-Gasp Victory for the Italians." *New York Times.* July 6, 1994.

Vecsey, George. "Roberto Baggio Stops Ugly Trip Back Home." *New York Times.* July 6, 1994.

———. "No More Blasts from the Distant Past for Spain." Georgevecsey.com. July 1, 2012.

Yannis, Alex. "Italy Soars Aboard the Baggio Express." *New York Times*. July 10, 1994.

Fensom, Michael J. "Own Goal at 1994 World Cup Still Connects Slain Colombian Andres Escobar, Former U.S. Midfielder John Harkes." *Newark Star-Ledger*. June 22, 2010.

Longman, Jeré. "Only Romario Finds the Net, and Brazil Lands in Final." *New York Times*. July 14, 1994.

Yannis, Alex. "Italian Injury List Grows After Plane Ride." *New York Times*. July 16, 1994.

Thomsen, Ian. "Brazil, Forced into Shootout, Wins 4th Title." *New York Times*. July 18, 1994.

Bertucci, Frank. "Baresi Champ in Loss." *Philadelphia Daily News*. July 18, 1994.

Vecsey, George. "Italy's Coach Seems Straight from Fellini." *New York Times*. July 10, 1994.

10. AMERICA'S FIRST SOCCER CHAMPION

Bondy, Filip. "U.S. Women's Team May Be World's Best." *New York Times*. June 9, 1991.

Basler, Barbara. "U.S. Women's Soccer Team's Message: 'No One Will Get in Our Way.'" *New York Times*. November 29, 1991.

"Topics of the Times: America's First First." *New York Times*. December 3, 1991.

Vecsey, George. "Women's Soccer: 76,481 Fans, 1 U.S. Gold." *New York Times*. August 2, 1996.

Grisamore, Ed. "No Hedging on Georgia's Hedges." *Charlotte Observer*. January 10, 1996.

"It Was a Ho-Ax." Dawgsonline.com. February 27, 2008.

Lukacs, John D. "A Journey Back 'Tween the Hedges.'" ESPN.com. October 12, 2009.

Goldman, Tom. "40 Years On, Title IX Still Shapes Female Athletes." *New York Times*. June 22, 2012.

11. ALLONS, ENFANTS

Harkes, John, with Denise Kiernan. *Captain for Life: And Other Temporary Assignments*. Chelsea, Mich.: Sleeping Bear Press, 1999.

Longman, Jeré. "Enmity Past, U.S. Meets Iran and Suffers Bitter 2–1 Defeat." *New York Times.* June 22, 1998.

———. "They All Come to Play for America; Regis Is the Newest Citizen on Polyglot U.S. World Cup Soccer Team." *New York Times.* May 21, 1998.

Vecsey, George. "U.S. Team Is Secluded and Surly." *New York Times.* June 9, 1998.

———. "Harkes Still Roots for His Pals on the U.S. Team." *New York Times.* June 23, 1998.

———. "Defeat Is Apolitical as Yanks Lose to Iran 2–1." *New York Times.* June 22, 1998.

———. "Reyna Felt Game Plan Right in His Back." *New York Times.* June 16, 1998.

Wahl, Grant. "Digging Up a Painful U.S. Memory." *Sports Illustrated.* February 5, 2010.

Powers, Scott. "Playing Three Straight World Cups, Brian McBride Has Many Fond Memories." ESPNChicago.com. June 10, 2010.

Blum, Ronald. "John Harkes Affair? Soccer Captain Allegedly Slept with Teammate's Wife." Associated Press. February 3, 2010.

Château de Pizay: http://www.chateau-pizay.com/uk/index.php.

Vecsey, George. "A Time-Study Man Monitors the World." *New York Times.* June 28, 1998.

Longman, Jeré. "Harkes Is Dropped from U.S. Cup Team." *New York Times.* April 15, 1998.

"Les temps modernes." *Observer.* April 2, 2006.

"Ronaldo Talks About What Happened in World Cup 98." ronaldohome.com. May 15, 2009.

"World Cup Heartbreak for Ba and Anelka." www.hurriyet.dailynews.com. May 25, 1998.

Clarey, Christopher. "France's 'Foreign Legion' Hopes Hour of Glory Has Arrived." *New York Times.* June 8, 1998.

12. AMERICANS WIN WORLD CUP—AGAIN

Longman, Jeré. *The Girls of Summer: The U.S. Women's Soccer Team and How It Changed the World.* New York: HarperCollins, 2000.

Kiernan, Denise. "The Long Way Home: Women's World Cup '99, the Latest Stop on the U.S.'s Road to Glory." *Village Voice.* April 20, 1999.

Vecsey, George. "Backtalk; When Is It Gamesmanship, and When Is It Cheating?" *New York Times*. August 8, 1999.

——. "A Kickoff Brings Joy and Thanks and Roars." *New York Times*. April 15, 2001.

"China Suffers Grievous Losses from WWC 2003 Relocation." Peopledaily .com.cn. May 8, 2003.

Longman, Jeré. "1999 Women's World Cup: Beautiful Game Takes Flight." *New York Times*. May 20, 1999.

Vecsey, George. "Kristine Lilly: A Player with Caps." *New York Times*. June 13, 1999.

——. "For Chastain, an Error, Then a Goal." *New York Times*. July 2, 1999.

——. "Final Game Owes Great Debt to China." *New York Times*. July 10, 1999.

——. "No Goals Scored, Two Champions, a Bright Future." *New York Times*. July 11, 1999.

——. "Veteran Lilly Does Job." *New York Times*. July 11, 1999.

——. "Will Women Enjoy a League of Their Own?" *New York Times*. July 12, 1999.

Longman, Jeré. "Day in the Sun for the Girls of Summer After a Riveting Championship Run." *New York Times*. July 12, 1999.

The 99ers. Film documentary. Directed by Erin Leyden. Produced by Julie Foudy. ESPN Nine for IX series. August 2013.

13. THE YEAR OF THE OUTSIDERS

"Reyna Hurt. Celtic Fan Taunts U.S. Captain with Airplane Gesture." Associated Press. October 1, 2001.

Clarey, Christopher. "BackTalk; The Beautiful Game Gets a Black Eye." *New York Times*. May 12, 2002.

Peart, Harry. "Blatter Could Face Corruption Probe." BBC.co.uk. May 4, 2002.

"Zidane Injured." Paklinks.com. May 26, 2002.

"Blatter Jeered at FIFA Congress." Associated Press. May 28, 2002.

"Blatter, Sportsman or Dictator." Associated Press. May 28, 2002.

Vecsey, George. "World Cup Refs Crack Down on the Divers." *New York Times*. May 28, 2002.

——. "Yellow Card to Blatter for Smugness at Cup." *New York Times*. May 30, 2002.

——. "He's a Long Way from Long Island." *New York Times*. May 29, 2002.

———. "Bruce Arena Returns to Old Neighborhood." *New York Times.* June 16, 2004.

Brooke, James. "Legacy of World Cup May Be the Stadiums Left Behind." *New York Times.* June 2, 2002.

"10 Year Anniversary of USA vs. Mexico in Columbus, Ohio." Ussoccer.com. February 10, 2011.

Longman, Jeré. "Dream Ends in a Moment of Vulnerability." *New York Times.* June 22, 2002.

———. "Another World Cup, Another U.S. Crossroads." *New York Times.* June 23, 2002.

Pielke, Roger, Jr. "How Can FIFA Be Held Accountable?" *Sports Management Review.* January 2013.

Vecsey, George. "Brazil Is Still the Center of the Universe." *New York Times.* June 25, 2002.

French, Howard W. "Brazil Earns a Spot in Its Third Straight Final." *New York Times.* June 27, 2002.

Longman, Jeré. "Ronaldo's Sweetest Vindication." *New York Times.* July 1, 2002.

Vecsey, George. "No Drum and No Fancy Dance, but a One-Man Band Leads Brazil." *New York Times.* July 1, 2002.

Gibson, Owen. "João Havelange Resigns as Fifa Honorary President over 'Bribes.'" *Guardian.* April 30, 2013.

14. THE HOME I WAS ALWAYS SEEKING

Vecsey, George. "When Fans in Italy and Russia Held Their Collective Breath." *New York Times.* November 16, 1997.

———. "Goodbye to Corner Kicks and Cappuccinos." *New York Times.* April 26, 2008.

15. SCANDAL AND HEAD-BUTT

Furlong, Ray. "New Future for Nazi Stadium." BBC.co.uk. July 31, 2004.

"Emotional Moggi Resigns as Juve General Manager." ESPNFC.com. May 14, 2006.

Vecsey, George. "Winning Fans Is Easier Than Winning Games." *New York Times.* June 6, 2006.

———. "Cosmic Questions on a Journey of Discovery." *New York Times*. June 9, 2006.

———. "And in the End, Germany Always Wins." *New York Times*. June 15, 2006.

———. "Party Ends Sadly, and Suddenly." *New York Times*. July 5, 2006.

———. "French in the Final, as a Spirit Moves Them." *New York Times*. July 6, 2006.

———. "The Final: Good Vibrations, Grim Echoes." *New York Times*. July 9, 2006.

———. "Italy's Victory Is Clear, but Moral of Story Is Not." *New York Times*. July 10, 2006.

"Zidane Explains." Canal Plus, France. July 12, 2006. http://news.bbc.co.uk/sport2/hi/football/world_cup_2006/teams/france/5174758.stm.

Wahl, Grant. "Surreal World." *Sports Illustrated*. July 17, 2006.

Scott, Matt. "How Fifa Vice-President Jack Warner Failed to Deliver on Promises." *Guardian*. November 29, 2010.

Schaap, Jeremy. *Triumph: The Untold Story of Jesse Owens and Hitler's Olympics*. Boston: Houghton Mifflin Harcourt, 2007.

16. NELSON MANDELA MEETS FIFA

Mandela, Nelson. *Long Walk to Freedom: The Autobiography of Nelson Mandela*. Boston: Little, Brown, 1994.

"Timeline: Nelson Mandela: Key Dates in the Former South African President's Life." Usatoday.com.

Burns, John F. "South Africa's New Era: Mandela to Go Free Today; De Klerk Proclaims Ending of 'Chapter' After 27 Years." *New York Times*. February 11, 1990.

Keller, Bill. "Mandela Is Named President, Closing the Era of Apartheid." *New York Times*. May 10, 1994.

Simons, Bill. "Nelson Mandela, Arthur Ashe, and the Transformative Power of Sports." *Inside Tennis*. September–October 2013.

Longman, Jeré. "South Africa Is Favored to Win Cup Bid." *New York Times*. May 15, 2004.

Smith, David. "Danny Jordaan—from 'Coloured' Footballer to World Cup Main Man." *Guardian*. March 4, 2010.

Mitchell, Francesca. "Khoi-San Identity." Sahistory.org.za. 2012.

Vecsey, George. "South Africa's Long Journey to World Cup." *New York Times*. November 11, 2008.

17. SPAIN MAKES A BREAKTHROUGH

Longman, Jeré. "South Africa Is Favored to Win Cup Bid." *New York Times*. May 15, 2004.

Vecsey, George. "South Africa's Long Journey to World Cup." *New York Times*. November 6, 2008.

Longman, Jeré. "U.S. Advances to 2010 World Cup." *New York Times*. October 11, 2009.

———. "Desperate Hope, Dramatic Ending." *New York Times*. June 24, 2010.

Vecsey, George. "A Foreign Game Looks Very American." *New York Times*. June 24, 2010.

———. "Diplomatic Traveling Supporter of U.S. Team Sees the Big Picture." *New York Times*. June 25, 2010.

———. " 'Mixed Results' for U.S.; Uncertain Future for Coach." *New York Times*. June 29, 2010.

———. "Foot in the Door." *New York Times*. June 30, 2010.

Clarey, Christopher. "In the Arena: Migratory Wildlife and Migratory Fans." *International Herald Tribune*. July 1, 2010.

———. "Reporter's Notebook: Around South Africa, the Good, the Bad and the Biltong." *New York Times*. July 4, 2010.

Vecsey, George. "For Once, Soccer Gods Smile on Spanish." *New York Times*. July 4, 2010.

Beacom, Steve. "Holland Playing Total Football? Not As We Know It." *Belfast Telegraph*. July 6, 2010.

Marcus, Jeffrey. "A Dutch Great Helped Transform Spain's Game." *New York Times*. July 10, 2010.

Vecsey, George. "Celebrating South Africa and a Job Done Well." *New York Times*. July 11, 2010.

18. BLATTER SCORES AN OWN GOAL

Jennings, Andrew. *Foul! The Secret World of FIFA: Bribes, Vote Rigging and Ticket Scandals*. London: HarperSport, 2006.

Vecsey, George. "Kissinger's Soccer Diplomacy." *New York Times*. March 31, 2009.

————. "Back-Scratching with a Global Reach." *New York Times*. December 1, 2010.

————. "U.S. Should Know There's No Sulking in Soccer." *New York Times*. December 3, 2010.

————. "Outlook That Soccer Can Do Without." *New York Times*. December 18, 2010.

Longman, Jeré, and Doreen Carvajal. "Power Broker Steps Down After Years of Whispers." *New York Times*. June 21, 2011.

Carvajal, Doreen. "For FIFA Executives, Luxury and Favors." *New York Times*. July 18, 2011.

Radnedge, Keir. "The Truth Is Out There." worldsoccer.com. January 24, 2012.

Hughes, Rob. "Kickback Report Was No Surprise to World of Soccer." *New York Times*. July 12, 2012.

"FIFA Picks Ex-U.S. Attorney as Corruption Prosecutor." Associated Press. July 17, 2012.

Lichfield, John. "Nicolas Sarkozy 'Colluded' to Get Qatar 2022 World Cup." Independent.co.uk. January 29, 2013.

Dunbar, Graham. "Anti-Corruption Advisers Challenge FIFA to Change." Associated Press. February 8, 2013.

Pianigiani, Gaia, and Thomas Fuller. "Soccer Fixing Inquiry Hinges on a Shadowy Singaporean." *New York Times*. February 14, 2013.

"Fifa Ethics Chief Michael Garcia Confident About Investigation." BBC.com. March 27, 2013.

Ozanian, Mike. "Soccer's Most Valuable Teams: At $3.3 Billion, Real Madrid Knocks Manchester United from Top Spot." Forbes.com. April 17, 2013.

"Jack Warner, Chuck Blazer 'Fraudulent' at Concacaf." Sportsillustrated.com. April 19, 2013.

Kennedy, Paul. "Gulati Wins Executive Committee Seat in 18–17 Vote." Socceramerica.com. April 19, 2013.

Settimi, Christine. "The World's Best-Paid Soccer Players." Forbes.com. April 17, 2013.

Hughes, Rob. "One by One, Those atop FIFA Are Falling." *New York Times*. May 7, 2013.

Gibson, Owen. "Sepp Blatter: How Fifa's Great Survivor Has Stayed on Top." *Guardian*. May 30 2013.

Hughes, Rob. "A Lecture FIFA Didn't Need to Make." *International Herald Tribune*. June 21, 2013.

Gibson, Owen. "Sepp Blatter Admits Qatar World Cup Error and Backs Winter Switch." *Guardian*. September 9, 2013.

Hughes, Rob. "Qatar World Cup: A Little Late for Common Sense." *International Herald Tribune*. September 10, 2013.

Borden, Sam. "Talk of a Cooler 2022 World Cup Heats Up." *New York Times*. September 11, 2013.

Average Weather in Doha, Qatar: weatherspark.com.

Bell, Jack. "Loss of '22 World Cup Bid Still Rankles Head of U.S. Soccer." *New York Times*. October 9, 2013.

19. THE AGE OF KLINSMANN

Vecsey, George. "Soccer Must Keep the Ball Rolling." *New York Times*. June 30, 2002.

Hersh, Philip. "Bringing the Sun of California to Germany." *Chicago Tribune*. May 27, 2005.

Goff, Steven. "World Cup Bonuses, Employee Salaries Listed in U.S. Soccer Federation Tax Document." *Washington Post*. February 14, 2012.

Hughes, Rob. "Spain's Destruction of Italy Silences the Doubters." *New York Times*. July 2, 2012.

Futterman, Matthew. "Jurgen Klinsmann Sounds Off." *Wall Street Journal*. January 22, 2013.

"FIFA Will Use Goal-Line Technology at 2014 World Cup." Associated Press. February 19, 2013.

Straus, Brian. "Friendly Fire: U.S. Coach Jurgen Klinsmann's Methods, Leadership, Acumen in Question." Aol.sportingnews.com. March 19, 2013.

Borden, Sam. "The Missing Piece." *New York Times*. March 20, 2013.

Longman, Jeré. "For U.S., Tie in Mexico Feels a Lot Like Victory." *New York Times*. March 27, 2013.

Baxter, Kevin. "Back from Sabbatical, Landon Donovan Determined to Regain Spot on U.S. Team." *Los Angeles Times*. March 28, 2013.

Hughes, Rob. "Champions League Final Does Not Mark Start of a German Era." *New York Times*. May 24, 2013.

Borden, Sam. "Strolling Crisply Past Panama, U.S. Settles into Driver's Seat." *New York Times*. June 12, 2013.

———. "To U.S. Soccer Team, Home Field Is an Ever-Changing Thing." *New York Times*. June 16, 2013.

"100 Years of Soccer." Ussoccer.com.

Hughes, Rob. "For David Villa, Change Might Be a Good Thing." *New York Times.* July 10, 2013.

Woitalla, Mike. "Dynamic Donovan Leads USA to Rout over El Salvador." *SoccerAmerica Daily.* July 22, 2013.

The Player (Anonymous). "The Power of Negative Thinking." *Howler Magazine.* Summer 2013.

Strauss, Ben. "One Goal, but Plenty for U.S. to Celebrate in Gold Cup Final." *New York Times.* July 28, 2013.

Vecsey, George. "Back Home, Still Taking on the World." *New York Times.* August 12, 2013.

Mahoney, Ridge. "Is MLS Brazil-Ready?" *Soccer America.* August 28, 2013.

Bagli, Charles V. "Soccer Club's Latest Stadium Proposal Would Give the Yankees a New Neighbor." *New York Times.* August 29, 2013.

Woitalla, Mike. "Mission Accomplished: Landon Donovan Leads USA to Brazil." *Soccer America.* September 10, 2013.

Keh, Andrew. "U.S. Wins and Secures Spot in World Cup." *New York Times.* September 11, 2013.

"Test for Klinsmann Will Be at the World Cup." Associated Press. September 11, 2013.

Kennedy, Paul. "Klinsmann Shakes Things Up." *Soccer America.* September 11, 2013.

Borden, Sam. "A Winter World Cup? Gulati Says Not So Fast." *New York Times.* September 13, 2013.

Lavin, Christine. "Sensitive New Age Guys." Video: http://www.youtube.com /watch?v=xWuJi8gO-sc.

Gibson, Owen. "Qatar World Cup 'Slaves': Fifa's UK Representative 'Appalled and Disturbed.'" *Guardian.* September 26, 2013.

Borden, Sam, and James Montague. "In FIFA Politics, Blatter Is the Consummate Player." *New York Times.* October 1, 2013.

Montague, James. "Changes Slowly Coming to FIFA as Problems Put It on the Defensive." *New York Times.* October 3, 2013.

———. "FIFA Will Study Winter Move for World Cup." *New York Times.* October 4, 2013.

Borden, Sam. "Unlucky Bounce for U.S." *New York Times.* December 7, 2013.

Bell, Jack. "Coach Named for New York M.L.S. Team." *New York Times.* December 10, 2013.

Bagli, Charles V. "Deal for Bronx Soccer Stadium in Works as Clock Ticks." *New York Times*. December 11, 2013.

Belson, Ken. "The Power Behind Manchester City Is Content to Stay Out of Sight in New York." *New York Times*. May 24, 2013.

Keh, Andrew. "Seeking Bigger Role, Bradley Invests His Future in M.L.S." *New York Times*. January 13, 2014.

Montague, James. "Pelé Backs Frenchman for FIFA Presidency." *New York Times*. January 20, 2014.

ACKNOWLEDGMENTS

When I decided to write about my eight World Cups, my agent, Esther Newberg of ICM Partners, came through, as always. She connected me with Paul Golob of Henry Holt and Company, who has been a wise and proactive editor. I also thank Alex Ward, the editorial director of book development at the *New York Times*, as well as Zoe Sandler of ICM and Emi Ikkanda, Jason Liebman, and Brooke Parsons of Holt.

It would be quite enough for Marianne Graham Vecsey to be the talented and pretty artist I met in college, but she also gave me her valuable reactions to this manuscript as it developed. Our oldest, Laura Vecsey, poet and journalist, also read the manuscript, and our two other journalist-children, Corinna V. Wilson and David Vecsey, are always there for counsel.

I thank the sports editors at the *New York Times* who encouraged my soccer jones over the years—LeAnne Schreiber, Joe Vecchione, Neil Amdur, and Tom Jolly—and I thank Jason Stallman, Jay Schreiber, Fern Turkowitz, Terri Ann Glynn, and so many other colleagues for making my ongoing association with the *Times* so enjoyable.

The photo search has been made easier by nice people out there: Jeff Roth at the *Times* morgue, who was invaluable in selecting photos; John

McDermott, whose great photographs grace this book and whose insights were invaluable; and Claudia Brose. (Yes, that is Roby Baggio's low-key voice on John's cell phone.) George Tiedemann, another great photographer on World Cup sidelines. Esther Montoro. Peter Schols. Carolyn Carbery and the Borghi and Keough families of St. Louis. Annette Shelby of International Sports Images. Matthew Lutts of AP Images. Nancy Glowinski of Reuters. David R. Zukerman.

The soccer press-box regulars and irregulars are part of this book, part of my life. Maybe it's because we help each other get through the exotic travel, sometimes huddling to re-create key plays, but I don't know any other sport where reporters like each other as much. (At least, I think they do.) I hope I am remembering all the soccer lifers and other friends who helped me with this book:

Greg Amante, Jack Bell, Ken Belson, Paola Beretti, Peter Berlin, Ronald Blum, Filip Bondy, Bob and Debbie Chalfin, Sean Clancy of Foley's, Christopher Clarey, Roger Cohen for his death-defying ride on the ottoman to celebrate a Chelsea goal, Rebecca Collet, Charlie Competello and all my pals from the *Times*' technology department for keeping me going, Pino DiBartolo, *tanti dolci ricordi*, Edward Lewin, M.D., Kenneth Ewing, M.D., former captain of Guatemala. Three nice people from FIFA over the years—Guido Tognoni, Andreas Herren, and Keith Cooper.

Paul Gardner, for blazing a trail in the New World, and for being my friend. Brian Glanville—not just for *Goal!* but for all the great words over the years and his advice on this book; Sunil Gulati, from the days when we watched Columbia matches in the bleachers; Sam and Jennifer Guttenplan, my Euro rellies, *merci beaucoup*; Colonel James Hackett, former chief of detectives in St. Louis, for memories of his playing days in that great soccer city; Phil Hersh, trilingual internationalist.

Rob Hughes, for his informed pieces in the *New York Times* and his counsel; Duncan Irving and Lawrie Mifflin, soccer authorities, Arsenal fanatics, coffee maker (Duncan), and, most important, great friends; Andrew Jennings: I would not want him to be on my case; Denise Kiernan; Becky Lebowitz; Michael Lewis of Big Apple Soccer; Ellis Levine.

Douglas Logan, who helped build a big-time league; Jeré Longman, that great reporter, for the enduring clips that inform many chapters;

Massimo Lopes Pegna, American correspondent for *La Gazzetta dello Sport*; Major League Soccer: Commissioner Don Garber, Dan Courtemanche, and Will Kuhns; Mel Mandell, for memories of old-time East Coast soccer; Jeffrey Marcus. With fond memories, the Professor—Julio Mazzei.

Addio, Joe McGinniss. Omar Minaya, and our friends from Mama's in Corona, Queens—Marie, Carmela, and Irene—as we watch the Azzurri in the back room. Robert Mindelzun, M.D.; Mac Nwulu, ESPN.

George Quraishi of *Howler Magazine*; Keir Radnedge, for tracking down the Boniek yellow card and for being one of the great voices in the sport; Alan Richman and his son Lincoln Richman, who found copies of *Goal!* and other World Cup documentaries; Ray Robinson, writer, editor, and friend, a wise sounding board for the process we both love; Riccardo Romani; Alan Rubin; Stratos Safioleas; Jeremy Schaap; Tom Schwarz, for introducing me to Harry Keough just in time; and so many other new friends in St. Louis.

Bob Seel, the captain; Ina Lee Selden, Altenir and Celia Silva in Rio; Dana Silverstein, Brad Smith, Clemson Smith Muñiz, Mark Starr, who always knew a good restaurant on the road; Hank Steinbrecher, Sue Sutera; Tom Timmermann, Sam Toperoff, Jamie Trecker, Jerry Trecker, Jim Trecker; Ahmet Bob Turgut, for his e-mail insights into Turkish soccer; the United States Soccer Federation: Jim Moorhouse, Neil Buethe, David Applegate, Aaron Heifetz, and Michael Kammarman, all a pleasure to work with over the years. Margaret S. Vecsey, for the astute questions; Randy Vogt, Grant Wahl, George Wilson, for riding shotgun to the tripleheader in 2010.

INDEX

ABOUT THE AUTHOR

GEORGE VECSEY is the anthor of more than a dozen books, most recently the bestseller *Stan Musial: An American Life*. He joined *The New York Times* in 1968, wrote the "Sports of the Times" column from 1982 to 2011, and is now a contributing columnist. He was honored in 2013 by the National Soccer Hall of Fame for his contributions as one of the first columnists at a major U.S. newspaper to cover the sport. He lives in Port Washington, New York.